THE BOOK OF 1930's BRITISH MOTORCYCLE ENGINES

A.J.S. - Ariel
B.S.A. - Calthorpe
Douglas - J.A.P.
Levis - Matchless
New Hudson - New Imperial
Norton - Panther
Raleigh - Royal Enfield
Rudge - Scott
Sunbeam - Triumph
Velocette

A Floyd Clymer 'Motorcyclist's Library' publication
Published in 2018 by: www.VelocePress.com

All rights reserved. This work may not be reproduced or transmitted in any form without the express written consent of the publisher. © 2018 Veloce Enterprises Inc.
San Antonio, Texas, U.S.A.

INTRODUCTION

Welcome to the world of digital publishing ~ the book you now hold in your hand, was printed using the latest state of the art digital technology. The advent of print-on-demand has forever changed the publishing process, never has information been so accessible and it is our hope that this book serves your informational needs for years to come. If this is your first exposure to digital publishing, we hope that you are pleased with the results. Many more titles of interest to the classic automobile and motorcycle enthusiast, collector and restorer are available via our website at www.VelocePress.com. We hope that you find this title as interesting as we do.

NOTE FROM THE PUBLISHER

The information presented is true and complete to the best of our knowledge. All recommendations are made without any guarantees on the part of the author or the publisher, who also disclaim all liability incurred with the use of this information.

TRADEMARKS

We recognize that some words, model names and designations, for example, mentioned herein are the property of the trademark holder. We use them for identification purposes only. This is not an official publication.

INFORMATION ON THE USE OF THIS PUBLICATION

This manual is an invaluable resource for those interested in performing their own maintenance. However, in today's information age we are constantly subject to changes in common practice, new technology, availability of improved materials and increased awareness of chemical toxicity. As such, it is advised that the user consult with an experienced professional prior to undertaking any procedure described herein. While every care has been taken to ensure correctness of information, it is obviously not possible to guarantee complete freedom from errors or omissions or to accept liability arising from such errors or omissions. Therefore, any individual that uses the information contained within, or elects to perform or participate in do-it-yourself repairs or modifications acknowledges that there is a risk factor involved and that the publisher or its associates cannot be held responsible for personal injury or property damage resulting from the use of the information or the outcome of such procedures.

WARNING!

One final word of advice, this publication is intended to be used as a reference guide, and when in doubt the reader should consult with a qualified technician.

ASSOCIATED BOOKS & INDEX

There are two additional publications in this same series they are:

BOOK OF 1930's BRITISH MOTORCYCLE CARBURETTERS AND ELECTRIC COMPONENTS which includes detailed overhaul, repair, adjustment and maintenance information on AMAC, AMAL, BINKS and VILLIERS carburetters and B.T.H., LUCAS, MILLER and VILLIERS electrical components .... ISBN 9781588501837

BOOK OF 1930's BRITISH MOTORCYCLE GEARBOXES AND CLUTCHES which includes detailed overhaul, repair, adjustment and maintenance information on ALBION, B.S.A., BURMAN, DOUGLAS, NEW HUDSON, RUDGE, SCOTT, STURMEY-ARCHER and VELOCETTE gearboxes and clutches .... ISBN 9781588501813

In addition, there are a number of PITMAN 'BOOK OF' series published by Floyd Clymer (USA) under an arrangement with Pitman (UK) plus original factory or authorized manuals that include additional overhaul, repair and maintenance information for the entire motorcycle that would compliment the appropriate engine section in this publication, they are:

A.J.S. 1932-1948	ISBN 9781588501257
ARIEL 1932-1939	ISBN 9781588500922
ARIEL 1933-1951	ISBN 9781588500717
B.S.A. up to 1926	ISBN 9781588501790
B.S.A. up to 1935	ISBN 9781588501868
B.S.A. 1936-1939	ISBN 9781588500465
B.S.A. 1936-1952	ISBN 9781588502179
DOUGLAS 1929-1939	ISBN 9781588502186
J.A.P. ENGINE1927-1952	ISBN 9781588501394
MATCHLESS up to 1933 inc. 1936 supplement	ISBN 9781588501905
NEW IMPERIAL 1935-1939	ISBN 9781588501899
NORTON 1932-1939	ISBN9781588500700
NORTON 1932-1947	ISBN 9781588501288
NORTON 1938-1956	ISBN 9781588502063
PANTHER (Lightweight) 1932-1958	ISBN 9781588501875
PANTHER (Heavyweight) 1938-1966	ISBN 9781588501882
RALEIGH up to 1933	ISBN 9781588501806

ROYAL ENFIELD 1934-1946	ISBN 9781588501455
ROYAL ENFIELD 1937-1953	ISBN 9781588501219
RUDGE 1933-1939	ISBN 9781588501820
SUNBEAM 1928-1939	ISBN 9781588501387
TRIUMPH 1935-1939	ISBN 9781588500663
TRIUMPH 1935-1949	ISBN 9781588501424
TRIUMPH 1937-1951	ISBN 9781588500649
VELOCETTE 1925-1970	ISBN 9781588501684

INDEX

A.J.S.	Page 1
ARIEL	Page 14
B.S.A.	Page 36
Calthorpe	Page 54
Douglas	Page 58
J.A.P.	Page 64
Levis	Page 90
Matchless	Page 110
New Hudson	Page 121
New Imperial	Page 131
Norton	Page 135
Panther	Page 150
Raleigh	Page 161
Royal Enfield	Page 174
Rudge	Page 191
Scott	Page 200
Sunbeam	Page 214
Triumph	Page 225
Velocette	Page 238

NOTES

NOTES ON REPAIRS TO A.J.S. MOTOR-CYCLES

By W. STEVENS (*A. J. Stevens Ltd.*)

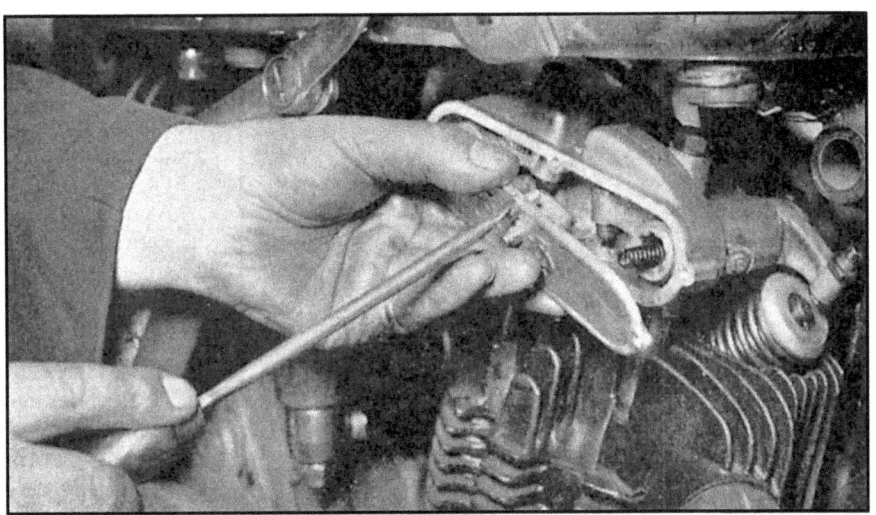

Fig. 1.—REMOVING ROCKER-BOX COVER.

Showing an o.h.v. engine with the push rods removed. It will be noticed that two springs are fitted behind the cover to prevent side movement of the rockers. Whilst taking out the last pin from the rocker box, press on the cover to relieve the pressure of the springs on the latter.

ENGINE

VARIOUS changes in design have been made from time to time, embodying detachable cylinder heads; plain, roller and ball main bearings; plain and roller big-end bearings; semi-automatic, mechanical, dry and wet sump lubrication systems.

Cylinder Heads

On engines up to 1927 both cylinder and head were held down by means of a bridge piece across the cylinder head and two long bolts attached to the crankcase; or, in the case of the o.h.v. models, with a stirrup strap for the head, and left- and right-hand thread sleeve nuts between the former and studs in the crankcase.

NOTES ON REPAIRS TO A.J.S. MOTOR-CYCLES

In these cases, when removing or tightening down the head ease or tighten the nuts evenly, and do not screw the head down too tightly, only sufficient to make compression tight.

On later models the cylinder barrel was held down from the foot by means of four studs and nuts on the crankcase, and the head on the cylinder barrel by four or more pins screwed into the latter.

Fig. 2.—Rocker-box Cover removed for Inspection of Rocker Studs and Push-rod Ends.

Removing Cylinder Head

The simplest method of removing a detachable head, after the holding-down attachments, etc., have been removed, is to insert a screwdriver or similar tool between the top cylinder fin and the head, prising the latter carefully off the cylinder from both sides—prising upwards, not downwards, or the radiating fins may be broken (Fig. 3).

O.H.C. Models—Most Important

In the case of overhead camshaft engines, when the cylinder or head only is removed, it is important that the camshaft sprocket and driving chain should be supported and not allowed to drop in the chain cover while the engine is being revolved. A piece of wire to prevent this happening can be hooked through the sprocket and fastened to one of the sprocket-cap pins screwed into the top of the chain cover (Fig. 5).

In removing the cylinder or head on these engines, it is first necessary, after taking away the exhaust pipe, carburetter, oil pipe to cambox, etc., to remove the cap secured to the top of the chain cover by four pins. Take out the split cotter from the nut on the camshaft, remove the nut and washer, and after removing the four pins holding the cambox on to

*Fig. 3.—*Method of removing Cylinder Head.
Prise off with a screwdriver. This should be done from both sides of the head, prising upwards not downwards.

the head, carefully take away the former whilst the sprocket is being steadied.

An assistant will be useful during this operation.

The sprocket and chain should then be supported by the method already mentioned (Fig. 5).

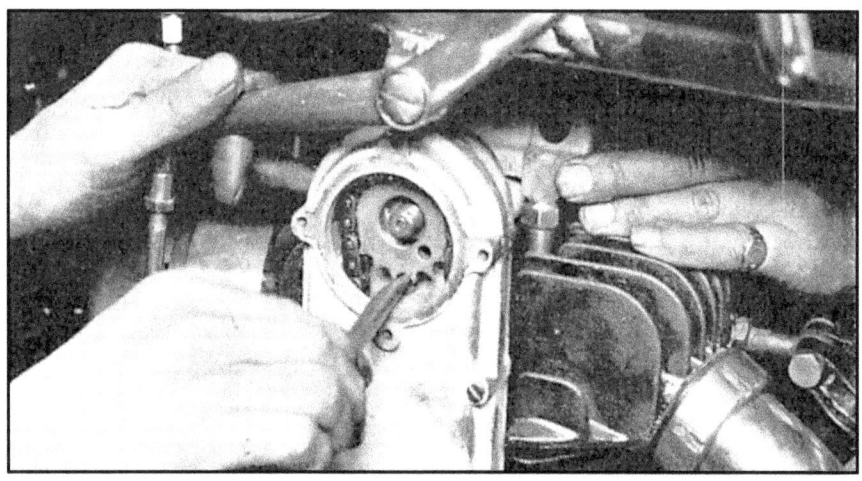

*Fig. 4.—*Removing O.H.C. Cambox.
The camshaft chain and sprocket in the timing cover should be steadied when doing this.

NOTES ON REPAIRS TO A.J.S. MOTOR-CYCLES

Compression Ratio should be altered only by changing Piston

It will not be out of place here to point out that on camshaft engines the compression should not be raised by taking any metal from the bottom or top of the cylinder, or the compression lowered by fitting a thicker washer to the cylinder foot, as this will alter the camshaft driving-chain centres. The makers' advice should be sought on this matter, as special pistons are supplied by them for the above purpose.

Making a Head Joint

Where cylinder heads are held down by means of pins screwed into the top of the cylinder barrel, refitting of the head will be simplified if the head washer is coated with a thin film of oil or vaseline and placed in position on the top of the cylinder. This will prevent the washer moving about during the fitting of the head, and possibly damaging the former when the holding-down pins are inserted.

Fig. 5.—WITH OVERHEAD CAMSHAFT ENGINES. Chain and camshaft sprocket securely supported by a wire hook to prevent them falling in the timing cover should the engine be revolved.

O.H.V. Tappet Tubes

On o.h.v. engines where rocker boxes are fitted, the push rods are enclosed by tubes, and to get at the former the lock nuts on either end of the latter are unscrewed and the tubes telescoped one inside the other.

To remove the push rods on all o.h.v. engines, special extractor tools are supplied by the makers. Two types have been used (see Fig. 8).

Pistons

On engines where cast-iron pistons have been used, the gudgeon pin was held in position by a thin steel band fitting in a groove.

On earlier models with aluminium pistons the gudgeon pins were held in position with a split cotter, and on later models with aluminium pistons

NOTES ON REPAIRS TO A.J.S. MOTOR-CYCLES

*Fig. 6.—*Cambox Cover removed for Inspection.

by means of small spring retaining rings inside the gudgeon-pin hole on either side of the piston.

In assembling care should be taken to see that in the case of the steel band fixing, this is below the outside diameter of the piston.

*Fig. 7.—*Removing Timing Cover.

Tap lightly at the back or on top with a mallet, at the same time pulling the cover away and keeping it square with the crankcase.

NOTES ON REPAIRS TO A.J.S. MOTOR-CYCLES

Always renew Gudgeon-pin Fixings

In the case of the split-cotter fixing, the original cotter should never be refitted. Always use a new one. The same applies to the spring-retaining rings where these are used, and special care should be taken to see that both these are fitted, as it is quite easy when repairs are being hurried forward for one to be missed. Also see that the retaining rings snap properly into their grooves, as if not, damage will be done by the gudgeon pin forcing the retaining ring against the cylinder wall.

Fig. 8.—Push-rod Extractor.

In the case of all gudgeon pins not held in position with retaining rings, the former are a force fit in the piston bosses, so that care should be taken to support the piston adequately when the gudgeon pin is removed or inserted.

Valve Timing

The correct setting for the valve timing on all A.J.S. engines is clearly marked on the timing wheels, as shown in Figs. 12 and 12A.

Singles

In the case of single-cylinder engines, the small timing wheel is stamped in one position with one dot, and in another position with two dots, these registering with similar marks on the inlet and exhaust camwheels.

Twins

In the case of twin-cylinder engines, there is an additional double camwheel which operates the two inlet valves. This double camwheel is marked with a

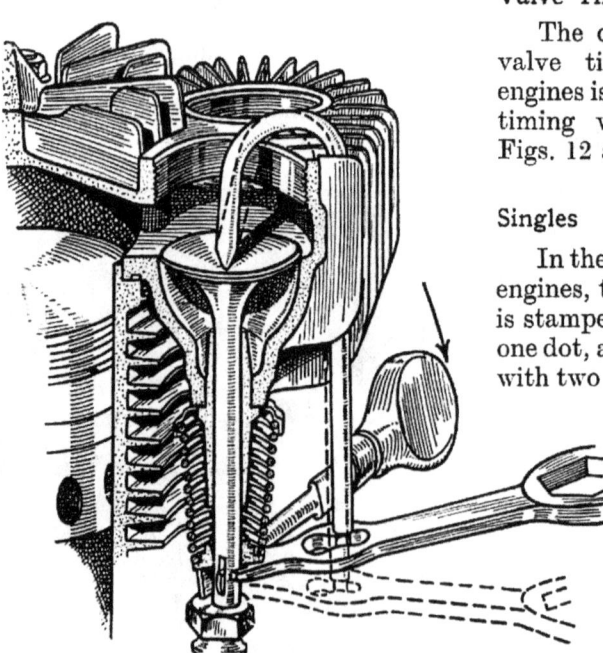

Fig. 9.—Using Valve Extractor.

This illustrates how to use a screwdriver in conjunction with the valve extractor to prevent the valve cone from canting on the stem. If this is not done an undue strain is put on the tool, which becomes distorted, as indicated by the dotted lines, and so loses its effectiveness.

NOTES ON REPAIRS TO A.J.S. MOTOR-CYCLES

Fig. 10.—Examining for Excessive Clearance between the Foot of the Tappet and the Stud at the Back by Twisting the Former with the Fingers.

"dash," which registers with a similar "dash" on the front exhaust camwheel.

O.H.C. Models

On overhead camshaft engines the small timing wheel is stamped with a dot which registers with a similar mark on the magneto driving sprocket. On this sprocket also is an arrow opposite the dot, which points to another arrow on the camshaft sprocket.

Main Bearings

Where plain bearings are fitted, and in case they have to be removed, first examine to see if a fixing screw is employed, as this should be taken out before the bush is driven out of the crankcase or otherwise damage may be done.

Big-end Bearing

If the flywheels have been completely dismantled, take

Fig. 11.—Making Airtight Joints on Twin Engines between the Induction and Inlet Pipes.

Slack off the locknuts on the inlet pipes which are screwed into the cylinder. Screw out the pipes until their faces are flush with those of the induction pipe, leaving no gap. The induction-pipe lock nuts should then be tightened up and afterwards the inlet-pipe nuts.

NOTES ON REPAIRS TO A.J.S. MOTOR-CYCLES

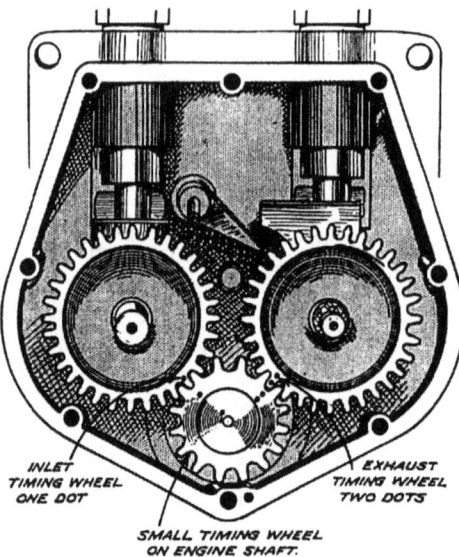

Fig. 12.—CORRECT SETTING OF TIMING WHEELS ON SINGLE-CYLINDER ENGINES.

care in assembling that a location peg is fitted to the crankpin, which registers with a slot in the flywheel. This is important, as the peg sets the position of holes drilled in the crankpin and up the web of the flywheel for oil feed to the big-end bearing.

Ignition Timing

All A.J.S. engines are provided with vernier adjustment. Fig. 14 shows this arrangement, a description of which might be useful.

The engine magneto driving sprocket is secured to its shaft by means of castellations which render wrong replacement impossible. The sprocket on the armature shaft of the magneto has a vernier adjustment which allows a very accurate and certain method of fixing the drive after the correct setting has been arrived at.

The setting of this vernier adjustment might sound a trifle complicated, but in reality it is quite simple. Fitted to the armature shaft on the magneto is a sleeve which has thirteen holes in a circle. Fitting over the collar on this sleeve is a magneto sprocket which has twelve holes similarly arranged.

On both the engine and the magneto sprockets will be found an arrow. These must point to each other when fitted in the chain. To do this, turn the engine

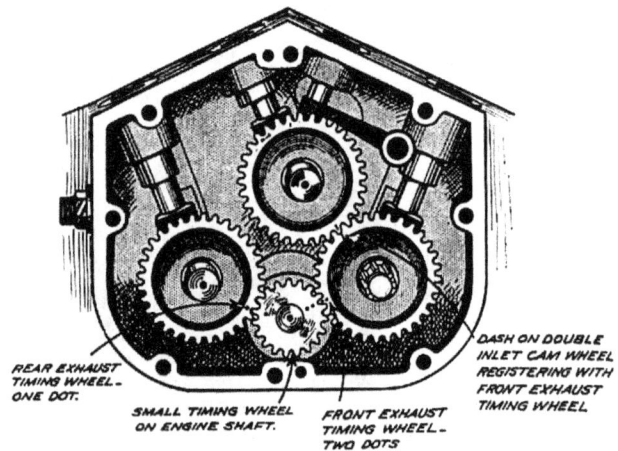

Fig. 12A.—TIMING-WHEEL SETTING ON TWIN-CYLINDER ENGINES.

over until the arrow on the driving sprocket is pointing directly towards the arrow on the magneto sprocket. The latter should be held free in the fingers, and moved

Fig. 13.—ADJUSTING MAGNETO CHAIN ON INCLINED ENGINES.

After the nuts on side of the platform have been slacked off, lever the latter up from the front. Note the chain inspection hole.

Fig. 13A.—ADJUSTING MAGNETO CHAIN ON VERTICAL ENGINES.

After slacking the pins under the magneto platform, lever with a screwdriver between the magneto and engine plates. No inspection hole and cover is provided on this model, but can be incorporated by the makers if required.

a tooth backwards or forwards in the chain until the correct setting is arrived at.

Having done this, place the magneto sprocket on the sleeve and turn the armature shaft of the magneto until the mark found punched over one

NOTES ON REPAIRS TO A.J.S. MOTOR-CYCLES

of the twelve holes on the sprocket registers exactly with a similar mark on the outside of the collar of the sleeve. It will now be found that the marked holes in the sleeve and sprocket respectively coincide, and the peg washer can be pushed into these holes, which effectively prevents the sprocket from moving from its correct setting when the sleeve lock nut is screwed up, without the possibility of the timing moving in the process, as is the case sometimes with other methods.

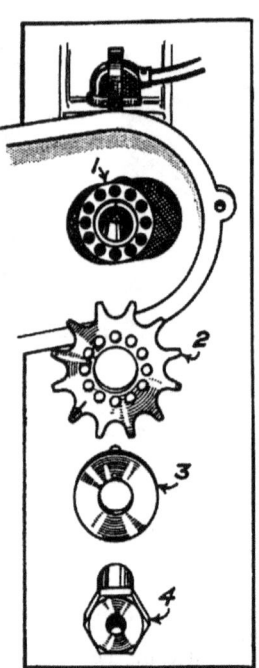

Fig. 14.—MAGNETO TIMING — VERNIER ADJUSTMENT.

1. Magneto sleeve.
2. Magneto sprocket.
3. Peg washer.　4. Sleeve lock nut.

As a means of verifying the timing, or if retiming is necessary on account of the sleeve having been disturbed, on the magneto armature shaft, the piston should be set its correct distance from the top of the compression stroke in the ordinary way, and the sleeve lock nut and peg washer should be removed. This will leave the armature shaft free from the engine drive, but still connected by the chain to the engine. See that the sprockets have their arrows facing each other, as previously mentioned, and that the marks on the sleeve collar and magneto sprocket register with each other. Set the contact-breaker points, fit the peg washer in the marked holes already mentioned, and tighten up the sleeve lock nut.

If the drive has been fixed up as before detailed, when dismantled at any time it can be put back without retiming.

If the one hole in the sleeve and in the magneto sprocket do not happen to be marked, it is well worth adding them, for reasons which will be obvious from the foregoing.

The vernier adjustment also provides a speedy means of altering the timing. First, remove the sleeve lock nut and peg washer from the magneto sprocket. Now, if the timing is to be advanced, fit the peg washer in the next hole to the left. This will advance the timing $\frac{1}{32}$ inch.

Fitting the peg washer in the next hole will give another $\frac{1}{32}$ inch, and so on.

To retard, work in the opposite direction.

TIMING CHARTS "A.J.S." ENGINES
1919–1928

MODELS.	INLET.		EXHAUST.		IGNITION MAX. ADV. Before T.D.C.	Tappet Clearance.	
	Opens before T.D.C.	Closes after B.D.C.	Opens before B.D.C.	Closes after T.D.C.		Ex.	In.
6 h.p., 1919-20 : Front Cylinder	0°	30°	54°	0°	35¼°	·008″	·006″
Rear Cylinder	0°	30°	50°	12°	35½°	·008″	·006″
3·49 h.p. Touring S.V., 1921	8½°	48°	58°	25°	37°	·008″	·006″
3·49 h.p. Sporting S.V., 1921	21½°	60°	60°	32½°	37°	·008″	·006″
3·49 h.p. Touring S.V., 1922-4	8½°	48°	58°	25°	37°	·008″	·006″
3·49 h.p. Sporting S.V., 1922-4	17½°	60°	53°	27°	42½°	·008″	·006″
7 h.p., 1921-8 : Front Cylinder	0°	27°	54½°	0°	34°	·008″	·006″
Rear Cylinder	0°	27°	51°	0°	34°	·008″	·006″
3·49 h.p. O.H.V., 1923-7	15°	58°	50°	25°	47°	·008″	·006″
3·49 h.p. Sporting S.V., 1925-7	15°	58°	50°	25°	37°	·008″	·006″
3·49 h.p. Touring S.V., 1925-7	15°	58°	50°	25°	38°	·008″	·006″
4·98 h.p. O.H.V., 1926-7	10°	33°	51°	5°	37°	·008″	·006″
4·98 h.p. S.V., 1927	15°	58°	50°	25°	38°	·008″	·006″
3·49 h.p. K3 S.V., 1928	20°	48°	48°	35°	34°	·008″	·006″
3·49 h.p. K4 & 5 S.V., 1928	20°	48°	48°	35°	43°	·008″	·006″
3·49 h.p. K6 O.H.V., 1928	20°	50°	50°	35°	46°	·008″	·006″
3·49 h.p. & 4·98 h.p. K7 & 10 O.H.C., 1928	30°	55°	50°	25°	52°	·018″	·016″
4·98 h.p. K8 O.H.V. & K9 S.V., 1928	20°	51°	61°	12°	37°	·008″	·006″
2·48 h.p. K12 S.V., 1928	17°	44°	41°	27°	39°	·008″	·006″

TIMING CHARTS "A.J.S." ENGINES
1929-1930

MODELS.	INLET.		EXHAUST.		IGNITION MAX. ADV. Before T.D.C.	Tappet Clearance.	
	Opens before T.D.C.	Closes after B.D.C.	Opens before B.D.C.	Closes after T.D.C.		Ex.	In.
9·96 h.p. M1 & 2, 1929	20°	51°	58°	13°	35°	·008"	·006"
3·49 h.p. M3 Touring S.V., 1929	20°	51°	50°	35°	37°	·008"	·006"
3·49 h.p. M4 & 5, Sporting S.V., 1929	20°	51°	50°	35°	40°	·008"	·006"
3·49 h.p. M6 O.H.V., 1929	20°	51°	50°	35°	45°	·008"	·006"
3·49 h.p. M7 Overhead Camshaft, 1929	30°	55°	50°	25°	53°	·018"	·016"
4·98 h.p. M8 O.H.V., 1929	20°	51°	50°	35°	37°	·008"	·006"
4·98 h.p. M9 Touring S.V., 1929	20°	51°	50°	35°	35°	·008"	·006"
4·98 h.p. M10 Overhead Camshaft, 1929	30°	55°	50°	25°	49°	·018"	·016"
2·48 h.p. M12 S.V., 1929	20°	51°	58°	13°	38°	·008"	·006"
9·96 h.p. R2 Touring S.V., 1930	20°	51°	58°	13°	35°	·008"	·006"
3·49 h.p. R4 & 5 Touring S.V., 1930	20°	51°	50°	35°	41°	·008"	·006"
3·49 h.p. R6 O.H.V., 1930	20°	51°	50°	35°	46°	·008"	·006"
3·46 h.p. R7 Overhead Camshaft, 1930	20°	55°	68°	25°	50°	·018"	·016"
4·98 h.p. R8 O.H.V., 1930	20°	51°	50°	35°	38°	·008"	·006"
4·98 h.p. R9 S.V. Touring, 1930	20°	51°	50°	35°	39°	·008"	·006"
4·95 h.p. R10 Overhead Camshaft, 1930	20°	55°	68°	25°	47°	·018"	·016"
2·48 h.p. R12 O.H.V., 1930	20°	51°	50°	35°	39°	·008"	·006"
1931							
9·96 h.p. S2 Touring S.V., 1931	20°	51°	58°	13°	35°	·008"	·006"
3·99 h.p. S4 S.V., 1931, & 3·49 h.p. S5 S.V., 1931	20°	51°	50°	35°	41°	·008"	·006"
3·49 h.p. S6 O.H.V., 1931	20°	51°	50°	35°	46°	·008"	·006"
3·49 h.p. S7 Overhead Camshaft, 1931	20°	55°	68°	25°	50°	·018"	·016"
4·98 h.p. S8 O.H.V., 1931	20°	51°	50°	35°	38°	·008"	·006"
4·98 h.p. S9 S.V., 1931	20°	51°	50°	35°	39°	·008"	·006"
4·98 h.p. S10 Overhead Camshaft, 1931	20°	55°	68°	25°	47°	·018"	·016"
2·48 h.p. S12 O.H.V., 1931	20°	51°	50°	35°	39°	·008"	·006"

1931

MODELS.	INLET.		EXHAUST.		IG-NITION MAX. ADV. Before T.D.C.	Tappet Clearance.	
	Opens before T.D.C.	Closes after B.D.C.	Opens before B.D.C.	Closes after T.D.C.		Ex.	In.
175 c.c. S.V. Standard 200 c.c. ,, ,, 250 c.c. ,, ,, 300 c.c. ,, ,, 350 c.c. ,, ,, 350 c.c. ,, "Aza".	12°	55°	50°	15°	35°	·006″	·004″
500 c.c. S.V. Standard 500 c.c. ,, Sports 550 c.c. ,, Standard 600 c.c. ,, ,, 600 c.c. ,, Sports	10°	50°	60°	20°	40°	·006″	·004″
680 c.c. S.V. Standard Twin 750 c.c. ,, ,, ,,	5°	40°	50°	25°	38°	·006″	·004″
980 c.c. S.V. A./C. and W./C. Twin	10°	50°	60°	20°	40°	·006″	·004″
980 c.c. S.V. 8-30 H.P. Twin	15°	60°	62°	22°	40°	·006″	·004″
175 c.c. O.H.V. Standard 200 c.c. ,, ,, 250 c.c. ,, ,, 300 c.c. ,, ,,	20°	60°	60°	25°	39°	·002″	·002″
350 c.c. O.H.V. Standard 350 c.c. S.V. Sports 400 c.c. ,, ,,	24°	55°	60°	30°	40°	·002″	·002″
500 c.c. O.H.V. Standard 600 c.c. ,, ,,	15°	55°	60°	22°	45°	·002″	·002″
500 c.c. O.H.V. Standard Twin 680 c.c. ,, ,, ,,	20°	50°	50°	20°	40°	·002″	·002″
1,000 c.c. O.H.V. Standard Twin 1,100 c.c. ,, ,, ,,	22°	60°	60°	20°	40°	·002″	·002″
175 c.c. O.H.V. Racing	20°	60°	60°	30°	35°	·002″	·002″
250 c.c. O.H.V. Racing 350 c.c. ,, ,,	24°	55°	62°	25°	40–48°	·002″	·002″
500 c.c. O.H.V. Racing 600 c.c. ,, ,,	22°	60°	60°	20°	38–50°	·002″	·002″
500 c.c. O.H.V. Racing Twin	24°	55°	62°	25°	42–50°	·002″	·002″
750 c.c. O.H.V. Racing Twin 1,000 c.c. ,, ,, ,, 1,100 c.c. ,, Sports W./C. Twin	22°	60°	60°	20°	38–50°	·002″	·002″

SPECIAL HINTS ON ARIEL MACHINES

By C. A. ELMHIRST BOOKER, M.Sc. (Eng.)

Fig. 1.—REMOVING THE CAMSHAFT SPROCKET.

The camshaft sprocket is threaded to take the extractor, which is shown being fitted; the nut is first removed. Pressure is brought to bear on the camshaft by the centre bolt of the extractor. The oil pump is at the bottom of the timing cover, where the three hexagon heads can be seen. The oil-inlet pipe is shown disconnected.

DISMANTLING ARIEL ENGINES

THE same method of dismantling can be followed for the side valve and overhead valve types of engine, the instructions given below dealing particularly with the o.h.v. model.

Taking down the Engine

After the engine has been removed from the frame, it should be cleaned down externally as far as possible, and then held in a vice by one of the crankcase lugs, the timing side of the engine being towards the mechanic. Normally, it will be found most convenient for the engine to be held by

SPECIAL HINTS ON ARIEL MACHINES

one of the rear lugs, so that it comes on the right of the vice. In the case of the 1929-31 250-c.c. engine, hold the crankcase by one of the front lugs.

Order of Dismantling

The most convenient order of dismantling is as follows:

First remove push rods by compressing the valve springs by means of a long screwdriver (placed over the rocker spindle greaser nut used as a fulcrum), the end resting under the rocker arm by the adjuster.

Fig. 2.—REMOVING THE CAM WHEEL. This will pull straight out as shown.

The Gasket

With the head off, prise up the copper gasket, using a penknife blade. If this gasket is removed carefully, it can be used over and over again, but should preferably be annealed on each occasion.

The Cylinder

The barrel is spigoted into the crankcase, but can be lifted straight off after the four cylinder-base securing nuts have been undone.

Removing " Square-Four " Cylinder Block

To remove the cylinder block on the " Square-Four " engine, take off the camshaft chain cover. Remove the camshaft driving sprocket, chain and spring-tensioning device. Next remove the front part of the magneto chaincase. The magneto drive can now be dismantled. The back half of the magneto chaincase is now quite free, and can be pulled off the locating spigot formed on the crankcase. Take off the magneto by undoing the securing strap. The eight cylinder-retaining nuts are now exposed, and when these have been removed the block can be lifted straight up.

Note that 1929-31 250-c.c. engines have five cylinder-retaining nuts—four in the conventional position in the cylinder flange, *and one inside the*

SPECIAL HINTS ON ARIEL MACHINES

tappet spring box. This latter nut is easily overlooked, and if any effort is made to prise up the cylinder before this nut has been undone, serious damage will result. Note also that the barrel on this engine is not spigoted into the crankcase, the retaining studs being used for locating purposes.

Piston

Remove the piston, which is secured to the connecting rod by a fully floating gudgeon pin.

Magneto Sprocket

Next take off the magneto chain cover and the magneto sprockets. If the sprockets have a thread cut for screwing on an extractor, use this (see Fig. 1); otherwise, prise off the sprocket by means of a couple of spanners, placed across a diameter at the back of the sprocket and used as levers. Both sprocket-securing nuts have right-hand threads.

Timing Cover

The timing cover is held by a number of cheese-headed screws, and can be pulled off when these have been removed. Do not forget to undo the two nuts securing the magneto platform to the front end of the chaincase, if the engine plates have not been taken off. The whole of the timing gear will then be exposed.

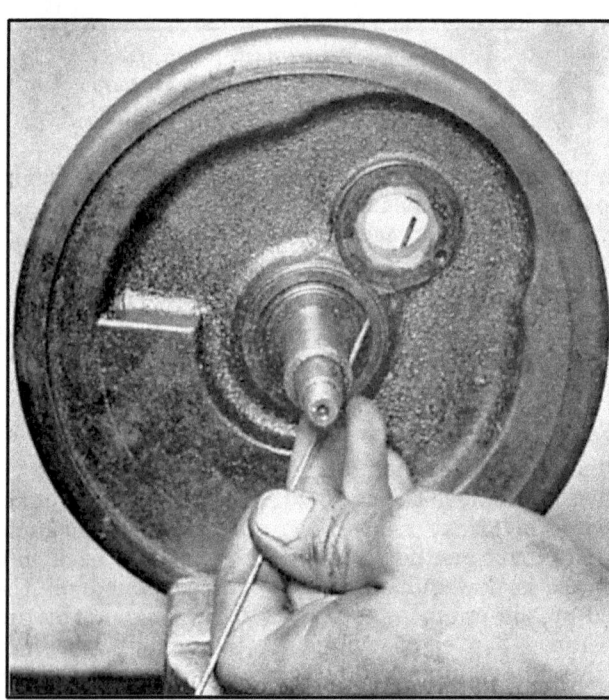

Fig. 3.—THE TIMING-SIDE FLYWHEEL (1926).
A spoke is used to make sure that the oil hole from the collector groove is clear.

Removing the Timing Gear

The cam wheel will pull straight out, and the cam levers will also pull off the cam-lever pin (see Fig. 2). Take out the tappets, noting which is the inlet

SPECIAL HINTS ON ARIEL MACHINES

and which is the exhaust. The oil pump, and part of the exhaust-valve lifter mechanism, will have come away with the timing case.

The timing pinion can be pulled off the mainshaft by means of the extractor. Note that the pinion-securing nut has a left-hand thread.

Removing the Shock-absorber Assembly

Turn the crankcase round in the vice, and remove the sprocket and shock-absorber assembly.

Fig. 4.—An Ariel Flywheel Assembling Jig in Use.

The two hollow mandrils are dead in line, and are also an accurate fit on the mainshafts, thus guaranteeing the mainshafts running true with each other. The right-hand mandril is adjustable sideways to allow the flywheel assembly to be slid in. The crankpin nuts are tightened by a long spanner against the " Vee " block placed between the flywheels.

Dismantling the Crankcase

Place the crankcase on the bench, and remove all the tiebolts holding together the two halves of the case, and tap outwards with a hide hammer one of the timing-side cylinder retaining studs. One or two gentle taps will be sufficient to free the spigot joint between the two halves of the crankcase without bending or damaging the threads of the stud.

Parting the Crankcase

On the " Square-Four " engine remove the large aluminium plate which carries the outer drive-shaft ball bearing. Undo the nuts, and then insert into three of the holes used for securing the primary chaincase three screws (¼ inch diameter × 20 t.p.i.), and screw these in so that their ends bear up against the crankcase and force the plate free. Now remove the

SPECIAL HINTS ON ARIEL MACHINES

plate which comes in line with the front crankshaft on the driving side. If the oil reservoir has not already been drained, do this now.

Now undo the set bolts, nuts, etc., holding together the two halves of the case, and take out the long bolt which screws up into the partition between the oil-reservoir and crankcase proper; this is located just in front of the drain plug. The top half of the case, complete with inner gearcase, crank assemblies, etc., can now be lifted clear.

The three big-end bearings working on overhung cranks can now be dismantled if required. The fourth bearing assembly follows normal single-cylinder engine practice where the flywheels are built up (Fig. 5).

Dealing with the Flywheel Assembly (Single-cylinder)

Lift off the timing side half of the crankcase. This leaves the flywheel assembly in the driving side half of the case. It will probably be found that the driving side mainshaft is sticking to the inner race of the ball bearing. Lightly polish, with a piece of fine emery cloth, as much of the mainshaft as is visible, so as to allow the ball bearing to slide freely once it has been moved on the shaft. If the shock-absorber spring collar did not come away with the other parts, remove it now. This collar fits into the case, up against the ball bearing, and has a shoulder on its outer face for the location of the shock-absorber spring.

Place a little oil and paraffin on the mainshaft. Hold the crankcase in both hands, horizontally, with the wheels above the case, and bump the end of the driving shaft downwards on to a block of hardwood. This should loosen the ballrace on the shaft, when the case can be pushed downwards, so sliding the bearing free of the shaft. If a little vigorous bumping does not move the inner race along the shaft, sterner measures must be employed. Get two blocks of wood, sufficiently thick to hold the flywheels and timing side shaft clear of the floor when the joint face of the crankcase is resting on their upper sides. This brings the wheels and half-case into a horizontal position, with the case on top, the case resting on the blocks, with the wheels held therein by the tightness of the ballrace on the shaft.

Place a soft metal drift on the end of the shaft, and give it a few vigorous blows with a fairly heavy hammer. This should free the bearing, when the wheels will drop out. A piece of wood placed on the floor just below the timing shaft will prevent any damage being done to the thread on the end of the shaft as the wheels drop clear.

Dismantling the Flywheels

To dismantle the flywheels, undo the lock screw and crankpin nut on the driving side, holding the wheels by the driving side flywheel only. Procure two solid blocks of wood, of equal thickness, and lay the flywheels, timing side wheel down, across the top of these two blocks. The blocks should be of such thickness that the timing side shaft does not rest

SPECIAL HINTS ON ARIEL MACHINES

on the bench. Now give a sharp blow with a hammer on the driving side flywheel, exactly opposite the crankpin, and near the edge of the wheel. One or two sharp blows given in this manner will break the taper joint between the flywheel and crankpin.

Special Note on decarbonising the " Square Four "

It is recommended that decarbonisation should be carried out about every 5,000 miles. This is perfectly simple, and is done as follows :

1. Remove the exhaust pipes, carburetter and sparking plugs.

2. Take off the distributer by pushing back the two spring clips.

3. Lift off the rocker-box cover ; this is held by four thumb nuts.

4. Disconnect the oil pipe to the rocker box at the point where it enters the oil restrictor ; this is attached to the front of the rocker box.

5. Undo the connection in the pressure pipe to the oil gauge : this connection is just above the rocker box.

6. Disconnect the camshaft drive.

Fig. 5.—" SQUARE FOUR" CRANKSHAFT ASSEMBLY.

The three connecting rods nearest the camera are the overhung type and the big-end bearings are dismantled by removing the nut and side plate. The one in the background is dismantled in a similar manner to the single cylinder type.

7. Remove the plug in the top of the chaincase.

8. Unscrew the camshaft-sprocket securing bolt and pull the sprocket off the shaft by means of the extractor provided.

9. Remove the two cheese-headed screws which are in line with the extractor.

10. Unscrew the head securing bolts and nuts.

11. Now carefully prise up the head from the barrel.

12. Put the head on the bench, taking care not to damage the distributor centre piece ; this is easily broken with careless handling.

SPECIAL HINTS ON ARIEL MACHINES

13. The carbon can now be scraped away from the combustion chambers, valve sprockets and ports.

The piston tops can be scraped by bringing each piston to the top of its stroke, and any carbon on the cylinder block can also be scraped away; take care not to damage the cylinder bores.

14. Reassemble in the reverse order.

REASSEMBLY WITH NOTES ON THE EXAMINATION OF PARTS
Mainshafts

If new mainshafts are being fitted, the chief point to watch is that the top face of the key is not touching the bottom of the keyway in the flywheel, or the shaft will pull up on this face and a small portion of the taper, the major portion of the taper not making contact. The two tapers must, of course, be clean, and the shaft should be pulled really tightly up into the taper hole in the wheel. A special long spanner is really required for this job, as there is insufficient leverage with the ordinary spanner; at the same time, do not overdo the tightening, or the centre boss in the wheel will probably crack (Fig. 8).

Assembling Flywheel—see to the Oilways

With 1929–31 vertical engines, the crankpin must be secured to the timing-side flywheel first, and the wheels can then be built up. Test the continuity of the oilways by forcing oil from an oilgun down the oilway in the timing-side shaft, and make sure that it exudes from the big end. Some crankpins have a peg projecting from the taper engaging with a keyway in the flywheel, so that oil-hole alignment is assured.

Con Rods and Crankpins

Having fitted the two shafts to their wheels, the crankpin should be secured to the timing side wheel. Assemble the rollers and connecting rod on to the big end, place the driving-side wheel on to the crankpin taper, and tighten up. If one of the Ariel flywheel assembling jigs (see Fig. 4) is not available, the usual method of lathe assembly must be followed.

When fitting Connecting Rod

When refitting the connecting rod, it is desirable to replace it the same way round; also, when pulling up the drive-side flywheel on to the crankpin taper, make sure that the connecting rod has from ·006 inch to ·012 inch sideplay. Taper joints will frequently pull up closer after being broken once or twice. If there is insufficient side clearance, the sides of the outer roller race should be carefully ground away.

On 1929–31 250-c.c. engines, should there not be the necessary side clearance, grind a little off the side of the connecting rod. Do not attempt

SPECIAL HINTS ON ARIEL MACHINES

Fig. 6.—Assembling the Shock Absorber.
The pressure of the spring is being held by one hand so that the sprocket binds on the shaft.

to fit distance shims on the crankpin. The connecting rod should be fitted so that the pinch bolt faces the front of the engine.

Examine the Cam-lever Pin

The cam-lever pin should be examined, and renewed if necessary. An examination of the inside of the crankcase will show that the end of the hole into which the pin is pressed, breaks through into the case. A small punch can therefore be used for driving out this pin. Sometimes this pin will be slightly loose in its housing. The remedy is to obtain a piece of steel tubing having a bore very slightly larger than the diameter of the pin, file off one end of the tube square, and to a sharp cutting edge, slip it over the pin, and drive it hard up against the face of the boss. This causes the aluminium to contract on to the pin, which is thus gripped tightly.

When fitting New Tappet Guides

When fitting new guides be careful not to drive them in to project below the inside face of the case.

SPECIAL HINTS ON ARIEL MACHINES

Timing Cover and Oil Pump

Before fitting the timing cover on the 1929–31 vertical engines see that the copper pipe which delivers oil into the hollow mainshaft is quite firm in the timing cover and is not bent at all (Fig. 13).

The joint between the cover and the crankcase is made with a paper washer, and it is most important to see that there is an *extra* paper washer, approximately ·005 inch thick, round the oil-joint pipe which projects from a boss on the crankcase and locates with an oilway in the back of the timing cover. The reason for this extra washer is to make quite certain that there is no air leak round this joint pipe.

With the 1929–31 250-c.c. engine see that there is an *additional* ·005-inch paper washer round the return oil connection; this is the short copper pipe which projects from the boss on the crankcase. The cover is not spigoted, but is located by two dowel pegs.

Now attend to the Oil Pump (Wet Sump Type)

Now examine the oil pump, which is fitted in the timing cover. The pump body is a light push fit into the cover, and is held in position by two small set screws. The inner end of the pump body is slightly taper, so that it slips easily into position until the flange is about an inch from the face of the cover. It should then require appreciable hand pressure to force the pump home. A loosely fitting pump will cause lubrication trouble. The single-plunger pump can be dismantled by screwing off the cap at the plunger end; the plunger and spring will then drop out. It is most probable that any wear will have taken place mostly on the plunger, so that fitting a new plunger to a worn pump is frequently effective. This saves the cost of replacing the pump body. The pump may also be put out of action by wear on the end of the plunger where this bears on the camshaft eccentric. Wear here will seriously upset the opening and closing of the ports in the pump body. This will naturally cause inefficient working of the pump. To avoid trouble see that the non-return valve or valves are kept free from dirt. With the disk type of valve make sure that the disk is flat, and that the coil spring is not bent or seriously weakened; also, note particularly that the valve seat in the pump body is perfectly flat.

Little need to dismantle Gear-type Pump

The oil pump on 1931 " Sloper " and " Square-Four " engines is of the gear type. This type of pump should neither be removed from the crankcase nor dismantled, unless either of these courses is obviously necessary. But if it is taken out, the most practical way of replacing it is to strip down the engine, part the crankcase, put the pump into position, and then insert the flywheels into the timing side of the crankcase. When fitting or taking out a pump, push straight in, or pull straight out, as the case may be. *Do not attempt to rotate it.*

SPECIAL HINTS ON ARIEL MACHINES

Now is the time to Reamer Main Bearings if Necessary

If a new timing side mainbush has been fitted, it will almost certainly require reamering. This is best done by bolting up the two halves of the case, and then inserting a special long reamer through the drive-side ball bearing; the axes of the two bearings will then come dead in line. If such a reamer is not available, the bush must be reamered out on its own, ignoring the possibility of a slight error in the alignment of the two shafts. This possible error will almost certainly be very small. Allow ·002 inch to ·003 inch clearance for the mainshaft. If the engine is to be carefully run in, and driven easily for some considerable time, the clearance can be slightly finer than this, but if it is to be used for hard work, get well up to the higher limit. The pressure of the boss on the bearing is likely to cause slight contraction of the bush when it heats up.

Fig. 7.—An Alternative Method of Truing Flywheels.

The periphery of the wheels is being rough-trued against a straight edge. These should afterwards be checked between centres of a lathe.

Reassembling the Crankcase

Lay the wheels, face downwards, on the bench, drive side on top; if there is a hole in the bench, so that the mainshaft can be slipped therein, allowing the wheels to lie flat, it will be found very useful. If there is no hole, use the wooden blocks, previously mentioned.

Now take one of the special hardened steel shims supplied for the purpose, and slip it over the drive side mainshaft; it will drop down into a small recess in the face of the flywheel. The shim must be of sufficient thickness to stand proud of the face of the boss, or a false clearance for the mainshaft endplay in the case will be obtained.

Next take the driving half crankcase and place it over the wheels, giving the case one or two gentle taps with a hide hammer, to make sure that the bearing has gone right home on the shaft. Hit the case outside the bearing housing, and close up to the shaft. Turn the wheels and case over, so that they are lying with the case downwards.

SPECIAL HINTS ON ARIEL MACHINES

Now take the other half of the crankcase, see that the two joint faces are perfectly clean, place the timing half case into position, and bolt the two halves together.

Stand the case upright and, using the hide hammer, tap the end of the timing shaft; this ensures that the wheels are hard over against the drive side ball bearing. Measure the distance along the drive shaft from the face of the crankcase to the shoulder at the outer end of the splines. Now give the end of the drive shaft several light blows along its axis; this drives the wheels over to the timing side main bearing.

Measure along the shaft again; the difference in the readings gives the endplay on the mainshaft. This should be approximately from ·008

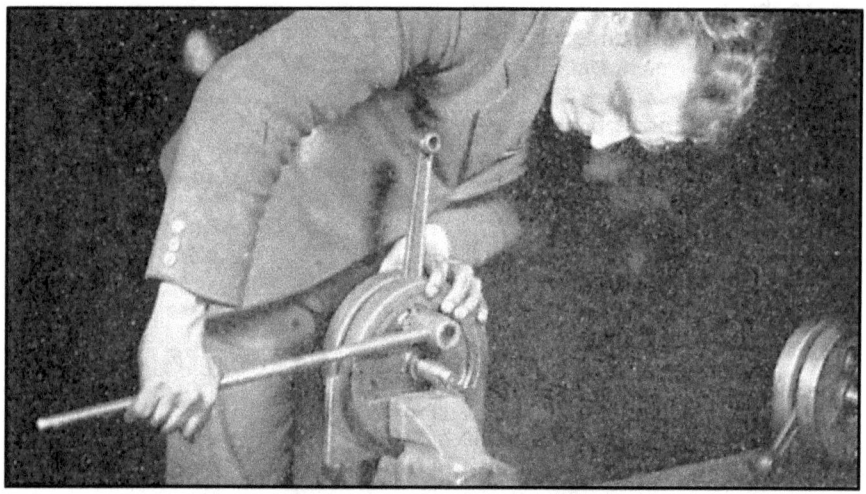

Fig. 8.—Crankpin being tightened up.

This takes place after the flywheels are trued. A long spanner is used, and a distance piece is placed between the flywheels to prevent straining the crankpin bosses.

inch to ·012 inch. If the clearance is less than this, a thinner mainshaft shim must be inserted. Recollect, however, that this shim must be thick enough to stand proud of the face of the flywheel boss. If it does not, the boss may rub against the outer race of the ball bearing.

If sufficient clearance cannot be obtained by means of this shim, it shows that the shoulder on the timing side bush was slightly thick, and the inner end of this bush must be faced down.

Correcting Excessive Endplay

If, however, as is probably the case, the end movement is excessive, correct by inserting a thicker or an additional shim. These shims are obtainable in seven thicknesses, gauges 12–17 and 27. When the correct

SPECIAL HINTS ON ARIEL MACHINES

end clearance has been obtained, carefully bolt up the two halves of the crankcase, making the joint with some suitable jointing compound. The manufacturers use this in preference to a paper washer. Be careful not to get a step between the two halves of the case, on the face on which the cylinder barrel seats. Place a straightedge over the joint, and, if necessary, give one side of the case one or two gentle taps with a hide hammer, so as to rotate the half case, relative to the other half, so bringing the two halves properly into register.

With the wheels correctly assembled in the case, the connecting rod will come practically in the centre of the aperture into which the barrel fits. Should the connecting rod be appreciably to one side or the other, the error must be corrected.

Piston

Test the fit of the piston in the barrel. Standard clearances with new piston and new barrel on 1926–28 engines are as follows :

Ring land	·016 to ·018 inch
Below rings, s.v. . . .	·007 ,, ·009 ,,
,, ,, o.h.v. . . .	·008 ,, ·010 ,,
Bottom of skirt	·010 ,, ·012 ,,

Test the fit of the piston rings, both in the barrel and in the piston-ring grooves. The correct gap between the ends of the rings when they are tried in the barrel should be from ·006 to ·008 inch, when new. The rings should fit in the piston-ring grooves freely, but without perceptible up-and-down play. The gudgeon pin should be just a free fit in the small-end bush, but can be inclined to tightness in the piston bosses, as the expansion of the aluminium piston when the engine becomes warm will give the necessary working clearance. It is imperative to see that the gudgeon-pin end pads are tight in the pin ; a loose pad *must* be replaced, or it will certainly break up inside the engine, resulting, probably, in the scrapping of the piston and cylinder. If a new pad is fitted, test the endplay of the pin in the cylinder bore : there must be a slight clearance. If it is necessary to remove metal from the end pad to prevent binding in the cylinder bore, it should be taken off the back of the shoulder before fitting, as the outer face of the end pad is carefully machined, to correspond to the contour of the barrel. The gudgeon-pin end pad of the " Two-Port " engine is not interchangeable with that of " Single-Port " engines.

Where to measure Oval Pistons

The 1930 and 1931 vertical engines are fitted with pistons which are slightly oval, the difference in the diameters of the piston when measured in line with the gudgeon-pin hole and on an axis at right angles to this is approximately ·010 inch ; therefore, always measure piston clearances on

SPECIAL HINTS ON ARIEL MACHINES

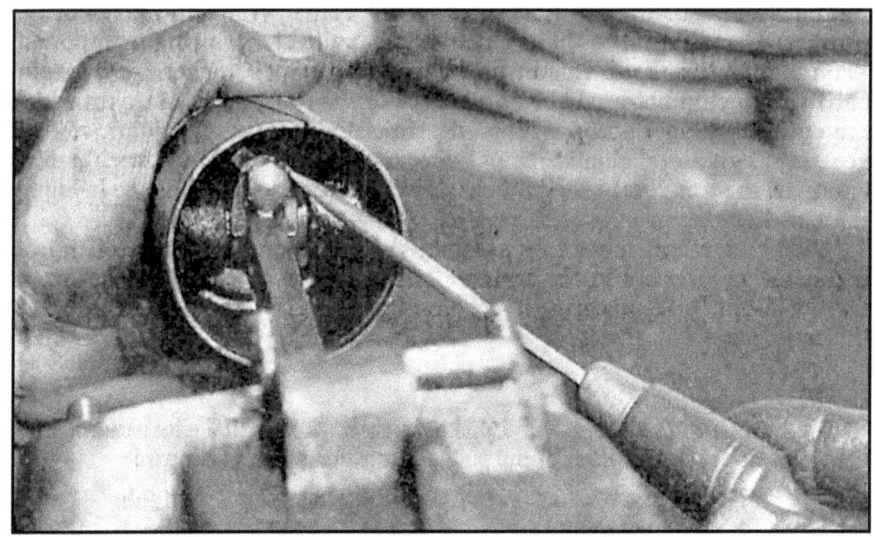

Fig. 9.—Removing the Piston (250-c.c. Engine).
A screwdriver is used to prise up the locking-washer ear, and the bolt can then be unscrewed, after which the gudgeon pin will push out.

the bearing faces of the piston, i.e. on the axis at right angles to the gudgeon pin. The correct clearances with new piston and cylinder are as follows:

	Std. S.V. and O.H.V. engines.	H.C. Piston for O.H.V.
Ring land	·025 to ·027 inch	·025 to ·027 inch
Below rings	·009 ,, ·011 ,,	·011 ,, ·013 ,,
Bottom of skirt	·004 ,, ·006 ,,	·004 ,, ·006 ,,

250-c.c. Engine Pistons

The latest oval-type piston, which is used on the 1930–31 models of the 250-c.c. engine, and which is being supplied for replacement purposes for the 1929 models, has, however, the following clearances, measured on an axis at right angles to the gudgeon pin :

Ring land	·018 to ·021 inch
For $\tfrac{5}{16}$ inch below bottom ring	·009 ,, ·011 ,,
Top of skirt	·007 ,, ·009 ,,
Bottom of skirt	·003 ,, ·005 ,,

The piston rings should be free in their grooves, but with no tendency to up-and-down movement, and the rings when tried in the cylinder should have from ·004 inch to ·006 inch clearance between their ends.

SPECIAL HINTS ON ARIEL MACHINES

Fig. 10.—The Pumps are driven from a Common Sliding Block.

The "Square-Four" Engine Pistons

The correct clearances of the aluminium alloy pistons on the "Square Four" are:

Ring land	·017 to ·019 inch
For ¼ inch below bottom ring	·007 ,, ·009 ,,
Top of skirt . . .	·006 ,, ·008 ,,
Bottom of skirt . . .	·004 ,, ·006 ,,

The pistons are numbered, and should always be replaced in their own cylinders, and the same way round.

The piston rings should have approximately ·001 inch up-and-down clearance in their grooves, whilst the gap between the ends of the rings when tried in the cylinder should be from ·004 inch to ·006 inch.

O.H.V. Barrel

Examine the barrel for scores due to piston seizures, and for ridges top and bottom due to ordinary wear. Ridges, if present, will be most noticeable at the top, about ⅛ inch below the spigot joint. Not infrequently a brightly polished mark will be found down one or both sides of the cylinder in line with the gudgeon pin. This is the result of the polishing action of the soft gudgeon-pin end pad, and, in general, does not indicate wear. If, however, dirt or grit has got into the hollow gudgeon pin, or has become embedded in the soft end pads, there may have been sufficient abrasion to cause a very serious groove. The standard works' oversizes

SPECIAL HINTS ON ARIEL MACHINES

Fig. 11.—REMOVING SUMP PLATE AND FILTER.

Undo the four bolts from the bottom of the crankcase. The oil pipe, drawing the oil for return to the tank, can be seen, and care should be taken that the pipe is inserted in the hole in the filter when the latter is refitted.

for reboring are ·020 and ·040 inch. See that the spigot-joint face is clean and not scratched. If gases have been blowing past, the joint face will have a blackened appearance. Examine the copper head gasket, and have it ready for replacement.

In fitting the cylinder barrel on to the crankcase, see that the gaps in the rings are diametrically opposed to one another. Use a paper washer and jointing compound between the cylinder base and the crankcase. Use a composition washer between the block and the crankcase on the " Square-Four " and smear both sides with jointing compound. Tighten down the retaining nuts evenly and firmly, working round the barrel, tightening each nut a little at a time, until all are secure.

S.V. Cylinder

Examine the barrel for wear, as described above, for the o.h.v. model. In this case, it will probably not be possible to feel a ridge at the top, as a result of wear, as the top piston ring should just touch the edge of the counterbore. Therefore, test for wear by means of a micrometer gauge. Valves should also be attended to (see notes under o.h.v. head). Originally, these valves were interchangeable, but in 1928 a better quality steel

SPECIAL HINTS ON ARIEL MACHINES

was introduced for the exhaust valve, and it is preferable to use this latest type valve for the exhaust. Inlet valves are stamped 2.S.11, while exhaust valves are stamped J.H.3.

O.H.V. Head

Examine joint face as for the barrel, and make sure that the top of the spigot on the barrel is not bottoming in the recess in the head into which it fits. There should be approximately $\frac{1}{64}$ inch clearance here, the joint coming on the wide faces above and below the gasket in the 1926 machines and a plain metal-to-metal joint for 1927. Use a jointing compound. Test the fit of the valves in the guides.

O.H.V. Rocker Gear

On 1926 engines, if a new rocker is tight between the plates, a small amount can be ground off the end, or, alternatively, should the rocker be slack, suitable pen-steel distance shims can be obtained to take up the clearance. Shoulders on the rocker spindles pull up against the inner faces of the side plates, so that if a shim is inserted, take care not to trap it between this shoulder and the plate.

In examining the rockers for wear, particularly note the condition of the end of the arm, where it bears upon the valve-stem end cap. If serious flats have formed, replacement is desirable; also, test the fit of the adjuster in the tapped hole through the outer arm. Any undue sloppiness may result in a stripped thread. In handling these adjusting screws, remember that they are hardened, and that the thread is therefore liable to chip if handled carelessly. The adjusting screw lock nut is normally placed above the rocker arm, but it is useful to remember that the placing of the nut below the arm will sometimes help out a loose thread until a replacement can be obtained. Make quite sure that the end of the rocker arm is striking the valve-stem end cap squarely, and that it is not to one side or the other of the cap when viewed from the front or rear.

If the rocker box on 1929–31 vertical engines becomes loose between the side plates through the compression of the fibre washers, it is quite sound to insert several thick brown-paper washers, between one of the fibre washers and the side plate, so as to take up the clearance.

Timing Gear

Before replacing the timing gear, carefully examine for wear, at the following places:

CAMS.—Along the track of the cam lever, particularly where the lever is on the lift; also examine the teeth of the cam wheel.

TIMING PINION.—Examine the teeth, especially those which are in mesh with the cam wheel when the cam levers are on the lift. This, of course, is during the period of greatest load.

SPECIAL HINTS ON ARIEL MACHINES

CAM LEVERS.—Examine the feet, where they are in contact with the cams. As wear takes place, a series of flats will form on the cam-lever feet, causing uneven valve action, and probably valve bounce at high engine speeds. Also examine the top of the cam lever where the tappet foot bears.

Reassembling Timing Gear

When reassembling the timing gear on 1926–28 engines, fit the inlet cam lever first, and then the exhaust cam lever. See that the oil hole for the cam-lever pin bearing comes on top ; this, incidentally, ensures that the cam levers are fitted the correct way up. Fit the timing pinion on to the mainshaft, seeing that the key is properly in position. Ignore, for the moment, the three keyways, and do not fit the securing nut : just drive the pinion home on to the taper. Insert the cam wheel so that the cam levers

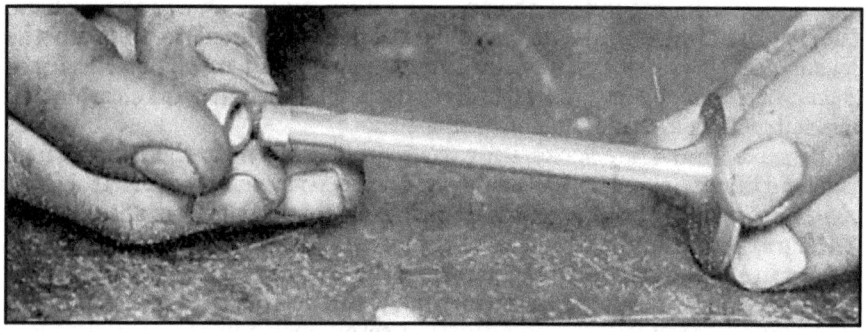

Fig. 12.—END CAPS TO VALVES.
Hardened steel end caps should always be fitted to the ends of the valves as shown.

are on the base of the cams, i.e. neither valve is on the lift, and drop the tappets into their guides. Slip the timing cover into position, and gently tap it home with a hide hammer. The cover is located on the face of the crankcase by means of a shallow spigot, so that it will be held in position.

Timing the Valves

Without rotating the engine, fit the push rods, and adjust the valve clearance so that the push rods will rotate freely but with no trace of up-or-down motion. In the case of s.v. engines give the inlet tappet ·002 inch, and the exhaust tappet ·004 inch clearance. Now pull off the timing cover, and rotate the engine until the inlet valve is just opening and the exhaust valve is just closing ; this is the period of overlap. Pull the timing pinion off the mainshaft, and then rotate the engine until the piston is at T.D.C. The valves, of course, have not moved. Refit the timing pinion, and replace the timing cover. Fit a timing disk to the

SPECIAL HINTS ON ARIEL MACHINES

drive-side mainshaft, and ascertain the valve timing obtained. Suppose the valve timing is, say, 25° early. Now the cam wheel has 40 teeth, while the timing pinion has 20; therefore, one tooth on the cam wheel is equal to 18° of rotation of the crankshaft, or, in other words, altering the mesh of the cam wheel with the timing pinion by one tooth alters the timing by 18°.

If the timing cover is removed, the cam wheel drawn out of mesh with the timing pinion, rotated clockwise one tooth, and then slipped back into mesh with the timing pinion, the timing will have been retarded by 18°, so that the error is now only 7°. Use can now be made of the three keyways provided in the timing pinion. These keyways are spaced equi-distantly, so that if one keyway is coincident with one of the timing pinion teeth, the next keyway will be $6\tfrac{2}{3}$ teeth away, and the re-

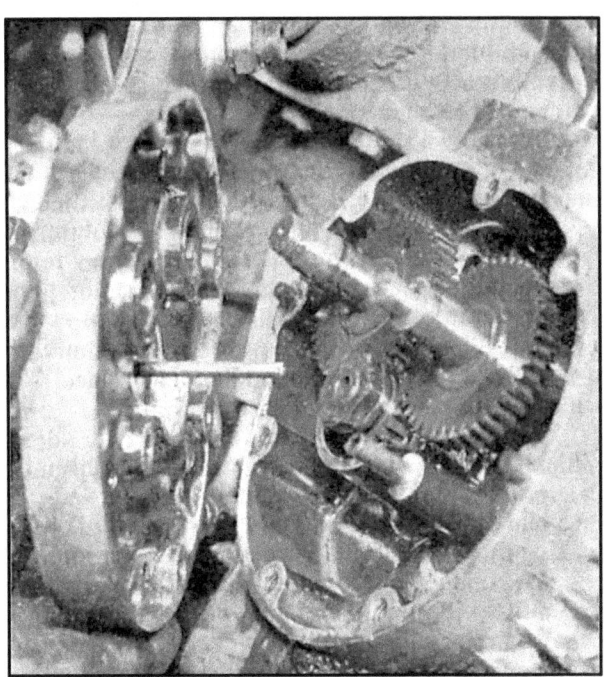

Fig. 13.—REPLACING TIMING COVER.

Make sure the oil pipe is tight in timing cover and carefully insert into the mainshaft. The return oil pipe can be seen projecting from the tiny case.

maining keyway $13\tfrac{1}{3}$ teeth away; that is to say, the keyway enables a variation of valve timing to be obtained of $\tfrac{1}{3}$ of a pitch on the timing pinion. With 20 teeth on the timing pinion, there are 18° per pitch, so that the keyways will vary in timing by 6°; therefore, the timing can be set to within plus or minus 3°. Suppose the pinion is withdrawn from the shaft and rotated one keyway clockwise, then to remesh with the cam wheel, the cam wheel must be rotated either $\tfrac{1}{3}$-pitch clockwise, which will retard the valve timing by 6°, or rotated $\tfrac{2}{3}$-pitch anticlockwise, which will advance the timing 12°. Similarly, if the pinion is rotated anticlockwise by one keyway, to remesh with the cam wheel, the cam wheel must be rotated by $\tfrac{1}{3}$-pitch anticlockwise, giving an advance of timing of 6°, or rotated $\tfrac{2}{3}$-pitch clockwise, which will retard the timing 12°.

SPECIAL HINTS ON ARIEL MACHINES

The error which remained was 7° early ; therefore, to get the valve timing as near as possible, it must be retarded by 6°, which will leave an error of only 1° early. From the summary above, it is seen that all that is required is to pull the timing pinion off the shaft, rotate one keyway clockwise, and then replace, at the same time rotating the cam wheel ⅓-pitch clockwise. It is most improbable that the points of opening and closing of each valve will come dead right, so that a slight compromise must be made, if necessary, the nearest correct timing being obtained. Actually a few degrees one way or the other will make no perceptible difference to the engine performance.

The valve timing of 1929–31 engines is not variable, as the correct cutting of teeth and keyways ensure that, with the timing marks in register, the valves are always correctly timed.

Timing of 1929–31 250-c.c. engines is obtained when the marked teeth on the inlet and exhaust cam wheels are brought into mesh with the corresponding marked teeth on the timing pinion. To set the valve timing, rotate the flywheels until the two centre dotted teeth on the timing pinion are pointing to approximately ten o'clock and two o'clock, regarding the pinion as a clock face. Then insert the two cam wheels, with the marked teeth meshing.

Before finally fitting the timing cover, do not forget to do up the pinion-securing nut, and see that the Tilson lock washer is replaced between the nut and the pinion. The turned-up tab on the washer fits into one of the keyways, and the other tab is then turned over on to the locking nut. The joint between the cover and the case is a plain metal-to-metal one ; therefore, see that the faces are perfectly clean and flat. Use a little jointing compound on the faces. Replace the cover and see that the cheese-head securing screws are done up deadtight. Goldsize is a very good jointing medium. If the oil pump has already been fitted to the timing cover, the following hint in connection with the fitting of the cover will be found useful. If, before any attempt is made to fit the timing cover, the engine is rotated so as to bring the highest part of the oil-pump drive eccentric on the camshaft to the extreme front of the engine, the oil-pump plunger will slip on to the base of the eccentric with the oil pump screwed right home in the timing case.

Special Note on " Two-Port " Timing Gear

For further tuning up of the 1927 " Two-Port " o.h.v. engine, the 1926 o.h.v. cam wheel can be fitted. The sides of the roller-ended cam levers will foul the cams at two points, and the cam levers must therefore be very slightly ground away, so as to give the necessary clearance. These points of contact come on the cam levers, just beneath the roller pins. The inlet cam lever fouls the exhaust cam, and vice-versa. This is due to the fact that the cam lever is wider than the cam, so that the inner side of the exhaust cam lever overhangs the inlet cam, and when the cams rotate,

SPECIAL HINTS ON ARIEL MACHINES

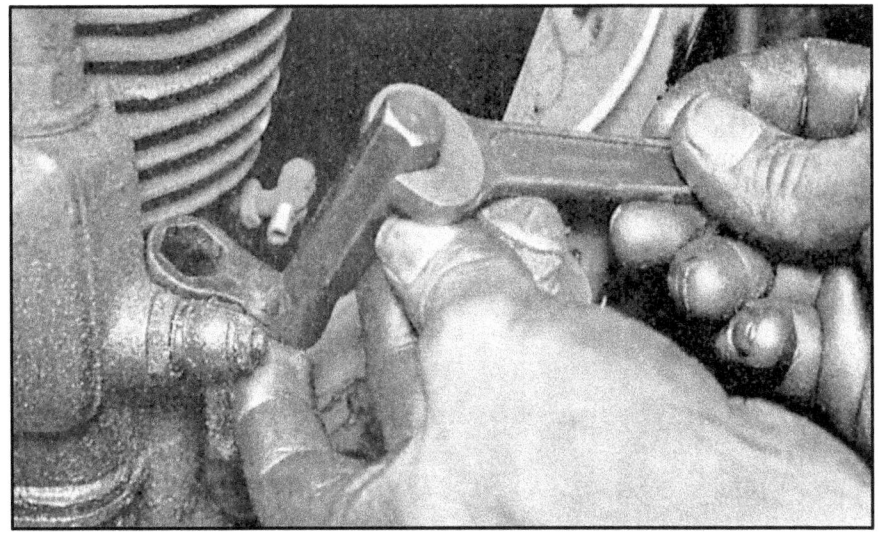

Fig. 14.—For Tight Corners.
A special spanner is used to undo the cylinder-base nuts behind the tappet case, which might otherwise be rather inaccessible.

there is one particular point where the inlet cam will foul the exhaust lever; similarly for the inlet lever. To ascertain just where this point of contact occurs, assemble the cam levers into the timing case, smear the cams with a little blue, insert the cam wheel into the case, and rotate; then see where the cam levers have been blued, and grind away a little metal at this point. It should not be necessary to grind away more than about $\frac{1}{32}$ inch.

Correct Valve and Magneto Timing

The correct valve and magneto timing is given on a separate chart.

Shock Absorber

If the engine-shaft shock absorber is of the spring-loaded, cam-faced type, the cam-faced slider is affixed to the mainshaft by means of splines and grooves. Examine these, and more particularly the points of the two cams which engage with recesses on the sprocket. Undue wear on either the cam face of the slider or the cam groove in the sprocket, will be liable to cause slip through these parts coming out of engagement. The correct order of reassembly is : (1) shock-absorber spring collar, with smaller diameter outwards, so that the shoulder forms an abutment for the shock-absorber spring; (2) dynamo driving sprocket, if fitted; (3) shock-absorber spring; (4) spring retainer, where fitted; (5) the slider; (6) the sprocket; (7) hardened steel washer; (8) nuts and washer.

SPECIAL HINTS ON ARIEL MACHINES

A little difficulty may be experienced in starting the first lock nut on the thread on the end of the mainshaft. The easiest method of fitting the nut is as follows (see Fig. 6):

With the engine in the vice, drive side outwards, stand squarely in front of the mainshaft. Have the washer and nut near to the right hand. Place the sprocket in position, and push it back on the mainshaft with both hands, slightly compressing the spring, so that the sprocket is pushed evenly on both sides. Then push hard with the left hand, taking the right hand away, and slip the washer on to the shaft and start the nut on the thread. The action of holding the sprocket with one hand only causes the sprocket to tip slightly on the shaft, so that it binds and is not difficult to hold with the one hand. Screw up the inner nut dead-tight, using a set spanner, and give the end of the spanner several sharp taps with a hammer to ensure its being screwed right home. Then do up the locking nut. Note that the washer between the inner nut and the sprocket is a hardened one, as it has to take the rubbing action of the sprocket, as this moves as a result of the power stroke and the restraining action of the spring. These locking nuts do *not* form a means of varying the shock-absorber springs tension. They must always be done up tightly so that the hardened washer is gripped up against the shoulder on the shaft. Grease the mainshaft, slider, cam face, sprocket, etc., before reassembling, and lubricate this part as frequently as possible.

Fig. 15—" Cut-away " View of the " Square Four."

Showing the general " lay-out." Note the magdyno and camshaft chains and the spring blade tensioning device to the latter. The gear pump at the base of the crankcase is also shown.

The order of assembly with 1931 " Sloper " engines is as follows: first, driving member on the mainshaft, then engine sprocket at the back of the driving member, sliding member, spring, spring collar and locking sleeve. It is not necessary to disturb the driving member to remove any parts of the shock-absorber assembly; just undo the locking sleeve and leave the driving member in position on the shaft. To remove the driving member use the extractor provided in the tool kit.

TIMING CHART FOR ARIEL MOTOR-CYCLES

1931

MODELS.	INLET. Opens before T.D.C.	INLET. Closes after B.D.C.	EXHAUST. Opens before B.D.C.	EXHAUST. Closes after T.D.C.	IGNITION MAX. ADV. before T.D.C.
LB31. 250 c.c. S.V.	5°	50°	55°	20°	42°
LF31. 250 c.c. O.H.V.	5°	50°	55°	20°	42°
SB31. 577 c.c. S.V.	5°	50°	55°	20°	38°
SF31. 499 c.c. O.H.V.	5°	55°	60°	20°	40°
SG31. 499 c.c. O.H.V.	22°	70°	70°	25°	40°
VB31. 557 c.c. S.V.	5°	50°	55°	20°	38°
VF31. 497 c.c. O.H.V.	5°	55°	60°	20°	38°
4F31. 497 c.c. O.H.C. 4-cyl.	10°	50°	55°	15°	35–40°

1930

LB. 250 c.c. S.V.	5°	50°	55°	20°	42°
LF. 250 c.c. O.H.V.	5°	50°	55°	20°	42°
E. 500 c.c. O.H.V.	5°	55°	60°	20°	38°
F. 500 c.c. O.H.V.	5°	55°	60°	20°	38°
G. 500 c.c. O.H.V.	22°	70°	70°	25°	42°
A. 550 c.c. S.V.	5°	50°	55°	20°	38°
B. 500 c.c. S.V.	5°	50°	55°	20°	38°

1929

LB. 250 c.c. S.V.	5°	50°	55°	20°	42°
LF. 250 c.c. O.H.V.	5°	50°	55°	20°	42°
E. 500 c.c. O.H.V.	5°	55°	60°	20°	38°
F. 500 c.c. O.H.V.	5°	55°	60°	20°	38°
A. 550 c.c. S.V.	5°	50°	55°	20°	38°
B. 550 c.c. S.V.	5°	50°	55°	20°	38°
Racing cam (for models E & F only).	22°	70°	70°	25°	42°

1928

A. 550 c.c. S.V.	5°	50°	55°	20°	38°
B. 550 c.c. S.V.	5°	50°	55°	20°	38°
C. 500 c.c. O.H.V. } 1-port engine	5°	50°	55°	20°	38°
D. 500 c.c. O.H.V. }	5°	50°	55°	20°	38°
E. 500 c.c. O.H.V. 2-port engine	5°	55°	60°	20°	38°
Racing cam (for model E only)	22°	70°	70°	25°	42°

TAPPET CLEARANCES

Correct running clearance for O.H.V. engines is nil when cold.*
Correct running clearance for S.V. engines is ·002" inlet, ·004" exhaust when cold.

* 4F31 inlet is ·002", exhaust is ·004".

REPAIRING B.S.A. ENGINES

By J. Earney, M.I.M.T.

UP to the introduction in the 1927 range of the sloping type o.h.v. engine, the B.S.A. design of engine might be said to embrace "accepted practice." With the exception of the 3·49-h.p. o.h.v., all models, both single and twin, were straightforward side-valve lay-outs, robust, sturdy, and generally considered very reliable. Consequently repairs and adjustments closely follow on the lines already dealt with in a general sense.

2·49-H.P. MODEL

Dismantling of the engine unit is quite a straightforward job. The exhaust pipe is pushed on the exhaust port stump, and is held in position by a half clip bolted on the lower crankcase bolt. The piston is aluminium alloy, and has three rings—the bottom one is chamfered and is an oil scraper returning surplus oil through the small holes drilled below the ring groove. The gudgeon pin is a push fit in the piston, and is fitted with end pads. These should always be examined, and if loose be replaced by new ones.

Timing Gear

In detaching the timing cover it will be noted on later models that small lugs project beyond the faces of the joint. If a drift is carefully used behind these no damage can occur to the joint. The mechanical oil pump is fitted to the timing cover, and is driven by the magneto idler pinion, the shaft of which is slotted to engage with the flat tongue of the pump. This will be dealt with later. The magneto is driven by a train of gear pinions. The small one on the mainshaft is fitted with a key and is secured with a castellated nut and lock washer. The pinion is easily pulled off the parallel shaft after the lock nut and washer have been removed.

A Note in Passing

The valve timing is marked on all three pinions. The "dash" mark on the small pinion should mesh with the inlet cam pinion, whilst the dot mark on the inlet should mesh with the exhaust cam pinion. It sometimes happens that the timing mark on the small pinion is covered by the lock washer and nut.

*Fig. 1.—*Assembling the Cush Drive.
A simple tool as shown can be made to assist in compressing the spring, at the same time allowing clearance to fit the lock ring (the shouldered one first).

Fitting Tappet Guides

The tappet guides are pressed into the crankcase and secured by a plate which is in turn bolted to the crankcase. This plate also acts as a support for the exhaust lift lever. After the plate has been removed, the guides can be withdrawn by a long bolt and a piece of steel tubing as recommended for the removal of small-end bushes and valve guides. New ones are replaced by reversal of the operation.

Magneto Pinion

This is removed by a drawer. It will be noticed that there is an oil-retaining washer fitted to the case by three screws at the back of the pinion.

Removing the Cush Drive

The cush drive is most easily removed as a complete assembly. A hexagon-headed sleeve nut will be noticed almost hidden in the centre of the assembly; unscrew this and remove the cush drive.

Replacing the Cush Spring

Should it be necessary to replace the spring, refit the complete assembly temporarily to the shaft, doing up the nut finger tight, just sufficient to hold the cush steady. Undo the two lock rings, preferably using the special "Cee" spanner supplied in the tool kit. The assembly will then fall apart. When reassembling it may be possible to compress the new spring sufficiently with one hand to allow the first lock ring (note: the shouldered one) to be started on the thread. This depends, however, largely on the physical ability of the operator, otherwise a "jaw" can be easily made up of an odd length of steel bar about $\frac{3}{4} \times \frac{3}{16}$ inch. This device can be seen in use in Fig. 1. The remainder of the assembly is removed from the shaft, and if the new spring is fitted in conjunction with the jaw and compressed in a vice, plenty of thread is exposed to allow the shouldered lock ring to be screwed on several threads. The jaw is pulled out sideways after the assembly has been removed from the vice. The compression of the spring is adjustable by screwing the inner lock ring in the required direction. Always lock the outer lock ring tightly. Finally, pour a few drops of oil on the cam faces and the splines.

Main Bearings

On taking apart the crankcase it will be seen that the mainshaft bearing is a plain shouldered bush on the timing side and a ballrace fitted to the driving side. The ballrace can be replaced, as already advised for other makes of engines.

Rebushing the Timing-side Bearing

The method of rebushing is as usually applied when fitting a phosphor-bronze bush into an aluminium casting. The bush should be a good press fit into the housing, and needs the steady pressure of a hand press to force it into position. In cases where the bush has been loose in the aluminium housing, it will be necessary to have the housing turned true and an oversize bush specially made. The bush will also have to be reamered or scraped to fit the shaft, oilways cut and cleaned up as already directed in similar cases with other makes. The B.S.A. design uses a small dowel

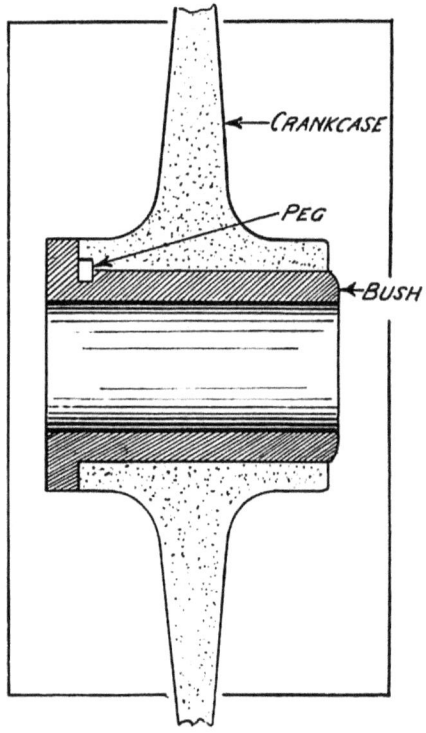

Fig. 2.—MAINSHAFT BEARING.
Note the small dowel peg which retains the bush.

REPAIRING B.S.A. ENGINES

peg to retain the bush. The bush is already partly drilled just behind the shoulder when purchased. The peg is fitted into this, and also registers with a hole drilled in the crankcase (Fig. 2). It is necessary, therefore, to see that the hole in the bush is in direct line with the one in the crankcase housing, and then, before the bush is pressed right home, the peg should be fitted (Fig. 3). Some fitters prefer to drill through the crankcase housing into the bush, tapping out 2 B.A. and fitting a brass screw, cutting off the head and filing down flush with the surrounding metal. Take care, however, the drill does not burst through the bush into the bore.

Fig. 3.—TIMING-SIDE MAIN BEARING (2·49 and 3·49 h.p.)
The main-bearing bush peg is being inserted in the bush before the latter is finally pressed home.

Allowing for End-play

When the bush has been fitted it is usually found that the shoulder is too "proud," i.e. too thick, thus causing end pressure on the flywheel assembly when the crankcase is bolted together. In some cases it may be found impossible to make the crankcase faces meet. The shoulder should be scraped to allow at least ·012 inch endplay. Do this very carefully, scraping the metal down evenly. Test the result by lightly smearing the shoulder with lampblack, refitting the flywheels and rotating them for a few revolutions. The shoulder should show contact with the flywheel boss for the whole of its circumference. In some cases it may be found that whilst the shaft is a good fit in the bush, excessive endplay has developed. This may be taken up by fitting ·005-inch shim washers, obtainable from any B.S.A. stockist (Fig. 4).

Big-end Bearings

These are roller type, the rollers being retained by flanges on the crankpin. Big-end bushes are not supplied under any circumstances by the makers, but worn connecting rods, provided they are sound, can be exchanged for a nominal sum from any stockist. The reason for this is owing to the bushes being ground after they are fitted to the connecting rod, an operation calling for elaborate plant and essentially a factory job.

Fitting Mainshafts

These are secured to the flywheels on all models by rivets. When fitting new shafts it is most important that they are a tight fit in the flywheel boss: do not depend on the rivets to hold the shaft. If there are any signs of looseness the flywheel should be scrapped. After the new shaft is riveted, check for truth between centres and again when the flywheels are assembled. On the later models the mainshaft on the driving side

Fig. 4.—How to reduce Excessive Endplay.

Thin shim washers are fitted on the mainshaft. Note the hole which registers with the main-bearing ballrace peg, which is also shown.

REPAIRING B.S.A. ENGINES

is drilled to lubricate the cush drive, and should be syringed through before reassembling.

Fitting Valve Guides

In all models valve guides are a driving fit in the cylinder. A length of steel tubing fitting snugly against the shoulder of guide should be used. Do not forget to replace the valve-spring cups.

Reassembling

This should not present any difficulty; it is, however, important to note the flywheel ballrace peg which locates with a slot in the inner bearing of the ballrace on the driving side (Fig. 4). If this is not correctly fitted to the slot, binding will be experienced when the crankcase is bolted together. Always fit the scraper ring with the chamfered edge uppermost. Make sure the mainshaft pinion lock washer is fitted and secured, also the felt washer behind the cush-drive assembly.

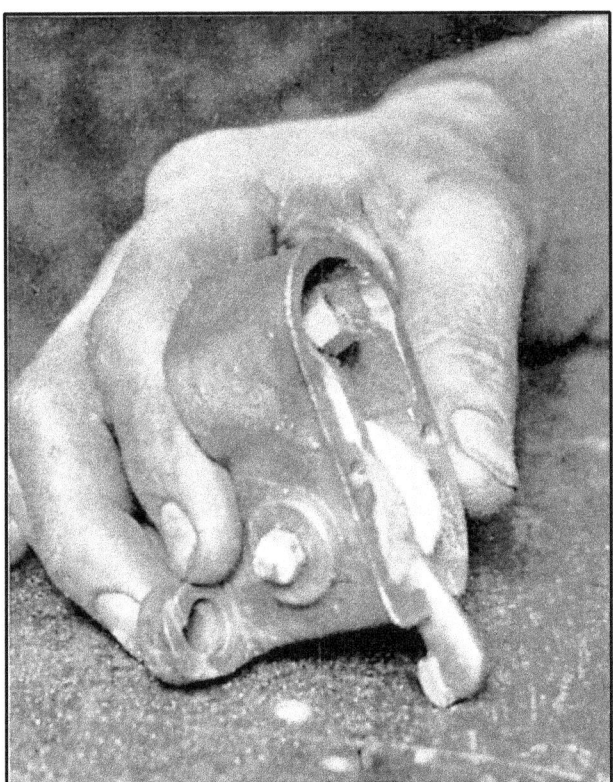

*Fig. 5.—*Result of a Worn Bearing.
Owing to play in the rocker bush the tappet-adjusting screw lock nut has been fouling the rocker box as shown, causing noise and rattle. Note the felt washers (3·49-h.p. model).

3·49-H.P. AND 4·93-H.P. SIDE-VALVE MODELS

These engines are very similar in many respects, and from a repair point of view are practically identical. The magneto, however, is driven by chain instead of gears. The adjustment is carried out by slackening the two bolts holding the magneto platform, which is slotted, and sliding this forward. The timing-side main bearing is a ballrace in the 4·93-h.p. model.

3·49-H.P. O.H.V. ENGINE

Two models of this type were made, the Standard and the Super Sports. The crankcase details are as already described, and the difference arises principally with the cylinder group. The valves are retained by the usual method of split collars, and two springs are fitted to each valve. Valve rockers are carried in separate boxes. These should be examined for wear on the rocker bearing (Fig. 5). On the standard model the rockers have plain bronze bushes; when replacing these leave sufficient metal to take up any sideplay on the rocker. Always replace the felt washers each side with new ones (Fig. 5). The rocker bearings on the Super Sports are cup-and-cone ball bearing, 13 ⅛-inch balls in each bearing—52 in all. These are adjustable.

Fig. 6.—Dismantling Rocker Box.

The cover has been removed, the two studs locking the spindles are shown on the right of the box. The rocker spindle is being unscrewed, and the adjusting sleeve is shown projecting from the opposite side. Note the felt washers.

Tappet-rod Ends

The tappet push rods should be examined for wear, usually detected by the adjusting screw sinking into the push-rod end cup. These ends are detachable, and can be replaced when worn at either end. File round

REPAIRING B.S.A. ENGINES

the end and drive out the rivet, when located, by a pin punch. Draw off the end, replace as necessary and always fit a new rivet (Fig. 7).

Avoid bending or flattening the rod. Note when assembling, the exhaust rod has a flange on one end that engages with the exhaust-valve lifter. Always replace the washers at the ends of the tappet-rod tubes on the Standard model, "Hallite" at the top and rubber at the lower ends.

5·57-H.P. ENGINE

This differs but very little from the previous models. Both aluminium and cast-iron pistons are fitted. In the latter type the gudgeon pin is secured by a patent split ring. Give special attention to the split-ring groove in the piston boss; carefully clean this out and make sure the ring slips into the groove when refitting the gudgeon pin.

Timing Gear

The mainshaft timing pinion is held on a parallel shaft by a right-hand taper-headed screw, which expands the mainshaft as in the twin-model engines (see Fig. 9).

A decompressor is fitted to aid starting; this is a small trip cam fitted to the exhaust rocker. The decompressor return spring should be tested, and if necessary replaced by driving out the two pins when the spring will be disclosed (see Fig. 8). Tappet guides are screwed into the crankcase, and it is a simple matter to replace these. The tappet rods have two small fillets which prevent the rod rotating when tappets are being ad-

Fig. 7.—FITTING PUSH-ROD ENDS (3·49-h.p. O.H.V.). These are secured by a small pin which is afterwards riveted over.

REPAIRING B.S.A. ENGINES

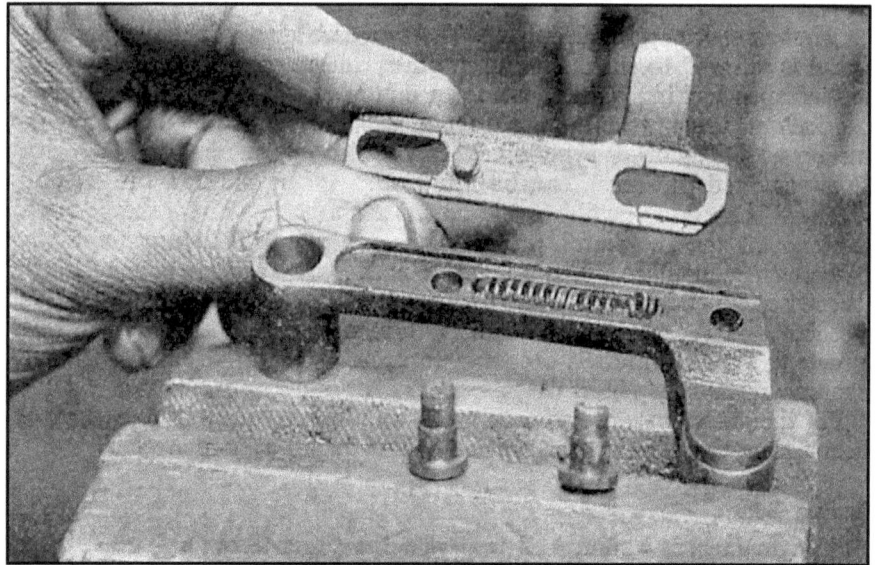

Fig. 8.—Where to find the Decompressor Spring (5·57-h.p. S.V.).

If the decompressor appears sluggish, the spring may be broken as shown. To examine or replace this it is necessary to drive out the two rivets, when the sliding lever can be lifted off.

justed. These fillets are very light, and both the tappet head and the locking sleeve must be held when being adjusted, otherwise the fillets will be sheared off. Timing-pinion bearings are ground-steel bushes. These rarely have to be replaced, and greater clearance is always allowed than with bronze bushes.

TWIN-CYLINDER MODELS

The 7·70-h.p. and 9·86-h.p. models incorporate the majority of the features dealt with in the preceding types. Dismantling is fairly obvious, and should be carried out on the lines already indicated. Both aluminium and cast-iron pistons are fitted, the latter having the B.S.A. split-ring type of fixing.

Removing Engine from Frame

When it is proposed to remove the engine completely from the frame, the difficulty sometimes arises with regard to the inside half of the front chaincase if the pressed metal type is fitted. This half is placed in position before the cush-drive assembly and the clutch are fitted, and in consequence these units must be removed before the half case can be taken away. It is not necessary to dismantle either of them. Remove the cush drive as previously advised in the earlier part of this section.

REPAIRING B.S.A. ENGINES

Detaching the Clutch Complete

First remove the clutch dome. There are two types of these: the early model is screwed to the outer clutch plate, and retained in position by a hook-shaped locking plate locating in one of the slots cut in the dome. The locking plate must be lifted out of the slot, when the dome can be unscrewed. The other type is held in position by four small nuts; with these removed the dome can be lifted off. When the dome is off two hexagon locking nuts will be seen on the mainshaft. These should both be removed and the clutch pulled off as one unit. This may require a little persuasion, although it is a simple matter with a chain wheel puller; otherwise, two large-type levers can be inserted between the large clutch sprocket and the chaincase, taking a bearing against the countershaft sprocket. If assistance is obtained to exert a steady pressure with the levers, whilst a sharp blow with a copper drift and hammer is given on the end of the mainshaft, the assembly will usually respond. The method of dismantling the clutch, etc., will be dealt with in a later section.

Timing Gear

The mainshaft pinion is fitted with the taper-screw fixing (Fig. 9). Note the position of the valve rocker levers when dismantling; also examine the rocker spindles—these are screwed into the case and are easily replaced (Fig. 9).

Rocker Rollers

These are replaceable if worn. The roller pin is shouldered and should be driven out from the side which has the smaller diameter; replace the roller and pin, and swell the latter with a centre punch on the side with the smaller diameter (Fig. 10).

Big-end Bearing

This is a double row of rollers, one row to each connecting rod, the latter being fitted side by side. It is important to note the small end of the rod is offset. The rods should be assembled so that they are offset towards each other, thus bringing the pistons in line when these are fitted (Fig. 11).

Fitting the Induction Pipe

This is a special B.S.A. feature, and is an important point. It will be noted that a flanged adjusting sleeve is fitted into the front cylinder inlet port. When reassembling, this sleeve should be screwed right into the cylinder. The induction pipe should be placed into position, and the narrow union nut on the pipe should then be fitted to the rear cylinder, just finger tight. The adjusting sleeve should then be screwed out until a good joint is made with the flange on the induction pipe. The

REPAIRING B.S.A. ENGINES

Fig. 9.—Removing the Mainshaft Pinion (Side Valve).
The taper-screw method for securing the pinion is shown being unscrewed, whilst the front inlet rocker spindle (with square shank) is also shown.

Fig. 10.—Fitting Rocker Rollers (Side Valve).
The pin is riveted by a centre punch after being fitted as shown.

REPAIRING B.S.A. ENGINES

Fig. 11.—CONNECTING-ROD ASSEMBLY (7·70 and 9·86 h.p.).
Showing how the connecting-rod small ends are offset, bringing the pistons in line.

wide union can then be screwed to the front cylinder and both unions finally tightened. It is well worth while paying special attention to fitting this part, otherwise airleaks are sure to occur.

Replacing Union Nuts

The special B.S.A. "Cee" spanner should always be used when adjusting the union nuts. There is a great temptation to use a chisel or punch instead of the proper tool, which usually results in splitting the nut. It will be noticed these are captive on the pipe owing to the flanged collars at the ends. They are screwed on the pipe, and have to be removed before the union nut can be replaced. Some difficulty may be experienced in unscrewing them, and rather than distort or flatten the pipe it is recommended to file a flat on either side for a spanner and fit a new collar: this only costs 6d., whereas a new pipe complete costs 14s. 6d.

THE 4·93-H.P. O.H.V. ENGINE

Removing the Rocker Box

Proceed in the usual way by detaching carburetter, plug, exhaust pipes, etc. The latter are pushed into the cylinder port and braced together by a tie bolt. Now undo the push-rod tubes; these are screwed on the tappet guides with a flat spring engaging with a notch on the tube. It is advisable to undo the push-rod tubes before removing the rocker box;

REPAIRING B.S.A. ENGINES

otherwise, the action of the return springs in the tube tend to bind the tube on the threads. Rotate the engine until the exhaust valve is open, when the ball nipple on the exhaust-lifter cable can be disconnected from the lever on the rocker box. Unscrew the cable adjuster and withdraw the cable entirely. Remove the two rocker-box holding-down bolts and the two horizontal bolts screwed through the yoke lugs. Disconnect the cylinder head steady strap and gently lever up the rocker box, sliding forwards at the same time. Take great care, as the yoke lugs are very easily fractured.

The Cylinder Head

Undo the four extended nuts holding the head and lever this off. It will be noted that the walls between the fins are thickened where the cylinder studs go through the casting, and a screwdriver should be carefully used at this point (see Fig. 12). The barrel can be lifted off after the four base nuts are removed. The gudgeon pin is a push fit in the piston.

Timing Gear

Take off the timing cover: the screws will be found to be very tight, and a good screwdriver will be necessary. For this reason it is well to take off the cover before taking the engine out of the frame. The cam

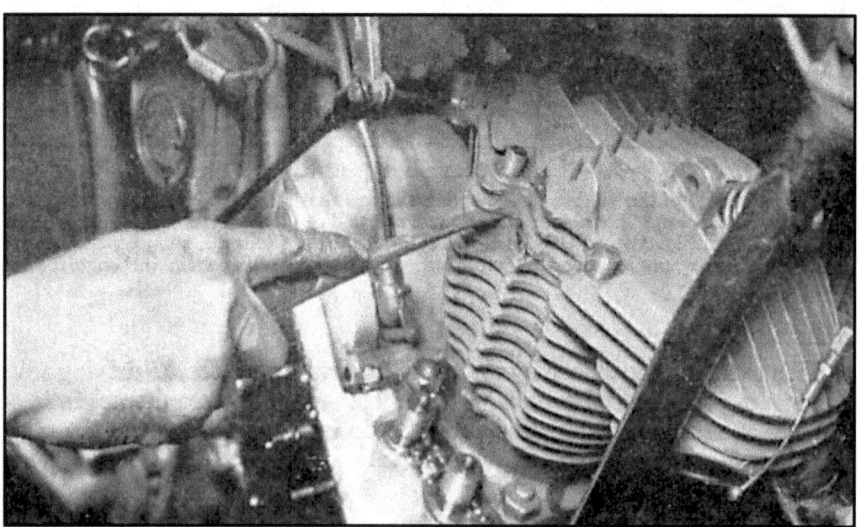

Fig. 12.—Ticklish but Safe.

Prise off the cylinder head by inserting a screwdriver and applying a twisting movement at the points where the cylinder studs come through the head. The casting is reinforced at these points (4·93-h.p. O.H.V.).

REPAIRING B.S.A. ENGINES

pinions revolve on stationary shafts. Check the shafts, which should be tight in the crankcase (Fig. 13). If these are found to be loose they should be taken out and the " Dee "-shaped ends copper plated to a thickness of ·004 inch and refitted. The timing cover should be placed in position to ensure the shafts lining up with the bushes in the cover. The main pinion is retained by a lock nut, washer and key on a parallel shaft. The tappets have large flat heads, and the guides have to be unscrewed from the crankcase before these can be withdrawn. The guides are locked by two small studs, which also go through the timing cover. The studs should be tapped to free the guides.

Fig. 13.—Testing Camshafts (4·93-h.p. O.H.V.).

A good picture of the timing case showing the camshafts being tested (they should be firm in the crankcase). A rod (the clutch push rod will do) is inserted in the hollow shaft to give additional leverage. One push-rod tube has been removed, showing the tappet guide. The two studs locking the guides can be seen projecting from the edge of the timing case.

Draining the Sump

This can be done either by undoing the drain plug on the driving side or removing the pump-base plate at the bottom of the crankcase timing-side half. The crankcase also should be drained by unscrewing the plug just above the sump plug, also on the driving side.

Taking the Crankcase from the Frame

If the front brake is foot operated, unhook pedal spring. Withdraw the long bolt through the footrests and rear-brake pedal. On later models the lug through which this bolt is fitted, on the right-hand side of the

REPAIRING B.S.A. ENGINES

machine, is loose and allows the pedal to drop down. Where this lug is fixed it will be necessary to slacken off the two front main frame bolts, allowing the lower cradle tubes to spring slightly. Note: there is a bush in the pedal bearing and a stop plate which is fitted against the engine plate. Take care of the distance piece on left-hand side of the machine. Disconnect clutch cable, gear rods, etc., remove the bolts from the rear engine plates and lift out the gearbox with the right-hand plate attached by the chain adjuster. Withdraw the front bolts and the crankcase can be lifted out from the left-hand side of the machine.

Crankcase Details

After the crankcase bolts have been removed the case can be taken apart. The main bearings are ballrace and roller bearing on the driving side, with a distance piece between them. The roller bearing is fitted first, i.e. nearest the driving sprocket. On the timing side there is a ballrace in the crankcase and a bush in the timing cover supporting an extension of the mainshaft. The big-end bearing is a double row of rollers accommodated in a single cage. Other details relating to fitting mainshafts, big-end bushes, etc., are as referred to with previous models.

When the crankcase is dismantled and taken apart, it is a good opportunity to clean the sludge that is trapped behind the bolt lugs in the sump.

Overhauling Rockers

These are dismantled by removing the rocker cover. Then unscrew the two $\frac{1}{4}$ nuts on the top of the box, giving the studs a tap to free the rocker spindles; these studs lock the rocker spindles when they are screwed up into position. Undo the two nuts that hold the rocker return springs, and unhook the springs. Remove the lock nut on the spindle where the grease nipple projects, then undo the adjusting sleeve and withdraw the spindle from the other side. The rocker can then be lifted out. Note the rollers in the rocker bearing, 11 each side in each rocker. Reassemble by reversing the order, taking up the endplay with the adjusting sleeve, and secure with the lock nut. Replace the felt washers as necessary.

Removing Valves

A special tool is supplied by the makers to facilitate this. The hook portion of the tool is inserted through the plug hole, and bears against the valve head; the levers are then brought to bear on the spring collar, enabling the split cotters to be removed.

Reassembling Points

Make a special feature of rejointing the crankcase, paying particular attention to the inner crankcase joint. Replace the felt washer on the timing-side mainshaft that fits against the timing-cover bush. Also the

REPAIRING B.S.A. ENGINES

main-pinion lock-nut washer. It is always worth while to replace with new, all felt washers and packings, the tappet-tube washers, etc., and do not forget the magneto-shaft oil-retaining felt washer. Piston rings should be fitted with ·008 to ·010 inch gap to the top ring and ·006 to ·008 inch to the lower ring. There is no scraper ring fitted. Valve clearances should be set at ·004 inch when cold. Timing pinions are all marked. Degree settings are given in detail on separate chart.

Compression Ratios

High- and low-compression pistons can be obtained and used in conjunction with a cylinder-base shim. The following choice of ratios is given:

Low-compression piston and shim	5·4 to 1 ratio
Low-compression piston without shim	5·8 to 1 ratio
High-compression piston and shim	6·4 to 1 ratio
High-compression piston without shim	6·8 to 1 ratio

Return Springs

These are fitted to the rockers and push rods. The rocker springs are adjusted by the nuts underneath the rocker box on the right-hand side. Turning the nut to the right increases the tension. The push-rod spring is adjusted by screwing the tube—downwards increases the pressure. It is recommended to tighten the springs fully when tuning for racing, but for normal purposes to slacken the springs right back.

Refitting the Rocker Box

Make sure the cams are off the lift with both the tappets down. Place the rocker box in position. The great point is to avoid straining the yoke lugs on the under side of the box. These must fit easily and the bolt holes line up. Tighten all bolts progressively.

Later Models

With the exception of minor details the foregoing remarks apply to later models. In the case of side-valve *de luxe* models, i.e. sloping engines, the crankcase details are the same as recommended for the 4·93-h.p. o.h.v. engine and the cylinder details as the standard side-valve engine. Whilst in the upright o.h.v. engines the crankcase features are as the standard models, the cylinder heads follow the 4·93 o.h.v. practice. The 1928 and later twin models are fitted with forked connecting rods with four rows of roller bearings in cages. In the 2·49-h.p. and the " light " o.h.v. models the push-rod tubes are not screwed to the tappet guides.

TIMING CHARTS "B.S.A." ENGINES

MODELS.	INLET.		EXHAUST.		IGNITION MAX. ADV. Before T.D.C.	Tappet Clearance.	
	Opens before T.D.C.	Closes after B.D.C.	Opens before B.D.C.	Closes after T.D.C.		Inlet. Inch.	Exhaust. Inch.
2·49 h.p., 1925–9	16° 42°	50° 78°	67° 90°	23° 50°	0	·014 ·004	·014 ·004
2·49 h.p. O.H.V., 1930 2·49 h.p. S.V., 1930	24°	65°	65°	25°	0	·003 ·004	·003 ·004
2·49 h.p. O.H.V., 1931	24°	65°	65°	25°	0	·003	·003
3·49 h.p. O.H.V., 1924–6	8°	40°	64°	10°	0	·004	·004
3·49 h.p. S.V., 1923–9	12°	51°	63°	13°	0	·004	·004
3·49 h.p. O.H.V., 1927, and super O.H.V., 1925–7	20°	40°	70°	20°	0 5°	·004	·004
3·49 h.p. S.V., 1930	24°	65°	65°	25°	0	·004	·004
3·49 h.p. O.H.V., 4·93 h.p. S.V., 5·57 h.p. S.V., 4·93 h.p. O.H.V., 1930	24°	65°	60°	20°	0	·003 ·004 ·004 ·003	·003 ·004 ·004 ·003
2·49 h.p. S.V., 3·49 h.p. S.V., 1931	25°	45°	65°	25°	0	·004	·004
4¼ h.p., 1915–20	–10°*	50°	53°	16°	0	·004	·004
4¼ h.p., 1921–3	–2°*	42°	67°	17°	0	·004	·004

* NOTE.—These settings are *after* Top Dead Centre.

TIMING CHARTS "B.S.A." ENGINES

MODELS.	INLET.		EXHAUST.		IGNITION MAX. ADV. Before T.D.C.	Tappet Clearance.	
	Opens before T.D.C.	Closes after B.D.C.	Opens before B.D.C.	Closes after T.D.C.		Inlet. Inch.	Exhaust. Inch.
4·93 and 5·57 h.p., 1924–5	8°	43°	62°	15°	0	·004	·004
4·93 and 5·57 h.p., 1927–9	12° / 25°	42° / 65°	65° / 85°	22° / 35°	0	·014 / ·004	·014 / ·004
3·49 h.p. O.H.V., 4·93 h.p. O.H.V., 5·57 h.p. De Luxe, 1927–9	24°	65°	60°	20°	0	·004	·004
4·93 h.p. O.H.V., 1929	24°	65°	60°	20°	0	·003	·003
4·93 h.p. S.V. Light, 1930	12° / 25°	42° / 65°	65° / 85°	22° / 35°	0	·014 / ·004	·014 / ·004
4·93 h.p. O.H.V. Light, 1930	24°	65°	60°	20°	0	·003	·003
4·93 h.p. Dirt Track O.H.V., 1929–30	24°	65°	60°	20°	5°	·004	·004
4·93 h.p. O.H.V., 1931	24°	65°	60°	20°	0	·003	·003
5·57 h.p., 1914–20	-10°*	50°	53°	16°	0	·004	·004
5·57 h.p., 1921–3	-2°*	42°	67°	17°	0	·004	·004
7·70 h.p., 1921–2	10°	50°	55°	15°	0	·004	·004
7·70 and 9·86 h.p., 1923–31	-3°*	40°	60°	14°	0	·004	·004

* NOTE.—These settings are *after* Top Dead Centre.

HINTS ON CALTHORPE MOTOR-CYCLES

FOR several seasons past, the Calthorpe Company have concentrated on the production of a 3·48-h.p. o.h.v. engine, and with the exception of detail improvements, the general features have remained unaltered, which emphasises the success of the design.

The Cylinder and Head

Dismantling is quite a simple job. The exhaust pipes are attached to the ports by clips in present models, and with a union nut in the earlier types. The next operation is to remove the push rods. Therefore, undo the nuts securing flanges at the top and bottom of the push-rod tube. The tube is in two halves, and these should be telescoped into each other. The tops of the push rods will then be exposed. Rotate the engine until both valves are closed. A tool is supplied with 1931 models to depress the valves, thus giving sufficient clearance to remove the push rods from the rocker cups. Each valve will, of course, have to be dealt with in turn. It is not necessary to remove the rocker-box cover. In any case, do not remove this unless the valves are closed, and then be careful not to rotate the engine whilst this is off, or there is a good chance that the rocker box will be broken. The cylinder head is held down by four long bolts which, although free to rotate, are held captive in the crankcase by screwed sleeves. Loosen these bolts by the hexagons immediately below the bottom fin on the cylinder barrel, giving a half turn at a time. When the bolts have been slackened right off, the head can be lifted off. This should be lifted as high as possible to clear the push rods. On no account should the screwed sleeves holding the bolts in the crankcase be removed before the holding-down bolts have been unscrewed from the head, or the thread will be stripped in the crankcase. Previous to 1930, the tappet rods were not interchangeable; therefore, these should be marked when taking down. The barrel can now be lifted off. The rings are fitted to the piston, the lowest one being a scraper ring. The gudgeon pin is retained by the usual circlips, and in consideration of the cost of these, it is worth while replacing them with new ones when overhauling. The earlier type was fitted with end caps to the gudgeon pin.

Rocker Box, etc.

This is easily detached from the head, when off the cylinder. Remove the two horizontal bolts and the holding-down bolt on the left-hand side.

HINTS ON CALTHORPE MOTOR-CYCLES

Take care to lift the box directly upwards. Any side strain may possibly fracture either of the forked yokes. If it is proposed to strip the box, the four castellated spindle nuts should be removed, and then the rocker return spring. If the cover bolts are now unscrewed, the cover can be lifted off, and the rockers can be lifted out. It will probably be necessary to give the rocker spindles a sharp tap to release the cones on the left-hand side of the box. The rockers are fitted with roller bearings at each end with a distance piece in between.

A thrust washer is fitted between the rollers and the rocker box. These should be replaced in cases of excessive endplay. *Note* the breathers fitted to the rocker-box cover.

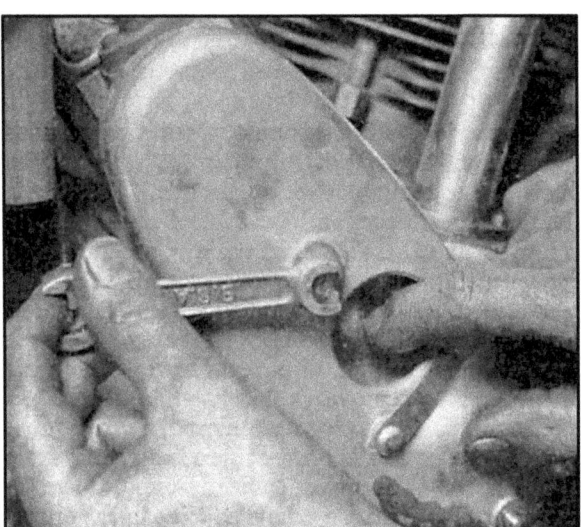

Fig. 1.—Adjusting the Magneto Chain.

First slacken the magneto holding-down bolts. Remove the inspection cover on the magneto chain case. Slacken off the lock nut on the centre spindle as shown. Then adjust the square centre spindle with the spanner, while feeling the tension of the chain through the inspection cover with your finger.

Valve Details

The valves are fitted with double springs and are retained by split collars or collets. Take care of the hardened-steel thimbles fitted on the ends of the valve stems. Replace with new ones if these are worn hollow, or the difficulty will be met with when checking the clearance of the rocker adjusting screw. Valve guides are detachable, and are pressed in the head. Always true the seatings when new guides are fitted.

Timing Gear

To examine the timing gear, the magneto chain cover should be taken off. Note the method of adjusting the magneto chain (see Fig. 1). The chain sprockets are fitted to tapered shafts. Undo the nuts and lift off the timing cover, taking care not to damage the joint. Disconnect the exhaust lifter and lever, take out the two cam rockers, and do not lose the two distance washers, either side of the rockers. The camshaft can then be withdrawn. On the 1930 model it is necessary to take off the pump cover before the camshaft can be taken out.

HINTS ON CALTHORPE MOTOR-CYCLES

Lubrication System (1930)

This model uses the camshaft and mainshaft pinions as an oil pump, drawing oil from the sump through a filter. This filter is located directly below the timing cover underneath the sump. A large hexagon plug will be found which, when removed, releases the filter gauze and incidentally drains the sump. Do not confuse this plug with the crankcase-drain plug, which is a little higher up on the side of the crankcase. The oil passes from the pump, forcing out a plunger-type indicator, to the mainshaft and the big-end bearings. The indicator is found on the rear of the timing cover, and is forced out about $\frac{1}{4}$ inch when the system is functioning correctly. Just above the indicator is a grub screw and lock nut which controls a bypass. Screwing this screw outwards allows the oil to pass straight to the sump, whilst screwing inwards forces the oil into the crankshaft assembly. The surplus oil is picked up by the flywheels, and as these revolve is deflected by a scraper into the sump.

1931 System

This is carried out by a separate gear pump, which is driven by a large pinion below the mainshaft pinion. Remove the lock nut, which has a left-hand thread, and insert two $\frac{1}{4}$-inch screws in the holes in the pinion. This will force the pinion off the shaft. Undo the screws, and the pump complete can be withdrawn (Fig. 2). With this system a pressure gauge is fitted instead of the indicator. This should be set by the control at the rear of the timing case to read about 5 lb. Always allow the engine to warm thoroughly before adjusting the setting, as oil always gives a higher reading when thick and cold.

Mainshaft Pinion

This is secured to the shaft by a left-hand thread. The keyways are provided, each giving a different position in relation to the tooth.

Engine Sprocket

Unscrew the lock nut, and the collars, shock-absorber spring and sprocket can be taken off. Note the balls between the sprocket and the sliding collar. If a dynamo is fitted, the sprocket for this unit will also have to be taken off. The crankcase can now be taken from the frame if desired.

Crankshafts

The main bearings consist of a double-row roller bearing to the driving side and a ballrace on the timing side. 1929 and earlier models have a phosphor-bronze bush on the timing side, and the mainshafts are fitted

HINTS ON CALTHORPE MOTOR-CYCLES

by taper and key. 1930 and 1931 mainshafts are pressed into the flywheels. A double row of rollers with a distance piece are fitted to the big-end bearing, and the crankpin is a taper fit into the flywheels. Always check the register of the oilways in the crankpin and the flywheel by forcing oil through with an oil gun.

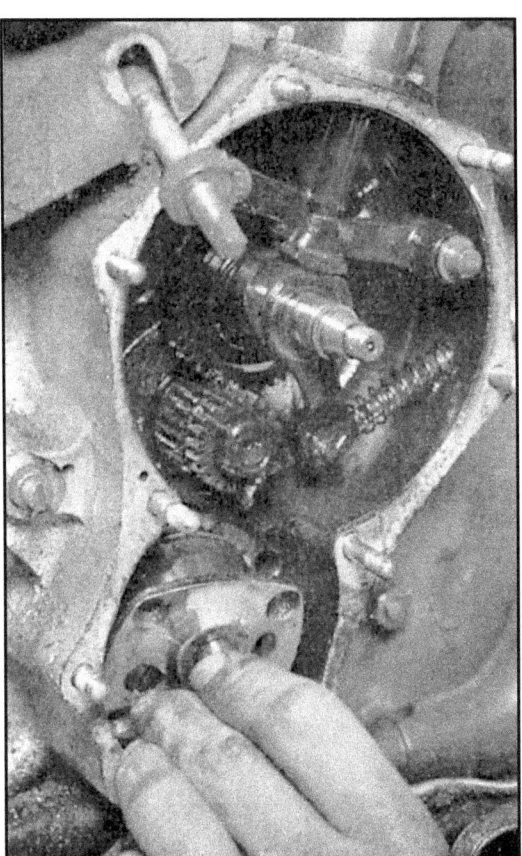

Fig. 2.—Taking out Pump—1931 Model.

Reassembling

When new tappet push rods are being fitted they are usually longer than necessary. They should be ground to the correct length before the hardened ball end is fitted. The overhead-rocker adjusting screws should be set to ·004 inch inlet and ·006 inch exhaust, when the engine is cold and both valves closed.

Coil Ignition

Some models are fitted with coil ignition. This is timed in a similar manner to the magneto. Slacken the setscrew holding the cam on the shaft, and draw this off the taper. Rotate the engine, and set cam with the contact points just opening, with piston top dead centre of the compression stroke, lever fully retarded. Then tighten the setscrew. The ignition gap should be ·012 inch for magneto and ·020 for coil ignition.

DOUGLAS ENGINE REPAIRS

By S. Gill

1926–1931 SIDE-VALVE ENGINES

Removing Engine from Frame

WHEN undertaking engine repairs (as apart from adjusting) the engine should be removed from the frame, an operation which takes some fifteen minutes, and only necessitates the removal of front chain cover and chain, disconnecting exhaust pipe and taking off engine bolts situated underneath the crankcase.

The dismantling of crankcase and removal of crankshaft calls for special tools, and should be carried out as follows:

*Fig. 1.—*CYLINDER AND DETACHABLE HEAD.
As fitted to the 350-c.c. model. Care should be taken not to strain the light barrel by over-tightening the nuts. If a leak is suspected, it is much better to make a new joint.

Dismantling Flywheel

In dismantling all that is necessary is to remove the adjusting nut, the springs and ring, and the flywheel lock nut. The flywheel, together with the remainder of the clutch, can then be removed from the shaft with the withdrawal tool. Screw the tool into the boss until it is against the end of the crankshaft. Hammer it round one turn or more, and then strike it sharply with the hammer, when the shock will loosen the flywheel from the taper of the shaft.

To remove flywheel from engines marked E.Q. and E.R., take off adjusting nut, cage and springs, and unscrew flywheel nut, which automatically comes up against the extractor ring, and so pulls the wheel from the shaft.

With all engines marked Y.E., E.H., E.R., E.N. and E.V., it is

DOUGLAS ENGINE REPAIRS

Fig. 2.—CONSTRUCTION OF CRANKSHAFT.
The timing-side web is removed to show the make-up of the big end on the crankpin. Note crankpin nut and washer.

necessary to remove the cam studs from the case before the cam wheels can be taken out. These studs are pressed into bushes, which are intercast with the case when it is made, and a special tool or attachment is required to grip the end of the stud for withdrawal.

The Crankshaft

This is built up in three sections—flywheel side, centre portion and timing side—the sides being pressed on to the crankpins, which are part of the centre, and are located by three dowel pins. The shaft must be pulled apart to renew big ends, which are made up as follows: crankpin bush, which is pressed on to pin; big-end bush, which is pressed into con. rod, and a single row of rollers. Great care must be exercised when fitting these bushes to avoid distortion. The

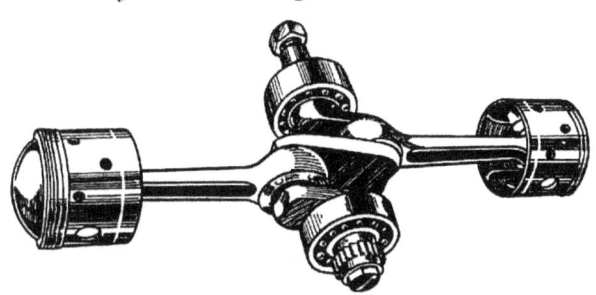

Fig. 3.—COMPLETE CRANKSHAFT RODS AND PISTONS WITHOUT THE BALANCE WEIGHTS.

shafts should be checked for alignment on assembly, and crankpin nuts locked quite tightly and secured with locking washer.

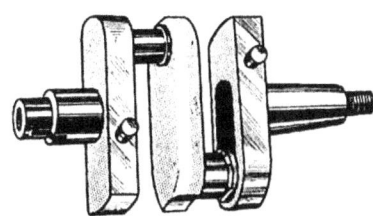

Fig. 4.—COMPLETE CRANKSHAFT WITH DETACHABLE BALANCE WEIGHTS.

Valve Timing

ENGINES MARKED Y.E., E.H., E.R., E.N., E.V.

Full details of timing for all Douglas engines are given on the separate timing chart.

When retiming, first fix the crankshaft pinion, place tappets in position, then place the cam wheels at correct setting according to marks, and finally press in the cam studs; on some models a binding plate is fitted, and this must be securely locked. The magneto should be set fully advanced with piston from 40° to 50° before top dead centre.

Valve Timing on Engines marked E.Q.

In setting this engine, the crankshaft should be set with the key for the timing pinion facing to the front instead of rear, when it will be found that by meshing the wheels according to their marks, the valve timing is in order.

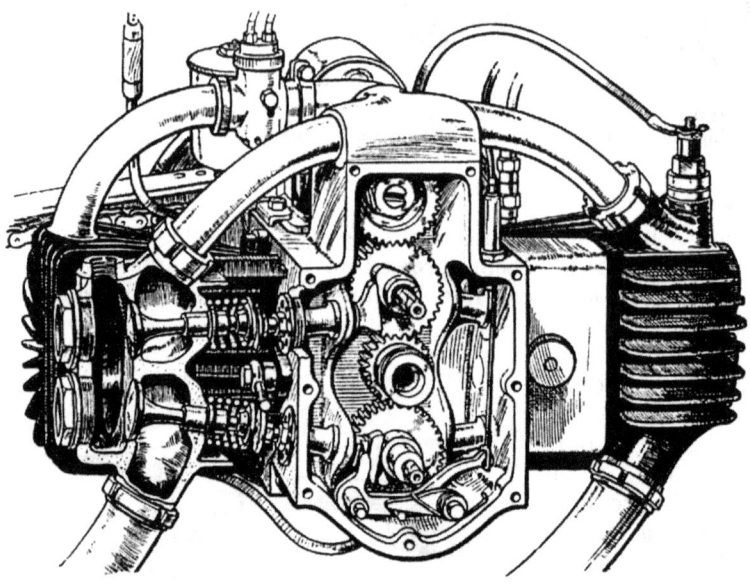

Fig. 5.—Showing the Timing Gear of the 350-c.c. Engine prior to 1929. The timing cover and oil pump have been removed, and the engine is in part section.

Magneto should be set fully advanced with piston from 34° to 37° before top dead centre.

Cylinder Barrels and Pistons on 350-c.c. Engines

Care must be taken in assembling these parts to avoid damage. The barrels are very light, and therefore any excessive straining on the bolts will cause the barrel to give, and when the engine is hot, the distortion will be so great that it will probably cause seizures. Whenever a leak at the joint is suspected, a new joint should be fitted to avoid over-tightening. In later models of this description, the makers have fitted a distance piece to prevent the heads being pulled too tight.

Engines Marked E.Q.—Valve Extracting and Adjusting

The valve-spring collar and end cap are screwed on to the valve stem ; these must first be unlocked. Then the valve may be removed by unscrewing it with a screwdriver engaged in the head of the valve.

DOUGLAS ENGINE REPAIRS

To adjust, first insert a feeler of the correct thickness between the tappet and valve-adjusting nut, then adjust the nut until it just holds this feeler in position, after which the valve-spring collar should be locked against this nut, and the feeler withdrawn. The adjusting nut and collar must at all times be securely locked together, otherwise the tappet adjustment will quickly vary and possibly cause damage to the valve stem.

1926–1931 O.H.V. ENGINES

These engines are of entirely different construction to the side-valve models, with the exception of the flywheel clutch, and the information given will be found to be generally applicable to all Douglas o.h.v. sports, racing and dirt-track machines. The general principle remains the same, with the exception that the magneto is of the opposite rotation.

Crankshaft—Removal and Assembly

To remove, first take off flywheel, timing cover, and take out the whole set of crankcase bolts. Ease the shafts from the main ball-races, when the whole assembly can be withdrawn. The assembly is made up of a one-piece two-throw crankshaft, connecting rods with solid ends, big-end rollers which run in cages, and two balance weights.

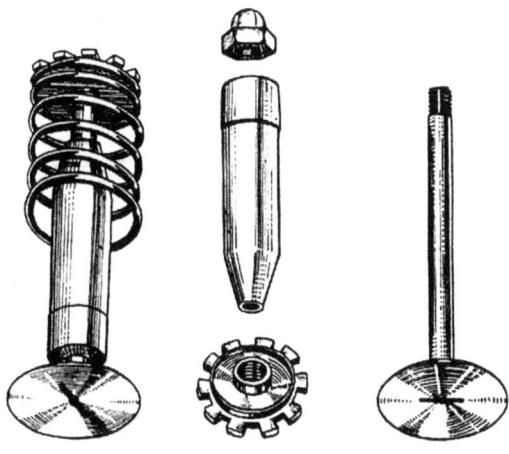

Fig. 6.—VALVE COMPLETE WITH GUIDE (E.Q. ENGINE).

The construction is such that the assembly must be made in the following order. Take the bare crankshaft, place connecting rod in its correct position over the journal, insert the rollers and cages into the big end and fix into position according to the means provided. This differs in various models. Finally, press the balance weight into position and lock with pin. The face of this balance weight acts as a location for the big-end bearing.

Camshaft

This runs on ball bearings, and is held in position by a locking plate fixed behind the cam wheel.

O.H.V. Rockers

These are made up in one piece, being hollow, and mounted on hardened steel sleeves, which are kept in position by rocker spindles

DOUGLAS ENGINE REPAIRS

passed through the rocker standard, which is cast with the head. An oil box is fitted to the top of the spindle, through which lubricant passes to the ball end of the push rod. Owing to the high speed at which these parts operate, they must be kept well lubricated, and if for any reason a failure occurs, the hardening of the parts will have suffered, and new parts will have to be fitted.

Valve Timing

All camshafts on this type of engine are marked in degrees, and the various types of engine differ to some extent. As, however, it is a one-piece camshaft, it will usually be found that if the overlap of exhaust and inlet are made to balance on top dead centre, the timing will be according to the marks fixed on the train of timing wheels. The correct setting on engines marked O.E. and E.D. is: exhaust opens 50° before bottom dead centre, closes 17° after top dead centre. Inlet opens 10° before top dead centre, closes 45° after bottom dead centre.

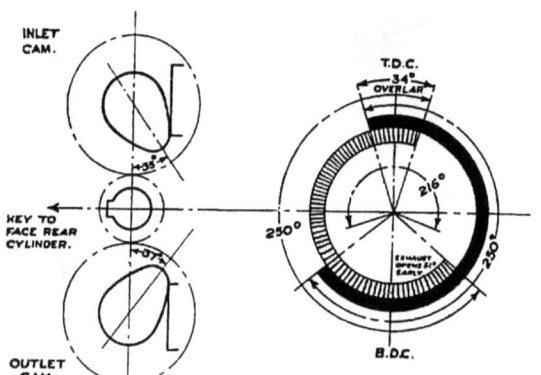

Fig. 7.—DATA FOR VALVE TIMING OF O.E. AND E.D. O.H.V. ENGINES.

The tappets are held in position by an aluminium clamp plate, and are themselves prevented from turning by the machining of the valve guide, it being essential, when assembling these parts, to see that they are placed in position with the foot of the tappet the correct way up, as this foot lies at an angle to the stem. This can easily be seen by holding the stem in line with a valve push rod on engine and noting when the foot is absolutely perpendicular.

Attention to Valves—Special Note

This should be the same as on all types of engines, but special note should be made that when replacing valves they should be put into their original position. This especially affects dirt-track and racing machines, as these valves are different in the diameter of the head, the difference being so minute that the valve may be placed into the wrong seat without being noticed, but it would naturally soon bring about trouble, as the small valve would drop much too low in the large seat.

The valve-spring pressure on this type of engine varies considerably,

DOUGLAS ENGINE REPAIRS

being approximately 80 lb. for a touring engine, up to 120 lb. for a racing engine.

The recommended tappet adjustment is ·002 inch, to be set when the engine is hot.

TIMING CHART FOR DOUGLAS ENGINES, 1926-1931

MODELS.	INLET.		EXHAUST.		IGNITION. MAX. ADV. Before T.D.C.	Tappet Clearance.	
	Opens before T.D.C.	Closes after B.D.C.	Opens before B.D.C.	Closes after T.D.C.		Inlet.	Exhaust.
Y.E., E.H., E.R., E.N., E.V. (S.V.) . . .	15°	50°	50°	15°	40°-50°	·006"	·006"
E.Q. (S.V.)	5°	45°	60°	20°	34°-37°	·006"	·006"
O.E., E.D. (O.H.V.) . .	10°	45°	50°	17°	35°-40°	·002"	·002"
E.L. (O.H.V.) . . .	10°	50°	63°	20°	45°-50°	·002"	·002"
E.U., E.T. (O.H.V.) . .	10°	50°	63°	20°	38°-40°	·002"	·002"

REPAIRING AND OVERHAULING J.A.P. ENGINES

By STANLEY GREENING, A.M.I.A.E. (*J. A. Prestwich Ltd.*)

NOTES ON DECARBONISING

Removing S.V. Cylinder

REMOVE exhaust-pipe nuts and valve caps. Disconnect petrol pipes and take off carburetter from induction pipe. On twin engines the induction pipe is fitted with two taper collars, the nuts being bored with a corresponding taper. These must be removed, both being right-hand threads.

Valve Caps

It is advantageous to remove the valve caps while the cylinder is fixed on the crankcase, as there is then less likelihood of damaging the base. Should the exhaust-pipe nuts and valve caps be difficult to remove, run the engine a little to warm it up, then work a little paraffin down the threads. If the valve caps are of aluminium it is better to let the engine cool down again before removing them, as the contraction and expansion of aluminium is much greater than that of cast iron.

Take off cylinder fixing nuts, removing them diagonally across the base in order to prevent throwing undue strain on one side.

Taking off Cylinder

The cylinder can now be taken off, but care must be exercised when doing this to see that no strain is thrown on the connecting rod. It is easier if the piston is practically on bottom dead centre of the stroke with machine in gear, not forcing the cylinder in any way, but gently levering it to the best position so that it will lift off easily.

Decarbonising

Now place a rag under piston and pack it round tightly so that no dirt or carbon can get into the crankcase. The piston top can then be scraped clean, but see that the crown is not scratched badly when doing this operation. Do not remove the rings unless you suspect

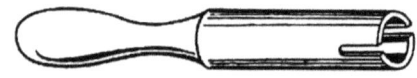

Fig. 1.—A USEFUL TOOL FOR REMOVING VALVE SPRINGS ON J.A.P. ENGINES.

REPAIRING AND OVERHAULING J.A.P. ENGINES

that they require renewing, as they will be nicely bedded in, and there is a danger of distorting them if the operation is not performed very carefully.

Fig. 2.—A Useful Tip for handling a J.A.P. Engine when it is removed from the Frame.
A wooden block bolted to the bench by the side of the vice, as shown above, will enable the engine to be conveniently supported.

Removing Valves

The valves can be removed from cylinders; the best method, if a special tool is not available, is to place the cylinder upside down on the bench, placing a packing piece under the valve heads so that when compressing the spring the valve will be prevented from being forced out.

If a slot is cut in a piece of tube as shown in Fig. 1, this can be placed over the stem of the valve, then the spring compressed and cotter removed, leaving the spring and collar free, when valve can be taken out.

Grinding in Valves

The valve heads and cylinder can now be scraped free of all carbon and the valve seatings reground by placing a little valve grinding paste on the seats, rotating the valve with a screwdriver, and during the operation turning the valve in a clockwise and anticlockwise direction and periodically lifting the valve in order to prevent scoring

65

REPAIRING AND OVERHAULING J.A.P. ENGINES

Fig. 3.—REMOVING THE BEVEL DRIVE.

In the case of engines fitted with the bevel-drive magneto, the drive is dismantled as follows : first remove the three bevel cap-cover screws, next shift the magneto to the left, now remove the bevel fixing nut, using a box spanner. Finally, use a brass punch, as shown above, to loosen the bevel wheel from its spindle.

REPAIRING AND OVERHAULING J.A.P. ENGINES

the seats. Do not place too much pressure on screwdriver, but turn sharply backwards and forwards.

Reassembling

The valves can now be reassembled in the cylinder after cleaning everything very thoroughly. It must be borne in mind that absolute cleanliness is essential in anything appertaining to engine work, and too much stress cannot be laid upon this point. Should the valve grinding compound get into the cylinder bore it will harm the latter and probably be washed into the bearings and quickly wear them out.

The springs, cotters and collars can be replaced with the special tool, and cylinder refitted. Care must be taken to see that the piston does not foul the connecting rod. The ring gaps should be evenly spaced and the gap held closed on the piston while cylinder is gently pushed down over them. There is a big chamber on the mouth of J.A.P. cylinder bores which facilitates this operation.

No paper washers are used on any J.A.P. engines, but if the faces are

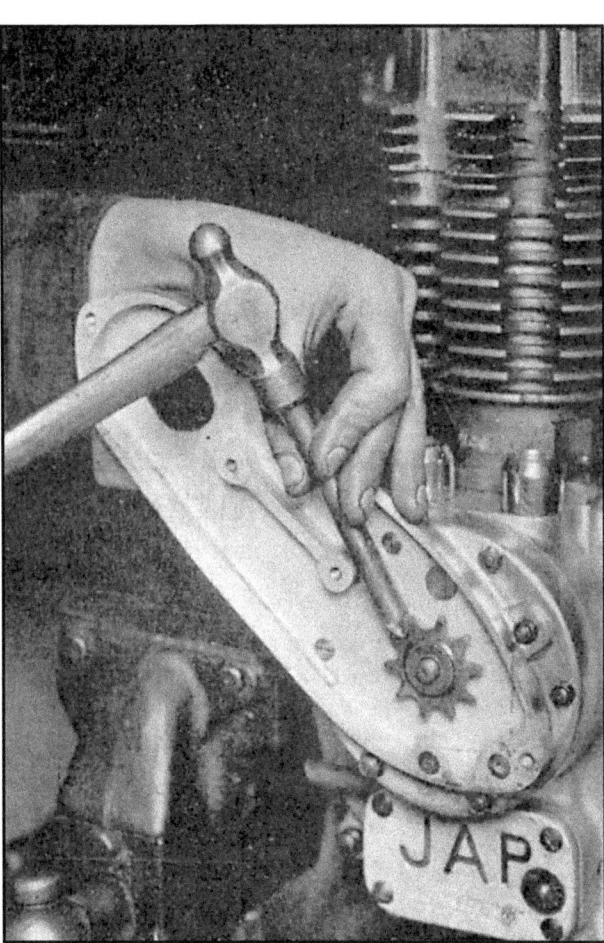

Fig. 3A.—REMOVE THE SPROCKET WHEEL.

First remove the chain cover, next remove the sprocket nut, then use a brass punch and hammer to loosen the sprocket, as shown above.

REPAIRING AND OVERHAULING J.A.P. ENGINES

damaged the burrs can be eased off with a fine Swiss file and a little goldsize smeared on cylinder base.

When replacing the fixing nuts tighten them finally a little at a time at opposite corners.

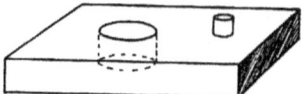

Fig. 4.—This illustrates a cast-iron block used in dismantling the Flywheels.

COMPLETE OVERHAUL OF SINGLE AND TWIN S.V. ENGINES

Taking off Cylinders for a Complete Overhaul

After taking out the engine from the frame it can be conveniently held in a vice if a wooden block is fixed to the bench as shown in Fig. 2.

Grip the middle left-hand lug in the vice with the gear side facing forwards, keeping the bolt fixed in the opposite lug and resting the bottom lug on the right-hand side of engine on the wood block. Cylinders can now be dismantled, taking precautions to see that the pistons are not forced against connecting rod in so doing.

Piston Rings

Remove the rings by inserting three feeler pieces between the rings and piston, spacing them at equal distances and sliding the rings over them. There is a very good instrument called the "Brico," manufactured by the British Chuck and Piston Ring Co., for this purpose.

Lay the rings aside so that they are fitted in their original grooves.

Taking off Sprocket

Next remove the chain-cover fixing screws and take off cover. The sprocket on the half time shaft can now be dismantled by a sprocket drawer or may be tapped at the *bottom* of the teeth with a brass punch and a hammer. A sharp blow will remove this from the taper after the fixing nut has been taken off. It will be unnecessary to take off the magneto sprocket unless the magneto requires attention.

How to take down the Bevel Drive

Various engines are fitted with a bevel drive magneto. It is first necessary in this case to remove the three bevel cap-cover screws, when the bevel fixing nut on the cam-wheel spindle will be in view. This must be removed with a box spanner, after having taken off the magneto from its base so that the nut is easier to get at. A sharp tap with a brass punch on the bottom of the teeth in an anticlockwise direction will remove the bevel from the taper.

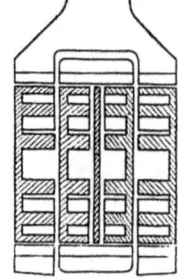

Fig. 5.—Big-end Assembly.

Note position of roller cages.

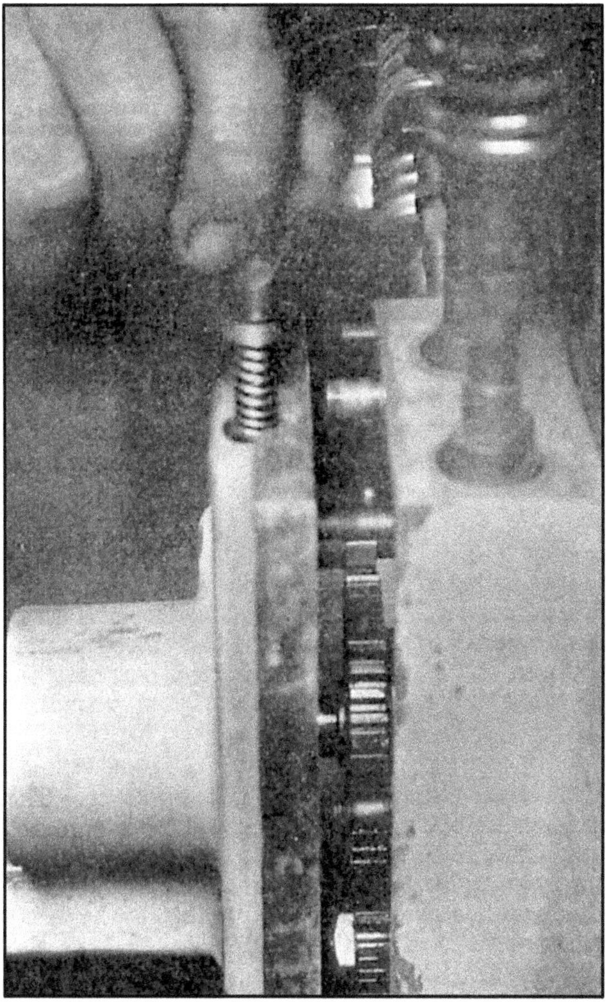

REPAIRING AND OVERHAULING J.A.P. ENGINES

Exhaust Lifter and Chain Drive or Timing Cover

Now take off the nipple, nut and guide from the exhaust lifter spindle. Remove the nuts from the gear drive and gently tap off the drive. Do not place a lever between the drive and crankcase, as damage will most likely result. While tapping off the drive make sure that the exhaust lifter cam is free, by pulling the spindle up and finding the free position (see Fig. 6). Take out cam wheel and levers, and place the levers on one side in their correct positions. They

Fig. 6.—Remember this when removing the Timing Cover.
Before removing the timing cover the exhaust valve lifter must be raised as shown.

can be refitted incorrectly, and it saves time to have them in correct order (see Fig. 8).

Removing Pinion

Place two dead-flat pieces of material on top of crankcase (see Fig. 16), and bring the piston

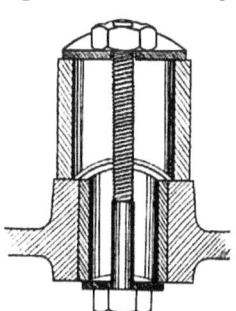

Fig. 7.—A Useful Workshop Tool for Withdrawing or Inserting Plain Bushes.

REPAIRING AND OVERHAULING J.A.P. ENGINES

down on to these. The piston must be brought to rest by turning the engine in the direction in which it runs, and the nut can be removed from the pinion, remembering that this has a LEFT-HAND thread.

Remove the pinion from the taper, noting the keyway which is connected with the key on the gear spindle, as there are three keyways on the pinion, each one giving a variation in the valve timing. The very early type pinions were screwed on the shaft with a *left-hand* thread and had no fixing nut.

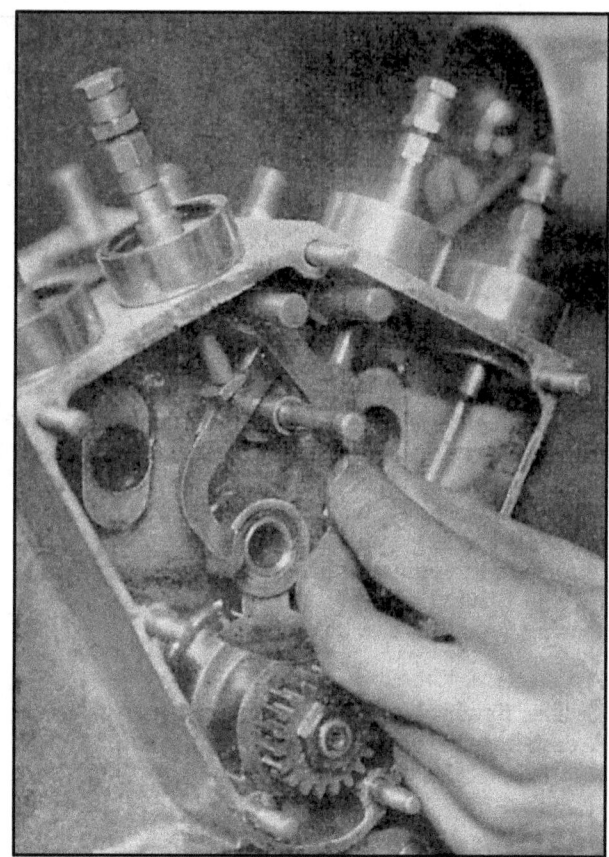

Fig. 8.—INSPECTING THE CAM GEAR.
After examining the teeth for backlash, remove the pinions and examine the levers for wear on the pads and on the cam-lever spindles. This picture also shows the order in which the levers should be replaced on their spindles when reassembling.

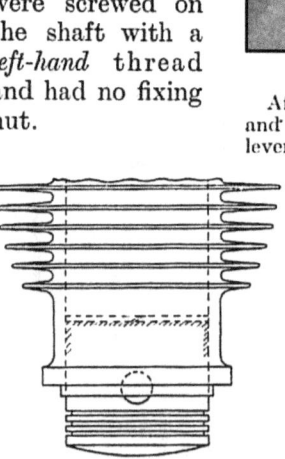

Fig. 9.—CHECKING PISTON-RING GAP.

Removal of Gudgeon Pin and Piston

In all standard engines prior to 1925 the gudgeon pins were a driving fit; aluminium pistons up to year 1928 were a fully floating fit with end pads in the gudgeon pins. After this date all J.A.P. pistons are fitted with circlips, which can be removed by compressing the two tail pieces and working outwards. Remove pin and take off

REPAIRING AND OVERHAULING J.A.P. ENGINES

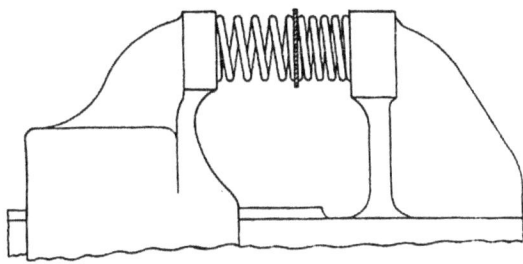

Fig. 10.—TESTING VALVE-SPRING TENSION.

piston, marking the side which is facing the front and replacing in the same position.

Parting Crankcase

Now take all the fixing bolts from the crankcase, and the halves can be parted by gently tapping the projecting lug evenly with a lead hammer or mallet.

Main Bearings

Practically all types of J.A.P. engines are of the roller-bearing type on the main driving-shaft side, and plain phosphor bronze bush on the gear side.

On 8-h.p. side-valve twin engines the driving side was of the double-row ball-bearing type since the year 1920, and roller bearing on the smaller twin engines, such as 680 c.c. and 750 c.c.

The driving side must be gently tapped off the shaft if of the ball-bearing type, but can be easily lifted off the roller type.

Flywheels

The flywheels can now be taken apart for examination of big end. A cast-iron block is used as shown in Fig. 4, with a hole for the main-

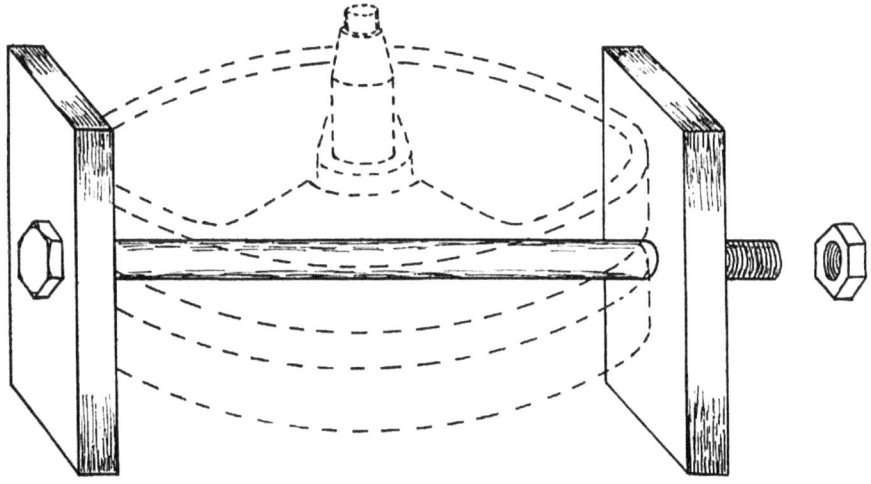

Fig. 11.—TRUING FLYWHEELS.
This useful workshop tool ensures that both flywheels are flush with one another.

REPAIRING AND OVERHAULING J.A.P. ENGINES

Fig. 12.—Driving in the Liner of a Big End.
Note the distance piece placed between the jaws to prevent damaging the big end, and the mild steel bar interposed between the hammer and the liner to avoid damaging it.

shaft and a projecting peg which rests against the counter weight and prevents the flywheels from turning when taking off the crankpin nut. The block should be held in a vice with the peg uppermost.

After the nut is taken off, tap the flywheel a few times on the rim on opposite sides of the crankpin. This will loosen the flywheel and allow it to be withdrawn from the crankpin.

Big-end Bearings

The single-cylinder side-valve engines have a double row of rollers in separate cages, the twins have one in each side of the fork rod and two on the centre rod.

Inspection for Wear

All the parts should be inspected for wear and renewed as found necessary. No hard-and-fast rule can be applied to the parts that should be replaced. It must rest entirely upon whether the owner requires the engine to be made as new or if he requires as little as possible expended on replacements. However, where the mainshaft and big end are concerned, it is false economy not to renew the parts showing any wear at all, as it will necessitate the whole engine again being stripped for renewals. Should only one roller be scored or flaked, it will be policy to replace all of them, as only under microscopical inspection can it be proved if the others are affected, and as a rule they are, and the race also. The liners are pressed into the rod and can be tapped out, not forgetting to support

REPAIRING AND OVERHAULING J.A.P. ENGINES

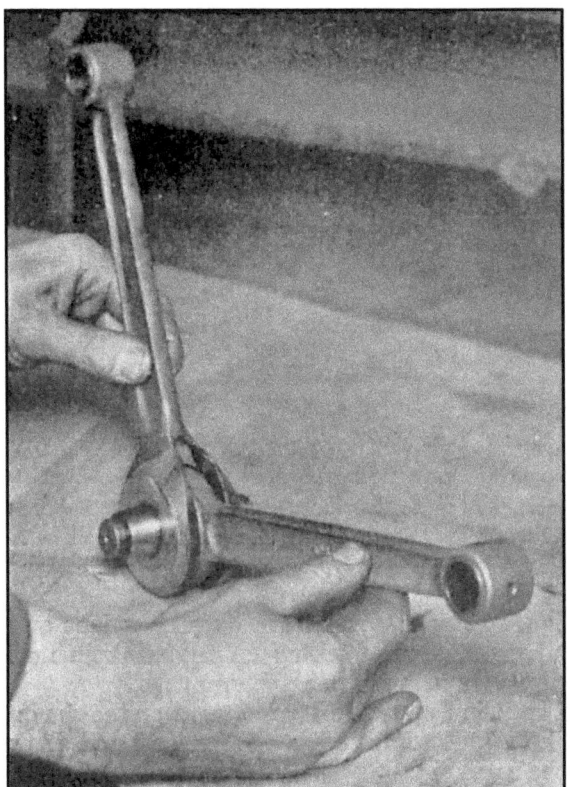

Fig. 13.—CON-ROD ASSEMBLY FOR TWIN J.A.P. ENGINE. Note the extended slot which must be on the *inner* side of the forked rod.

each half of the fork rod. Look to small end for wear in the bush. If requiring renewal, these and all plain bushes can be removed by the bolt and distance piece (see Fig. 7), or a suitable punch with pilot a good fit in the bush.

Cam Gear

Inspect cam gear: (1) teeth for back lash (oversize pinions can be had from makers); (2) levers for wear on the pads, or in case of roller cam levers on the outside diameter of rollers and on roller spindle. There should be appreciable up-and-down movement of the cam rollers on their bearings to allow for lubrication; (3) wear on cam-lever spindles and in bore of cam lever (a slight up-and-down movement is permissible here); (4) the exhaust lifter cam should show little sign of wear; (5) wear of cam-wheel spindle and bushes. It is best to place the cam wheels in the bushes, and after placing on the drive, test by trying to move the spindle up and down.

Cylinders and Pistons

Taking now the cylinders and pistons. Should the bore be badly stepped where the rings travel, it is advisable to have the cylinders reground and new pistons and rings fitted by the makers. This, however, should not be apparent until after several thousand miles running.

On 70 m/m bore and under the bottom of skirt clearance is approximately ·004 to ·006 inch. Above this diameter it is from ·007 to ·009 inch.

REPAIRING AND OVERHAULING J.A.P. ENGINES

Rings can be tried for width of gap by placing the rings in the bore where it is not unduly worn and squaring them by placing the piston in the bore and pushing the rings down a little (see Fig. 9). These should be renewed if the gap exceeds $\frac{1}{32}$ inch. A fair average gap for all standard types of engines is ·005 per inch of bore diameter.

Piston-ring grooves should be tried by placing the ring in the groove and noting the amount of side play. When new this is ·002 to ·003 inch. It should not be excessive, as once it gets bad the groove very quickly wears by the change

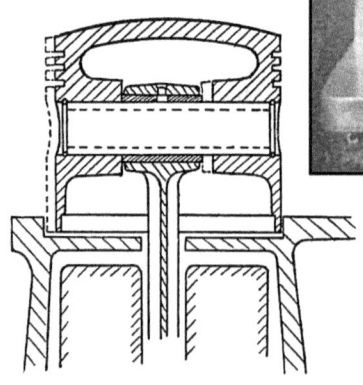

Fig. 15.—CENTRALISING PISTON IN SPIGOT.

Fig. 14.—HOW J.A.P. PISTONS ARE TESTED FOR WEAR.

The above gauge is used for measuring the diameter of a piston accurately at different points round the circumference. The large disk seen above the piston is hollow, and is closed by a flexible diaphragm which has a pointer touching the piston. The disk is connected to a thin tube, and both are filled with liquid. A slight movement of the diaphragm is magnified many times in the tube.

REPAIRING AND OVERHAULING J.A.P. ENGINES

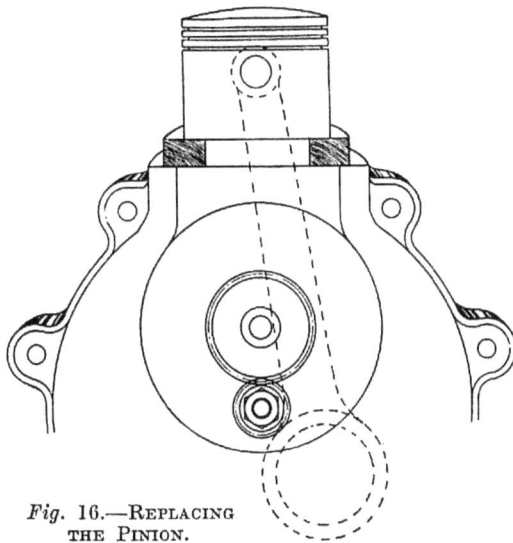

Fig. 16.—Replacing the Pinion.

The piston should be brought down on to two flat blocks to enable the fixing nut to be tightened up. Position of rod shown is for unscrewing nut which is L.H. thread.

An Ingenious Instrument

Fig. 14 shows a very interesting instrument which is used in the factory for measuring the diameter of a piston at different points. Although this instrument is too elaborate for use in an ordinary repair shop, the principle is thought to be of sufficient interest to warrant the following description.

Essentially the apparatus consists of a surface plate having an upright arm attached to it. On the upright is carried the measuring appliance. The latter consists of a fine tube filled with liquid communicating on its lower end with a large flat circular vessel. The lower end of this vessel is closed by a flexible diaphragm with a pointer attached to the centre. The piston is placed on the surface plate, and the pointer adjusted so that it just touches the side of the piston as shown in Fig. 14. The piston can then be moved along underneath the pointer and also twisted round. Any variation in diameter will, of course, cause a slight movement of the pointer and diaphragm.

A simple calculation will show that if the diameter of the diaphragm is 3 inches and the internal diameter of the tube say one-tenth of an inch, the movement of the pointer will be magnified 900 times in the tube.

Valve Seatings, Guides and Springs

Valve seatings in cylinders should not be worn or badly pocketed. Valve-seating cutters can be obtained from the manufacturers, but new valve guides should first be fitted, as the pilot of the cutter would otherwise be loose and cut the seating out of alignment.

Valve guides must be replaced if any sign of wear is apparent, as heavy petrol consumption and erratic running can often be traced to this cause.

Valve springs can be inspected for loss of tension by placing a new one together with the old with ends butting in a vice (see Fig. 10). Screw up the vice, and if the old one closes up before the new one it is as well to renew it.

REPAIRING AND OVERHAULING J.A.P. ENGINES

BIG ENDS AND GUDGEON BUSH

Assembling

Liners are replaced by pressing same in their housings. It is best to place a piece of flat metal underneath and either press or tap the liner until it is flush with side of rod. Great care must be exercised to see that the liner enters dead square, as if the alignment is bad a seized bearing will quickly result owing to the rollers tending to run up the crankpin. Small end can be replaced as shown in Fig. 7.

It may be found necessary to reamer out the bush after fitting same, as it will close in a little after drawing it in the housing.

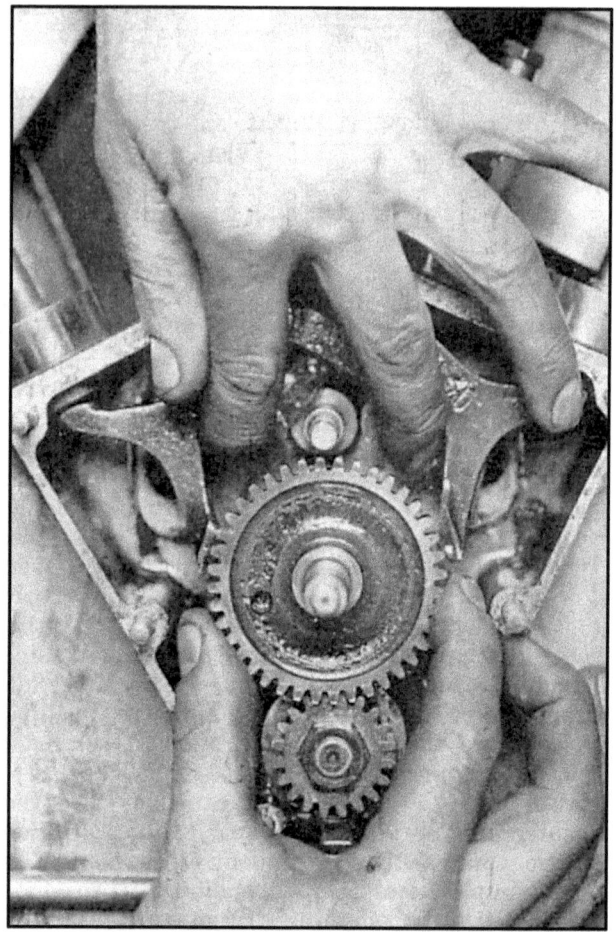

Fig. 17.—Replacing the Timing Wheels.

Force the cam lever apart with the fingers as shown, and insert the timing wheel so that the centre-punch marks on the wheel and pinion correspond.

Having the crankpin in position in one side of flywheel, the rollers and cages can be put into correct position (see Fig. 5), and bearings placed over the crankpin. Place a little oil on all bearings before refitting parts.

Assembling Flywheels

If the connecting rod is from a twin engine be sure and place the inner rod the correct way. A small slot will be noted extending up the fork rod from the gash; this must be placed on the inside, so that the angle of the cylinders may be obtained (see Fig. 13). The fork is connected to the

REPAIRING AND OVERHAULING J.A.P. ENGINES

front cylinder. Now place other flywheel on the crankpin after having thoroughly cleaned the tapers with petrol for preference, in order to prevent any oil film remaining which might cause the flywheels to shift. Tighten up the flywheels in the flywheel block, but the outside diameters must be flush one with another for truing purposes. A very excellent little tool for this purpose is given in Fig. 11. It consists of a piece of round mild steel (which will go in between the flywheels) threaded at either end and two flat pieces of metal of about 5 inches long, 1½ inches wide and ⅜ inch thick, drilled in the centres to just clear the spindle, and two large nuts with the faces dead true with the thread.

If the spindle is placed in between the flywheels and the nuts tightened on the small blocks, the flywheels will be in most cases brought dead true and the crankpin nuts can be finally tightened.

Afterwards check them by revolving them in between lathe centres.

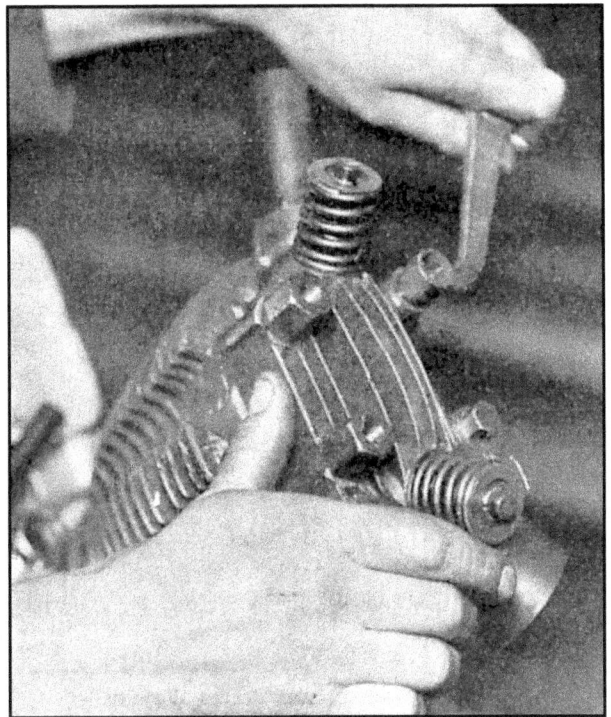

Fig. 18.—DISMANTLING A CYLINDER HEAD.
Note that a special angle box spanner must be used for undoing the fixing studs.

Assembling Flywheels in Crankcase

Now replace the roller bearing in driving side, the first roller cage being placed with the rollers facing the outside and back of cage facing towards flywheels. Then place the thick washer and after this the second cage of rollers, the back of cage facing the back of first cage. Now place the thin washer which butts against flywheel.

Place the flywheel in crankcase, and after placing the case in the vice on left-hand lugs and resting on wood block, fit a bolt in opposite lug and try for end play. There should be approximately ·008 inch, and any excess

77

REPAIRING AND OVERHAULING J.A.P. ENGINES

can be taken up with shims on the driving-side. Do not move the gear-side bush to take up the play, as this centralises the flywheels in crankcase.

On some later type engines the driving side-bearings have no cages: there are long rollers which must be packed in position with a little grease.

Fitting Pistons

Refit the pistons according to the marks made on taking same off. If of the end plug gudgeon type, the pins only require to be placed in the piston, but on circlip type the circlips need to be replaced. Take care to see that they are well bedded down in their grooves, or the pin may work the circlips out and score the cylinder.

If a new gudgeon bush has been fitted, test the piston for being central in the spigot of crankcase. This can be done by pushing the boss up against the bush and noting the clearance between piston and spigot. Repeat this operation on opposite side (see Fig. 15). Should this not be central draw the gudgeon bush as necessary.

Fitting Cam Gear

Place the levers on their respective pivot pins: in the case of twin engines with plain levers, the first lever to be fitted is the (1) rear inlet, which goes on the front pivot pin, (2) front inlet on rear pivot pin, (3) exhaust cam levers with the extension of pad facing outwards.

Pinion

Replace pinion on correct keyway. Bring piston down to rest on block or two flat pieces of metal, and tighten up fixing nut (left-hand thread).

Fitting Cam Wheel Exhaust Lifter and Drive

Now hold the levers apart with the fingers and place cam wheel in bushes, noting that the centre-punch marks correspond on the pinion and cam wheel. Place the distance piece over the lifter spindle. In some engines the distance piece is fitted before the exhaust lifter and in others the order is reversed. This is obvious by the position of lifter cam.

If new cam bushes have been fitted, the end play must be adjusted with the cover in position: ·008 inch is allowed, but must be adjusted by shifting the bushes in the drive. If new cam levers are fitted, see that the pads are square on the cam faces by placing a little lamp black on the cams and rotating engine.

Fit the chain or bevel drive with the exhaust lifter on the bearing,

REPAIRING AND OVERHAULING J.A.P. ENGINES

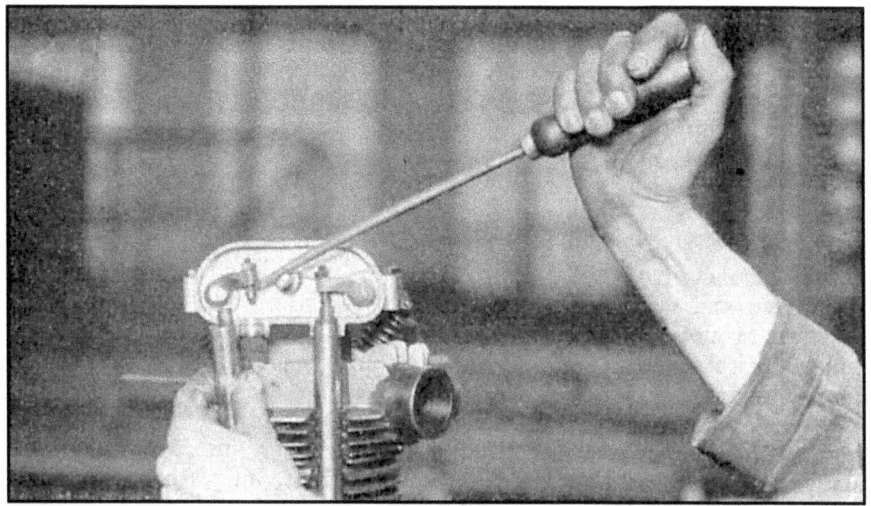

Fig. 19.—DISMANTLING THE HEAD.
First remove the push rods by levering the valves open.

and spindle protruding through the lifter guide hole in drive. As the drive is pushed over the studs, the lifter should be worked up and down to find the correct position for the lifter cam. It will slide on easily if care is taken to see that the cam is placed correctly to go between the lifter

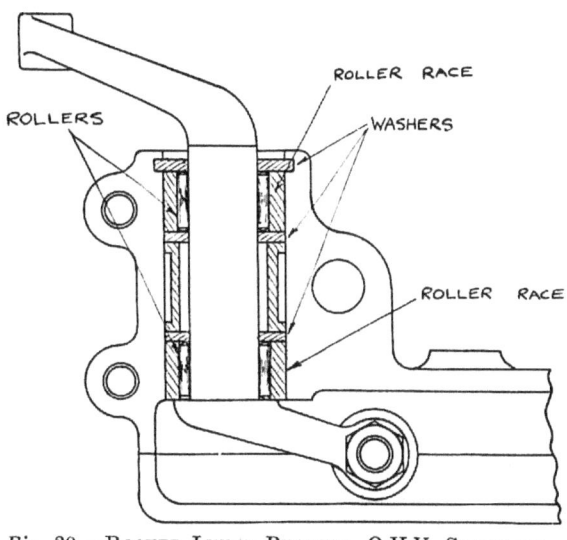

Fig. 20.—ROCKER LEVER BEARING, O.H.V. STANDARD.

Fig. 20A.—PUSH ROD AND ENDS.

REPAIRING AND OVERHAULING J.A.P. ENGINES

heels on the cam levers. Before placing on cylinders put about half a teacupful of oil in the crankcase.

Cylinders

Fit on the cylinders and adjust the tappets to ·004 inch clearance inlet and ·006 inch exhaust. Fit the exhaust lifter spindle guide, replace washer, nut and brass nipple. Adjust the nut so that there is a full $\frac{1}{32}$ inch free movement of spindle before lifter heel engages with cam lever and lifts exhaust tappet.

Fig. 21.—DISMANTLING THE HEAD.
After disconnecting the push rods unscrew rocker box fixing bolts and take off the rocker as shown above.

Valve Timing

The valve timing should be correct if the gear spindle has not been moved in the flywheels and instructions have been followed regarding replacement of pinion and cam wheel. Roughly, if the inlet valve opens slightly before top dead centre, the timing should be correct. In the case of engines with two separate cam wheels, take care to see that the front and rear inlets are not open at the same time.

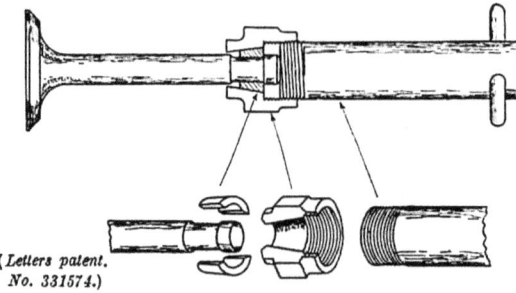

(*Letters patent.* No. 331574.)

Fig. 22.—VALVE GRINDING TOOL.

REPAIRING AND OVERHAULING J.A.P. ENGINES

This cannot happen if they are replaced to the marks, but may do so if a new cam wheel is fitted.

Magneto Timing

Magneto sprockets and chain can now be refitted and timed so that the points on the contact breaker open when the piston is $\frac{7}{16}$ inch before top dead centre, piston going up on compression stroke and ignition lever fully advanced.

If bevel driven, the nut on bevel wheel on cam spindle is not tightened up, as it is necessary to get the piston in correct position, set the points on magneto just opening, then tap on the bevel with a brass punch and finally tighten the nut. Check over magneto timing afterwards to see that the bevel has not moved. With twin engines it is necessary to see

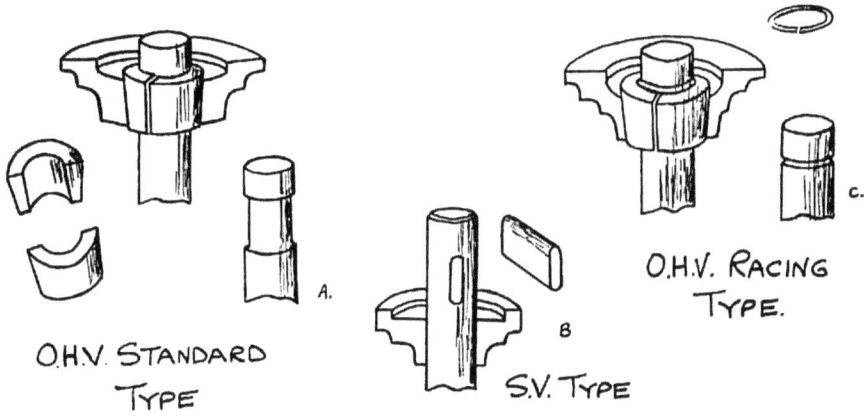

Fig. 23.—Methods of Valve Spring Fixing.

that No. 1 cam on magneto is timed to No. 1 cylinder. No. 1 cylinder is the left-hand one with cam gear facing forwards.

The complete valve and magneto timing for all types of engines is given on a separate chart.

OVERHEAD VALVE STANDARD ENGINES

The instructions given for the overhaul of side valve engines apply to the o.h.v., except for the difference on o.h.v. rocker gear and one or two small details.

Open Type Rocker Gear

To dismantle cylinder head a special angle box spanner is supplied for the fixing studs. It is a very difficult proposition to unscrew these studs without this spanner.

REPAIRING AND OVERHAULING J.A.P. ENGINES

Dismantling Head

First remove the push rods by levering the valves open. Up to 1928 the bearings were of the plain bearing type, after which they were roller bearing. The hinge pin screws into one side of the standard and is plain on the opposite side. It is first necessary to take out the split pin, unscrew nut, then unscrew the hinge pin from rocker standard, a screwdriver slot being provided for this purpose.

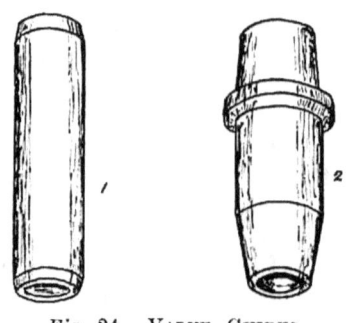

Fig. 24.—Valve Guides.
S.V. Type.   O.H.V. Type.

Do not attempt to drive out this pin after taking off the nut, otherwise a broken standard will result. In 1929 the enclosed rocker gear type was brought out.

To dismantle head first unscrew bell crank arm on front of rocker cover, take off cover. It is now possible to press down push rod cover, which will then pull forwards out of the spigot in rocker box. Disconnect push rods, and after taking off rocker fixing bolts the rocker box will be detached, leaving the head held by four bolts which can be taken out as explained previously. The rocker bearings will practically last as long as the engine. Do not worry about the endplay in rockers after dismantling the box, as this is positioned by the small pads on the rocker cover, therefore this must be in position when testing this.

If it should be more than a full $\frac{1}{84}$ inch, it can be adjusted by taking off the top half of the box and the roller races moved outwards, tightening the top half after adjusting.

In the direct attack type of push rod, the push rod rests in a recess in the cam lever, and there are no tappets. Be careful to see that the rods are replaced correctly with the loose ball engaging o.h. rocker.

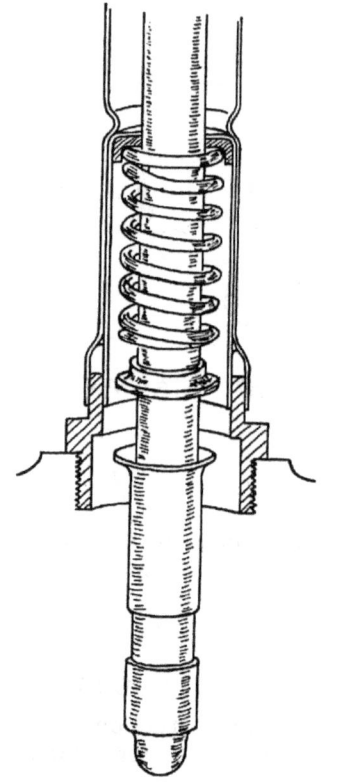

Fig. 25.—Push-rod Return Spring—O.H.V. Racing.

Taking out Valves

The valves are fitted with a split taper cone, and a tool is manufactured for taking these apart. It is similar to a carpenter's clamp, one end

REPAIRING AND OVERHAULING J.A.P. ENGINES

positioning under the valve head, the other resting on top of spring collar. This end is screwed, and by screwing same up it compresses the spring and the split cotters can be removed. Upon releasing this, the collar and spring can be taken off.

Grinding Valves

No screwdriver slot is provided in the head of o.h.v. valves, as it is detrimental, but a special tool is sold by the manufacturers, Messrs. J. A. Prestwich, which will take any size of valve and is extremely simple to use (see Fig. 22).

The split cotters fitted to the valve stem are placed in the tool, and by screwing up the nut, the valve can be held in exactly the same manner as on the engine.

Cylinder Barrel

The barrel is held on the base in the same manner as the side-valve cylinders.

All other details are similar to the side-valve engines.

INTERESTING FITTING DETAILS ON SIDE-VALVE AND O.H.V. ENGINES

Push rod ends are renewed by tapping off the end cap from push rod and pressing on the new cap. The detachable end is clearly shown by Fig. 20A.

When making up new complete push rods, care must be exercised when cutting the rod to length. The method is to place the bottom end on the tappet, or in the case of enclosed rocker gear, on the recess in the cam lever, and place the loose top end cup in position at the side of the push rod, when it will be evident how much is required to cut off before fitting the end cup.

Previously it has been mentioned that it was possible to adjust the end-play in rockers by moving the race. It will be clearly seen by Fig. 20 the position of the races in the rocker box.

On side-valve engines, valve guides are plain on the outside diameter and have no shoulders (see Fig. 24 (1)). The correct position of these can be taken from the old guide. When fitting these, which are a press fit in their housings, care must be exercised to see that they are not pressed in too far so that they foul the radius underneath valve head, or the valve will not seat. There should be $\frac{3}{32}$-inch clearance between finish of radius and end of valve guide.

Racing type valve guides have a shoulder which locates the position

REPAIRING AND OVERHAULING J.A.P. ENGINES

(see Fig. 24 (2)). Care is needed when tapping these in position. Too much force will result in the shoulder being fractured.

When refitting the split cotters and collars to valves, see that they are placed on the same valves from which they were taken off, as they will be nicely bedded in, and it is therefore essential that they are kept together. When fitting new split cotters they will be found to be split through one side, but only halfway through the opposite side. They need to be sawn right through this side before fitting. The reason they are delivered in this way is to be sure that the cone is a dead fit (see Fig. 23).

Side-valve Tappets

Tappets are supplied left long enough on the stem to take up wear. They therefore require to be cut off to correct length. The old-type stems required hardening on the ends after cutting to length by heating to a cherry red and quenching in oil, but the latest type are hardened and only require grinding to length.

On racing valves of the latest type a spring ring is incorporated with the split cotters. This is for locating the split cotters, and also acts as an extra safeguard for preventing the cotters moving. This ring fits in a groove in the valve stem, and on its outside diameter rests in a recess provided in the split cotters (see Fig. 23c). When dismantling the valve it is necessary to first remove the spring ring (after, of course, having compressed the spring), then the split cotters can be removed.

SPECIAL NOTES ON J.A.P. O.H.V. RACING ENGINES

Racing engines are manufactured in seven different types, comprising 175-c.c., 250-c.c., 350-c.c., 500-c.c., 600-c.c., 750-c.c. and 1,000-c.c. twin.

Compression Ratios

Pistons are supplied giving different compression ratios for petrol-benzol and alcohol fuels, and appended hereunder are suggested ratios for all engines.

		Piston for Petrol-Benzol.		Piston for Alcohol.	
175 c.c.,	53 × 78 mm.	With $\frac{1}{4}''$ plate = 9	to 1 ratio	$\frac{1}{32}''$ plate = 13	to 1 ratio
250 c.c.,	62·5 × 80 mm.	No plate = 8·2	to 1 ,,	No plate = 10·4	to 1 ,,
350 c.c.,	70 × 90 mm.	No plate = 7·4	to 1 ,,	No plate = 10	to 1 ,,
500 c.c.,	80 × 99 mm.	$\frac{1}{16}''$ plate = 7	to 1 ,,	No plate = 10	to 1 ,,
600 c.c.,	85·7 × 104 mm.	$\frac{1}{4}''$ plate = 6·6	to 1 ,,	No plate = 8	to 1 ,,
750 c.c.,	74 × 85 mm.	$\frac{1}{8}''$ plate = 7	to 1 ,,	No plate = 8·25	to 1 ,,
1,000 c.c.,	80 × 99 mm.	$\frac{1}{16}''$ plate = 7	to 1 ,,	No plate = 10	to 1 ,,

Special Piston for 600 c.c. Engine

With the 600-c.c. single a special H.C. piston can be supplied, giving 12 to 1 ratio. This, however, has been mainly used on the Continent for sidecar races.

REPAIRING AND OVERHAULING J.A.P. ENGINES

Engine for Dirt-track Machines

There is also a special 500-c.c. dirt-track engine which has a bore and stroke of 80 × 99 mm. This engine is considerably lighter than the standard racing engine, weighing only 57 lb., and developing 36 B.H.P. on alcohol fuel.

Timing for Dirt-track Engine

The valve and magneto timing is given on the separate chart for all racing engines, but does not include the dirt-track engine. This is as follows :

Inlet opens 39° before T.D.C. Inlet closes 64° after B.D.C.
Exhaust opens 66° before B.D.C. Exhaust closes 35° after T.D.C.
Magneto timing 37°, with ignition lever fully advanced.

Improving the Performance

There is very little work which can be put in to improve the performance of racing engines, as they are specially erected, and all the parts, such as ports, valves, head and piston crown are highly polished. It is necessary, however, when dismantling and re-erecting, to see that the parts are restored to their former condition by polishing the ports, head, valves, etc. Do not grind the valves unnecessarily with coarse grinding compound, but touch them up with a metal polish only, unless they are badly pitted on the seatings.

The piston ring clearance must not be as small in the gap as a standard engine, but should be about ·018 to ·020 for 60- and 70-mm. bores, and ·020 to ·025 for 80- and 85·7-mm. bore cylinders.

New copper gaskets should be fitted each time the head is taken off.

Regarding cam wheels, there are no special cams supplied other than those fitted to each engine.

Plugs

Recommended sparking plugs are :
KLG No. 348 or No. 341. The former stands more heat than the latter, but the latter will withstand more oil but less heat.
Lodge B.R. 19.

Carburetter Jets

Jet and choke sizes need considerable thought and experiment. It is impossible to lay down any hard-and-fast rule, but with a too large choke acceleration will suffer, and if too small the all-out speed will be restricted.

Too small a jet will quickly result in overheating and burnt exhaust valves, and with too large a jet the maximum revolution per minute will not be reached.

REPAIRING AND OVERHAULING J.A.P. ENGINES

Transmission Parts

When tuning for racing the engine very often receives all the attention, and vital parts, such as gearbox, wheel bearing, tension of chains, etc., are neglected. It is essential to have these parts free running, as a good deal of loss of speed can be traced to tightness in these fitments.

Gear Ratios

Gear ratios need a good deal of thought, and it is found in most cases that one is apt to overgear. This is very detrimental, as the engine can never reach its peak revolutions per minute.

For ordinary races, such as on give-and-take roads, the following gear ratios will be found about the best for solo work:

175-c.c.	250-c.c.	350-c.c.	500-c.c.	600-c.c.	750-c.c.	1,000-c.c.
7·3 to 1	6 to 1	5·3 to 1	4·25 to 1	4·25 to 1	4 to 1	3·25 to 1

Hereunder is a chart giving engine revolutions at various road speeds and gear ratios for 26-inch diameter road wheels.

Gear:	3½	3¾	4	4¼	4½	4¾	5	5¼	5½	5¾	6	6¼
m.p.h.				Engine Revolutions per minute								
5	226	242	258	275	291	307	323	339	355	372	388	404
10	452	484	517	549	581	614	646	679	711	743	776	808
15	679	727	775	824	872	921	970	1,018	1,066	1,115	1,163	1,212
20	905	969	1,034	1,099	1,163	1,228	1,293	1,358	1,422	1,486	1,551	1,616
25	1,131	1,212	1,292	1,373	1,454	1,535	1,616	1,697	1,777	1,858	1,939	2,020
30	1,357	1,454	1,551	1,648	1,745	1,842	1,939	2,036	2,133	2,230	2,327	2,424
35	1,583	1,697	1,810	1,923	2,036	2,149	2,262	2,376	2,488	2,602	2,715	2,828
40	1,810	1,938	2,068	2,198	2,326	2,456	2,586	2,716	2,844	2,972	3,102	3,232
45	2,036	2,182	2,327	2,470	2,617	2,763	2,909	3,055	3,200	3,345	3,490	3,636
50	2,262	2,424	2,585	2,747	2,908	3,070	3,232	3,394	3,555	3,716	3,878	4,040
55	2,488	2,666	2,844	3,022	3,199	3,370	3,555	3,733	3,910	4,087	4,265	4,444
60	2,715	2,908	3,102	3,296	3,490	3,684	3,878	4,072	4,266	4,460	4,654	4,848
65	2,941	3,150	3,360	3,570	3,781	3,991	4,201	4,411	4,621	4,831	5,042	5,252
70	3,167	3,394	3,620	3,846	4,072	4,298	4,524	4,752	4,976	5,204	5,430	5,656
75	3,394	3,636	3,878	4,121	4,362	4,605	4,847	5,091	5,331	5,576	5,818	6,060
80	3,620	3,876	4,136	4,396	4,652	4,912	5,172	5,432	5,688	5,944	6,204	6,464
85	3,846	4,118	4,394	4,671	4,943	5,219	5,495	5,771	6,043	6,316	6,588	6,868
90	4,072	4,364	4,654	4,940	5,234	5,526	5,818	6,110	6,400	6,690	6,980	7,272
95	4,299	4,606	4,912	5,214	5,525	5,833	6,141	6,449	6,755	7,061	7,367	7,676
100	4,525	4,848	5,170	5,494	5,816	6,140	6,464	6,788	7,110	7,432	7,756	8,080

In conjunction with above chart a suitable gear can be selected by studying where the engine peaks, as follows:

Engine	175-c.c.	250-c.c.	350-c.c.	500-c.c.	600-c.c.	750-c.c.	1,000-c.c.
R.P.M.	7,000	6,500	6,200	5,600	5,200	5,500	5,200
Brake horse-power	12	17·3	23	31	33	40	58

For 28-inch wheels multiply the revolutions by ·93, and for 24-inch wheels multiply by 1·03.

TIMING CHART "JAP" ENGINES
1926—1928

MODELS.	INLET.		EXHAUST.		IGNITION MAX. ADV. Before T.D.C.	Tappet Clearance.	
	Opens before T.D.C.	Closes after B.D.C.	Opens before B.D.C.	Closes after T.D.C.		Ex.	In.
175 c.c. S.V. Standard	5°	45°	65°	15°	35°	·006″	·004″
250 c.c. S.V. Standard	8°	52°	60°	20°	40°	·006″	·004″
250 c.c. S.V. Sports	5°	45°	65°	15°	40°	·006″	·004″
250 c.c. O.H. Standard	8°	52°	60°	20°	40°	·002″	·002″
250 c.c. O.H. Racing	15°	55°	65°	25°	40°	·002″	·002″
293 c.c. S.V. Standard	0°	30°	45°	25°	35°	·006″	·004″
300 c.c. S.V. Standard	8°	52°	60°	20°	35°	·006″	·004″
350 c.c. S.V. Roadster	8°	52°	60°	20°	35°	·006″	·004″
350 c.c. S.V. Standard	8°	52°	60°	20°	35°	·006″	·004″
350 c.c. S.V. Sports	8°	52°	60°	20°	40°	·006″	·004″
350 c.c. O.H. Standard	8°	52°	60°	20°	40°	·002″	·002″
350 c.c. O.H. Sports	15°	55°	65°	25°	40°	·002″	·002″
350 c.c. O.H. Racing	15°	55°	65°	25°	40°	·002″	·002″
500 c.c. S.V. Standard	15°	60°	62½°	22½°	40°	·006″	·004″
500 c.c. S.V. Sports	15°	60°	62½°	22½°	40°	·006″	·004″
500 c.c. O.H. Sports	15°	60°	62½°	22½°	40°	·002″	·002″
500 c.c. O.H. Racing	15°	60°	62½°	22½°	40°	·002″	·002″
600 c.c. S.V. Standard	15°	60°	62½°	22½°	35°	·006″	·004″
600 c.c. S.V. Sports	15°	60°	62½°	22½°	35°	·006″	·004″
4 h.p. S.V. Twin	0°	30°	50°	20°	38°	·006″	·004″
680 c.c. S.V. Twin	0°	30°	50°	20°	38°	·006″	·004″
980 c.c. S.V. Twin	0°	30°	50°	20°	35°	·006″	·004″
980 c.c. S.V. Twin, 1926	10°	50°	60°	20°	40°	·006″	·004″
980 c.c. S.V. Sports Twin	10°	50°	60°	20°	40°	·006″	·004″
8-30 h.p. Sports Twin	15°	60°	62½°	22½°	40°	·006″	·004″
980 c.c. O.H. Sports Twin	15°	60°	62½°	22½°	40°	·002″	·002″
1,100 c.c. O.H.W.C. Twin	15°	60°	62½°	22½°	40°	·002″	·002″

TIMING CHART "JAP" ENGINES
1929—1930

MODELS.		INLET. Opens before T.D.C.	INLET. Closes after B.D.C.	EXHAUST. Opens before B.D.C.	EXHAUST. Closes after T.D.C.	IGNITION MAX. ADV. Before T.D.C.	Tappet Clearance. Ex.	Tappet Clearance. In.
175 c.c. S.V., V.		5°	45°	65°	15°	35°	·006"	·004"
200 c.c. S.V., N.		8°	52°	60°	20°	32°	·006"	·004"
250 c.c. S.V., B.		8°	52°	60°	20°	40°	·006"	·004"
250 c.c. O.H.V., P.O. and P.O.Y.		20°	60°	60°	25°	39°	·002"	·002"
300 c.c. S.V., A.		8°	52°	60°	20°	35°	·006"	·004"
350 c.c. S.V., I.Y. and I.Y./M.		8°	52°	60°	20°	35°	·006"	·004"
350 c.c. S.V., I.		8°	52°	60°	20°	35°	·006"	·004"
350 c.c. O.H.V., I.O. and I.O.Y.	STANDARD	24°	55°	60°	20°	40°	·002"	·002"
500 c.c. S.V., K.Y.	STANDARD	15°	60°	62½°	22½°	40°	·006"	·004"
500 c.c. S.V., K.	STANDARD	10°	50°	60°	20°	40°	·006"	·004"
500 c.c. O.H.V., K.O. and K.O.Y.	STANDARD	15°	60°	62½°	22½°	45°	·002"	·002"
550 c.c. S.V., L.Y.	STANDARD	15°	60°	62½°	22½°	40°	·006"	·004"
600 c.c. S.V., U.	STANDARD	10°	50°	60°	20°	35°	·006"	·004"
680 c.c. S.V., G.T.	STANDARD	5°	40°	50°	25°	38°	·006"	·004"
680 c.c. O.H.Y., G.T.O.Y.	STANDARD	20°	50°	50°	20°	40°	·002"	·002"
750 c.c. S.V., M.T.	STANDARD	5°	40°	50°	25°	38°	·006"	·004"
980 c.c. S.V., K.T.	STANDARD	10°	50°	60°	20°	40°	·006"	·004"
980 c.c. S.V., K.T.W.	STANDARD	10°	50°	60°	20°	40°	·006"	·004"
1,100 c.c. W./C., L.T.O.W., L.T.O.W./C., L.T.O.W./R.		15°	60°	62½°	22½°	40°	·002"	·002"
350 c.c. O.H.V., S.O.C.	SPORTS	15°	55°	65°	25°	42°	·002"	·002"
500 c.c. O.H.V., K.O.C.	SPORTS	15°	60°	62½°	22½°	44°	·002"	·002"
980 c.c. S.V., K.T.C.	SPORTS	10°	50°	60°	20°	40°	·006"	·004"
8-30 h.p., K.T.C.Y.	SPORTS	15°	60°	62½°	22½°	40°	·006"	·004"
175 c.c. O.H.V., H.O.R.	RACING	20°	60°	60°	30°	35°	·002"	·002"
250 c.c. O.H.V., P.O.R.	RACING	24°	55°	62°	25°	48-50°	·002"	·002"
350 c.c. O.H.V., S.O.R.	RACING	15°	55°	65°	25°	48-50°	·002"	·002"
350 c.c. O.H.V., I.O.R.	RACING	24°	55°	62°	25°	48-50°	·002"	·002"
500 c.c. O.H.V., K.O.R.	RACING	15°	60°	62½°	22½°	38-50°	·002"	·002"
500 c.c. O.H.V., J.O.R.	RACING	20°	55°	65°	25°	38-50°	·002"	·002"
600 c.c. O.H.V., U.O.R.	RACING	15°	60°	62½°	22½°	38-50°	·002"	·002"
750 c.c. O.H.V., E.T.O.R.	RACING	15°	60°	62½°	22½°	38-50°	·002"	·002"
8-45 h.p. O.H.V., K.T.O.R.	RACING	15°	60°	62½°	22½°	38-50°	·002"	·002"
1,000 c.c. O.H.V., J.T.O. and J.T.O.R.	RACING	15°	60°	62½°	22½°	38-50°	·002"	·002"

TIMING CHART "JAP" ENGINES
1931

MODELS.	INLET.		EXHAUST.		IG-NITION MAX. ADV. Before T.D.C.	Tappet Clearance.	
	Opens before T.D.C.	Closes after B.D.C.	Opens before B.D.C.	Closes after T.D.C.		Ex.	In.
175 c.c. S.V. Standard 200 c.c. ,, ,, 250 c.c. ,, ,, 300 c.c. ,, ,, 350 c.c. ,, ,, 350 c.c. ,, "Aza".	12°	55°	50°	15°	35°	·006″	·004″
500 c.c. S.V. Standard 500 c.c. ,, Sports 550 c.c. ,, Standard 600 c.c. ,, ,, 600 c.c. ,, Sports	10°	50°	60°	20°	40°	·006″	·004″
680 c.c. S.V. Standard Twin 750 c.c. ,, ,, ,,	5°	40°	50°	25°	38°	·006″	·004″
980 c.c. S.V. A./C. and W./C. Twin	10°	50°	60°	20°	40°	·006″	·004″
980 c.c. S.V. 8–30 H.P. Twin	15°	60°	62°	22°	40°	·006″	·004″
175 c.c. O.H.V. Standard 200 c.c. ,, ,, 250 c.c. ,, ,, 300 c.c. ,, ,,	20°	60°	60°	25°	39°	·002″	·002″
350 c.c. O.H.V. Standard 350 c.c. S.V. Sports 400 c.c. ,, ,,	24°	55°	60°	30°	40°	·002″	·002″
500 c.c. O.H.V. Standard 600 c.c. ,, ,,	15°	55°	60°	22°	45°	·002″	·002″
500 c.c. O.H.V. Standard Twin 680 c.c. ,, ,, ,,	20°	50°	50°	20°	40°	·002″	·002″
1,000 c.c. O.H.V. Standard Twin 1,100 c.c. ,, ,, ,,	22°	60°	60°	20°	40°	·002″	·002″
175 c.c. O.H.V. Racing	20°	60°	60°	30°	35°	·002″	·002″
250 c.c. O.H.V. Racing 350 c.c. ,, ,,	24°	55°	62°	25°	40–48°	·002″	·002″
500 c.c. O.H.V. Racing 600 c.c. ,, ,,	22°	·60°	60°	20°	38–50°	·002″	·002″
500 c.c. O.H.V. Racing Twin	24°	55°	62°	25°	42–50°	·002″	·002″
750 c.c. O.H.V. Racing Twin 1,000 c.c. ,, ,, 1,100 c.c. ,, Sports W./C. Twin	22°	60°	60°	20°	38–50°	·002″	·002″

REPAIR NOTES ON LEVIS ENGINES

By W. S. BANNER (*of Butterfields, Ltd.*)

Fig. 1.—REMOVING THE FLYWHEEL—FIRST OPERATION.
Use a hammer and spanner as shown above to loosen the flywheel nut.

TWO-STROKE MODELS

WITH certain exceptions in the case of the "Six-Port" model, the methods of dismantling all Levis two-stroke models are almost identical.

How to remove the Flywheel

The first operation is to remove the flywheel, which operation should be performed in the following manner. After unscrewing the flywheel nut (ordinary right-hand thread), the end of the crankshaft should be given one or two sharp square blows with a fairly heavy hammer. At the same time, hold the flywheel firmly with one hand and pull away from the engine. At the first or second blow, the flywheel should come

*Fig. 2.—*Removing the Flywheel—Second Operation.
Tap the end of the shaft with a hammer, hold the flywheel firmly with one hand, and pull away from engine.

*Fig. 3.—*Replacing the Flywheel.
In this case the final tightening of the flywheel nut should be carried out as above, using the spanner and hammer.

REPAIR NOTES ON LEVIS ENGINES

away, and, if the blows are square and decided, no damage will be done to the threads on the end of the crankshaft, as the end of the shaft is toughened.

Dealing with Obstinate Cases

The flywheel should come off, however obstinate, if one person holds the flywheel firmly by its rim, at the same time pulling away from the engine, whilst a second person uses the hammer on the end of the crankshaft as mentioned above. It should be carefully noted that a hammer of less than $1\frac{1}{2}$ lb. is quite useless for this job.

No key is used to secure the flywheel to the shaft, the fixing relying solely upon the taper. This applies to all Levis two-stroke models, with the exception of a comparatively small number of machines turned out in pre-war days. These were fitted with keys, but it is recommended that the use of the key be discontinued, as it has no holding value. Quite obviously such a small key cannot possibly be expected to hold a flywheel of such weight and diameter.

If a Flywheel works Loose—a Warning

It is important to note that, in the case of trouble with the flywheel coming loose upon the taper, it is not of the slightest use to endeavour to secure it with the aid of a key. If this is attempted, all that will happen, when the engine is started up, is that the flywheel will shear the key, thus irreparably damaging both the taper of the crankshaft and the bore of the flywheel. In this case, the only remedy is new parts.

Removing the Cylinder

The removal of the cylinder does not present any difficulty, and in the case of all Levis models, the cylinder can be removed without taking the engine out of the frame. In the case, however, of those models where the tank is mounted on two detachable tubes, it is advisable to remove the tank first, as by doing this the job is made very much more easy and convenient. The time saved more than compensates for the time taken to remove and replace the tank, and moreover, there is far less danger of damaging the piston or straining the connecting rod than when trying to work in a confined space. In the case of recent models with saddle tank, the frame has a second rail upon which the tank is mounted, and in this case there is no advantage in removing the tank first.

An Important Precaution

When removing the cylinder, it is very advisable to stuff the inside of the piston with rag before the cylinder actually comes away. Otherwise the heavy deflector head of the piston will cause the skirt to come sharply in contact with the connecting rod immediately the cylinder is removed, and which is quite likely to crack the piston.

REPAIR NOTES ON LEVIS ENGINES

About Gudgeon Pins

There are broadly two different types of gudgeon pin in use in Levis two-stroke engines: firstly, a taper gudgeon pin of $\frac{7}{16}$-inch diameter; and secondly, a parallel gudgeon pin of $\frac{1}{2}$-inch diameter, the latter type being fitted to the recent models. The early $\frac{7}{16}$-inch taper gudgeon pins rely entirely upon the taper to secure them in the piston bosses, in which case, of course, the gudgeon pin is a rather tight fit in the piston. In the case of these, the utmost care must be used in dismantling to avoid distorting or breaking the piston. The gudgeon pin should be driven out with a hammer and a brass punch, whilst the piston is well supported on the other side. These taper gudgeon pins drive out towards the flywheel.

In the case of the $\frac{7}{16}$-inch taper gudgeon pins which have circlips in the piston bosses, these are not so tight, and removal is therefore not fraught with much difficulty or risk of damage. Wherever a $\frac{1}{2}$-inch gudgeon pin is fitted, it will be found to be parallel and a comparatively loose fit, so that it may be pushed out either way after, of course, the circlips have been removed.

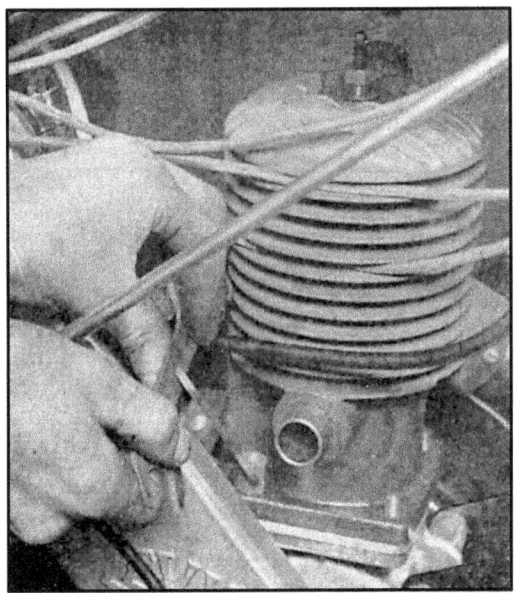

Fig. 4.—DEALING WITH AN AWKWARD NUT.
The cylinder base nut behind the magneto chain cover must be removed as shown above. Note that two thin spanners are required for this purpose.

Prising Crankcase Apart

After the piston has been taken off and the crankcase bolts removed, the crankcase halves should be carefully prised asunder. Use the handle of a hammer or a piece of wood between the two halves, or tap one of the cylinder base studs lightly with it. As crankcase compression is used in a two-stroke, care should be used to prevent damage to the faces of the crankcase halves whilst they are dismantled.

An Important Note for dismantling the Big End

The taking down of the big end will be obvious, but it should be noted that each time this operation is performed, new big-end pins will be

REPAIR NOTES ON LEVIS ENGINES

required. They are not intended to be used more than once, and new pins should be obtained before starting upon the job. The big-end bearing is plain and of phosphor bronze, being made in two halves. Shims are used to fill in the gap of the sawcut which has divided the bearing. After the big end has been dismantled, the engine will have been resolved into its component parts.

Examine Piston for Wear—a Cause of "Two-stroke Rattle"

When decarbonising, it is highly important to clean off every trace of carbon from the sides of the deflector head of the piston and from the cylinder walls inside near the top. Any sign of excessive wear or binding of the piston, especially the one side at the top and the opposite side at the bottom, indicates that the alignment of the connecting rod has suffered, and this should have the careful attention of a capable and experienced engine fitter, or the necessary engine parts returned to the makers for attention. These two items are sometimes responsible for the elusive "two-stroke rattle" which has given rise to so many discussions amongst motor-cyclists.

Re-erecting—the Big End

Let us now deal with the process of re-erecting. In assembling the big end and refitting same to the one-piece crankshaft, the two new big-end pins should be screwed up tight with a tubular spanner, and after they are home, split the threaded ends and splay same open slightly like a split pin. Also, do not forget to file off the corners of the hexagon heads of the big-end pins, as unless this is done there is not enough clearance in the crankcase.

Fig. 5.—METHOD OF REMOVING THE CYLINDER.

Observe that the inside of the piston is stuffed with rag to prevent it from becoming damaged by contact with the connecting rod when the cylinder is actually lifted off.

If it is necessary for a new big-end bearing to be fitted, it should be noticed that this has to be pegged and scraped in the usual way. Slight play can be taken up by filing the shims previously referred to. These should be secured on a board with short tacks or nails, the latter being

REPAIR NOTES ON LEVIS ENGINES

driven almost home so as not to project above the surface of the shim. The shims should then be filed until the play has been taken up.

Cleaning out Crankcase and Oilways

Before refitting the crankshaft in the crankcase, take the opportunity of swilling this out thoroughly in paraffin, so that the oilways may have a good clean. The crankshaft is drilled as part of the Levis lubrication system. The oilways in the crankcase bearings should also be similarly swilled.

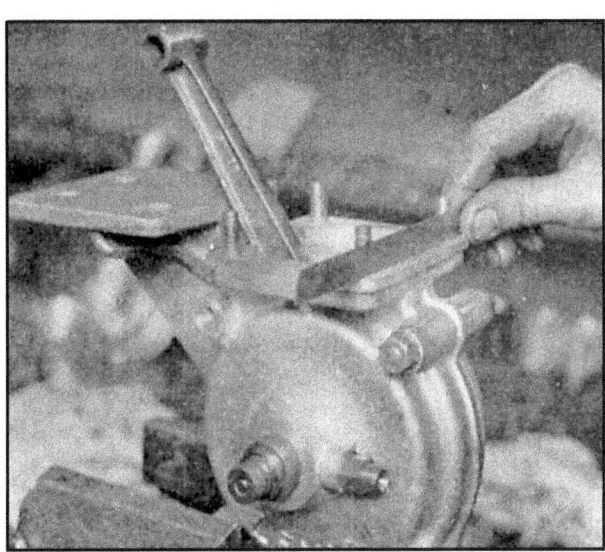

Fig. 6.—An Important Test when Reassembling a Levis Crankcase.

Lay a straightedge across the two halves to make sure that they are in line. A perfect joint is of first importance, because of the use of the crank chamber for compression.

Worn Main Bearings

The main bearings should be examined for play, and if this is only slight, renewal should not be necessary. Do not worry too much about crankcase compression as regards the bearings, as it has been proved time and again that the bearings invariably require renewal for mechanical reasons long before the loss of compression is sufficient to have any effect upon the efficiency or performance of the engine. If the main bearings are badly worn and really require renewal, it is advisable to return the crankcase to the makers to have this done, as few garages and still fewer owners are likely to have a line reamer such as is necessary to ensure that the main bearings are in alignment. With an ordinary reamer, it is quite possible for the bearings to be reamered individually, and each one apparently quite all right in its own half of the case, but all this is quite useless if by any chance the bearings should not be in alignment when the crankcase is bolted up. If it is impossible for the crankcase to be returned for this work to be done by the makers, then the utmost care should be taken to get everything as good as possible, and after the crankcase has been bolted up with the crankshaft in place, turn the

REPAIR NOTES ON LEVIS ENGINES

crankshaft round to make quite sure that it revolves freely when turned with the finger and thumb.

Fitting New Little-end Bush

With regard to the little-end bush, should this require renewal and a replacement part has been obtained from the makers, it will be found to be oversize. This is necessary, as a standard new bush would be slack in the hole in the top end of the connecting rod after the original bearing has been removed, as the hole is necessarily slightly enlarged in so doing. Before fitting, therefore, the bush should be turned to the correct size outside. As regards the inside of the bearing, if this is to fit a taper gudgeon pin, then a taper reamer is necessary in order to ensure a nice fit. When the gudgeon pin has been replaced, do not forget to fit two new circlips unless the gudgeon pin is of a very early type where circlips were not fitted.

Do not forget that when any or all of the three phosphor-bronze bushes are replaced, the new bush or bushes must be drilled where requisite with the necessary oil holes *after the bush has been fitted in place.*

Is Sideplay in Bearings Important?

No jointing washer is required between the two halves of the crankcase, but these should be scrupulously clean, and it is a good plan to paint the edges of the joint with goldsize before reassembling. One point that owners often raise is with regard to sideplay in the bearings, and it may be here stated definitely that sideplay alone is absolutely immaterial. In fact, a certain amount of sideplay is necessary, and unless there is an appreciable up-and-down play the bearings do not require renewal.

Refitting Cylinder

When the crankcase has been bolted together and before finally tightening everything up, put a straightedge across the top of the crankcase to ensure that this is absolutely level. Otherwise when you come to screw down the cylinder, there is a possibility of breaking it unless it beds down perfectly evenly on to the flat top of the crankcase.

The usual paper washer is required between the cylinder and the crankcase, and after making one for this purpose, *do not forget to cut out a hole to correspond with the transfer port!* The usual washer is also required between the exhaust port and the exhaust pipe in cases where the exhaust pipe is attached to the cylinder by means of either two or four pins. Obviously, in the case of those engines where the exhaust pipe is merely a push-in fit in the lug, no washer is required. In the case of the induction port (if the carburetter lug has been removed) no washer is required at this point; the surfaces should be absolutely clean and treated with goldsize before reassembling.

REPAIR NOTES ON LEVIS ENGINES

Fig. 7.—NOT A JOB FOR THE AMATEUR.
If the main bearings have to be renewed, it is best to return the crankcase to the makers. The process of reamering out the bearings can only be done by using the special line reamer shown above.

See if Valve is Gastight

Before refitting the release valve in the top of the cylinder head, it is as well to just inspect this and see that it is gastight. As the little valve is not exposed to the flame as regards the seating, except on very rare occasions, it does not require very frequent attention, but if it is pitted or obviously not making a gastight joint, it should be ground in in the usual way. If the little spring has lost its tension, it should be replaced.

Care in replacing Flywheel

When replacing the flywheel great care should be taken that both the end of the crankshaft and the hole in the flywheel are perfectly clean and free from grease or grit. The illustration (see Fig 3) shows the manner in which the flywheel nut should be finally tightened. It is not sufficient to merely pull up this nut as tight as possible with a spanner by hand. The special spanner supplied by the makers must be used, and the nut " jarred " up deadtight by hammering the end of the spanner as far as it will go. Take particular care that there is sufficient thread on the end of the crankshaft remaining below the face of the flywheel

REPAIR NOTES ON LEVIS ENGINES

Fig. 8.—TESTING THE BEARINGS.
The crankshaft should be capable of being easily rotated by means of the finger and thumb.

boss to allow the nut to force the wheel deadtight upon the taper without fouling the last thread. A movable spanner is not sufficiently strong for this job.

FOUR-STROKING—ITS CAUSE AND REMEDY

Four-stroking (unless caused by overoiling) is due to an excessively rich mixture, and if the float level is correct (easily checked by a reference to the maker's booklet), the remedy is to fit a smaller jet. The best way is to get several smaller jets and try them one by one, each smaller than the preceding one, till the engine two-strokes to your satisfaction. It must be remembered that the engine will two-stroke at walking pace, but to obtain this means using a smaller jet than is really advisable, as a certain amount of power at larger throttle openings would thereby be sacrificed. A setting which is a compromise to suit one's own taste can usually be obtained, and it is best to tolerate a little four-stroking downhill or at very low speeds.

THE " SIX-PORT " TWO-STROKE MODELS

The " Six-Port " engine differs from other Levis two-strokes in three main respects :

(1) It is the only Levis two-stroke engine with twin exhaust pipes.

REPAIR NOTES ON LEVIS ENGINES

Fig. 9A.—TIMING THE MAGNETO—FIRST OPERATION.
This shows the method of timing the magneto in the case of two-stroke models with the plug in the side of the cylinder. Operation 1.—Get the piston on top dead centre and put a chalk mark on the flywheel, together with one on the cylinder so that both marks are in line as shown above.

(2) It is the only Levis two-stroke engine wherein an aluminium alloy piston is employed; and (3) It is the only two-stroke model with a detachable head.

Points to Note when Decarbonising

As regards the general dismantling of the engine, this should be carried out on the same lines as the other two-stroke models, but in dismantling the cylinder, the head should be first removed. Owing to the superior performance of the "Six-Port" engine, it naturally requires more care and attention to keep it in tune than the ordinary models. Obviously, for the purpose of decarbonising only, it is not necessary to remove the cylinder barrel, as decarbonising can be done when the head has been taken off, but it is very advisable, whenever decarbonising is required, to take an opportunity to inspect the rings so that these may be freed, if they show a tendency

REPAIR NOTES ON LEVIS ENGINES

to stick, or replaced if obviously worn.

Do not remove the transfer passage cover: it should never be necessary to remove this. There is no object in breaking a good joint, but if this should be done inadvertently, note that a washer is required between the cover and the cylinder barrel.

Removing Carbon from Piston

Great care should be exercised in removing carbon from the piston of the "Six-Port" engine, as the aluminium alloy is very soft, and could be cut with a knife. Particular care is necessary in cleaning the ring slots so as not to damage them in any way.

Fig. 9B.—TIMING THE MAGNETO—SECOND OPERATION.
Place a second chalk mark on the cylinder where shown, and turn the flywheel back until the chalk mark on it is in line with the second chalk mark on the cylinder. The contact points should just be breaking with ignition lever set at full retard.

How to wreck an Engine

When replacing the piston, be careful not to put it on back to front, as owing to the shaped combustion head the engine will be wrecked if an attempt is made to even turn it round with the kick-starter. The gentle slope of the deflector head is towards the exhaust ports. In any two-stroke

REPAIR NOTES ON LEVIS ENGINES

model, care should be taken that the piston is put on the right way, but in the case of the other models nothing more serious than a loss of power will be experienced. With the "Six-Port," there is the above real danger, and therefore great care should be exercised not to make this mistake.

There is a plain copper washer between the head and the barrel, and this should be replaced if damaged. When fitting this copper washer, be careful to put it on with the hole in register with the release valve passage to the exhaust manifold. Also see that the passage in question is clear.

MAGNETO TIMING INSTRUCTIONS

Engines with the Sparking Plug in the Rear of the Cylinder

If with Variable Ignition.—Turn the flywheel until the piston is dead on top centre. This position can be seen by removing the plug and looking in through the hole. Place the "Advance" lever in "Fully Retarded" position, when the magneto points should just have broken.

If with Fixed Ignition.—Turn the flywheel forward till piston reaches top of the stroke; now turn flywheel backward until piston has descended $\frac{3}{16}$ to $\frac{5}{16}$ inch, according to the circumstances (for hilly country $\frac{3}{16}$ inch is recommended, whilst for a comparatively flat district $\frac{5}{16}$ inch may be used). The points should just be in the act of breaking.

Fig. 10.—Removing the Head of the Levis "Six-Port" Model.

Engines with the Sparking Plug in the Side of Cylinder Head

It must be carefully noted that this type of engine does not require, *and will not stand*, as much advance as the other models.

REPAIR NOTES ON LEVIS ENGINES

Fig. 11.—THE PISTON OF THE LEVIS " SIX-PORT " MODEL IN PLACE.
Note that the gentle slope of the deflector head of the piston is towards
the exhaust ports.

" Six-Port " Model

Get piston on top dead centre, and put a chalk mark on the flywheel. Then turn the flywheel back $1\frac{1}{4}$ inches. The points should be just breaking and the ignition lever fully retarded. This equals 2 mm. of advance with the ignition lever fully retarded or $7\frac{1}{2}$ mm. of advance with the ignition lever fully advanced. The ignition timing of the " Six-Port " engine is

REPAIR NOTES ON LEVIS ENGINES

of vital importance, and it will be found that it will stand much earlier timing than previous Levis models to advantage.

If slow running is required with even two stroking down to exceedingly slow speeds, and high speed is not of consequence, then the magneto timing may be set much later. The most suitable slow timing is best arrived at by experiment to suit the rider's requirements.

THE O.H.V. FOUR-STROKE MODELS

As the Levis models " A," " A1," " A2," " B " and " B Special " are all similar in design, the following remarks may be taken to apply to all the o.h.v. four-stroke machines made by this firm.

Dismantling the Cylinder

In order to dismantle the cylinder, slacken off the exhaust nut or nuts with the special spanner provided; it is not necessary to completely remove the exhaust pipes when decarbonising. In the case of models dated early 1930 or previously, the rocker-box lid is attached by five small set pins, and it is not necessary to remove the lid or other parts when dismantling. In the case of late 1930 and subsequent models, in which the rocker-box lid is attached by a spring or central bolt, it is essential to remove the rockers before the head can be

Fig. 12.—DISMANTLING THE CYLINDER HEAD OF THE LEVIS O.H.V. FOUR-STROKE—
FIRST OPERATION

After the rocker-box lid has been removed, and the rockers withdrawn, the nuts underneath the rockers must be removed with a tubular spanner as shown.

taken off, as there are two nuts underneath the rockers which have to be undone. Slacken off the bottom push-rod tube nut, and then the rocker box, together with the push-rod tube, may be lifted off completely by the tube. Be careful to disengage the two push rods out of the cup-ended tappets and the whole should come away. The push rods are marked "left" and "right" respectively, so that there is no need to take any steps to keep them separate.

Fig. 13.—SECOND OPERATION.
The rocker box and push-rod tube can then be taken off in the manner shown, the right hand disengaging the push rods out of the cup-ended tappets.

Fig. 14.—THIRD OPERATION.
Removing the cylinder head from the barrel

REPAIR NOTES ON LEVIS ENGINES

 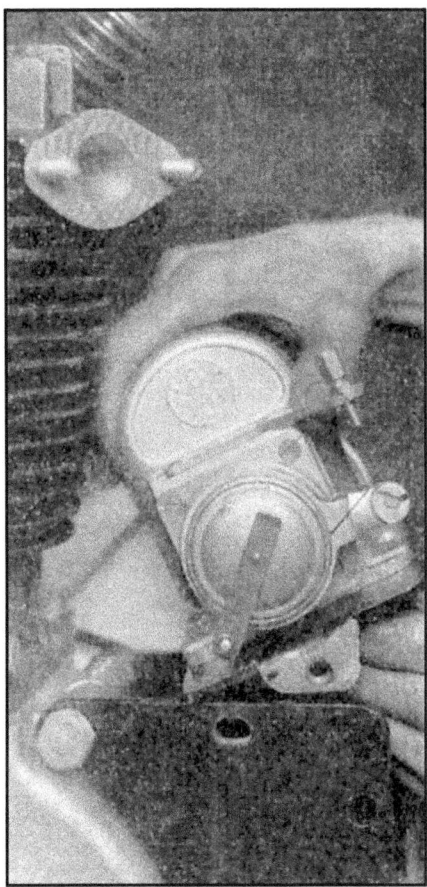

Fig. 15.—ADJUSTING THE MAGNETO CHAIN.
After the two nuts (one on each side) have been slackened, the magneto can slide on its platform until the chain is at the requisite tension.

Fig. 16.—METHOD OF REMOVING THE MAGNETO.
Observe that the magneto must be canted over towards the cylinder before it can be lifted off.

Procedure for Decarbonising

Undo the nuts that secure the detachable head to the cylinder, when same can be lifted off; if necessary, a little gentle prising will help. It is not necessary to remove the cylinder barrel except for examination purposes, and then only at fairly lengthy intervals. Even if the barrel is being removed, it is recommended that the carbon be removed from the top of the piston whilst the cylinder barrel is in position, as this greatly simplifies the work.

REPAIR NOTES ON LEVIS ENGINES

Useful Valve Removal and Grinding Tools

On the end of each valve will be found a small hardened cap, and care should be taken that these

Fig. 16.—REMOVING THE TIMING COVER FROM THE CRANKCASE.

This must be pulled away square, as shown, until the oil tube is free of the mainshaft.

caps are not lost whilst the parts are dismantled. The valve removal is simple and the method obvious, but

Fig. 17.—HOW TO RETIME THE VALVES CORRECTLY.

A flat is ground off one of the teeth of the small pinion, and this tooth should be meshed between two teeth which have been similarly treated on the large pinion.

REPAIR NOTES ON LEVIS ENGINES

a special removing tool, such as the Hickman, is necessary. A little device to assist in valve grinding can be obtained from the makers very cheaply.

Engine being Completely Dismantled

If, for any reason, the engine is being completely dismantled, the following notes should be most carefully observed. In order to remove the sprocket adapter from the mainshaft, always use a sprocket drawer. *Under no circumstances must the end of the shaft be hammered.* The mainshafts are a push-in fit in the flywheels on both sides, and if a hammer is used the result will simply be to drive the shaft through the flywheel and probably cause considerable damage. In any case, it will most certainly be a job for the makers.

Methods of parting the Crankcase

Fig. 18.—THE SPROCKET ASSEMBLY OF THE LEVIS O.H.V. FOUR-STROKE.

Items are shown in the correct order, i.e. driving sprocket, distance piece, dynamo sprocket and lock ring.

In the case of early 1931 and all previous models the mainshaft is mounted on a ball bearing on the timing gear side, and a roller bearing on the driving side. Later models have a roller bearing both sides. In the case of the models with the ball bearing on the timing side, some little difficulty may be experienced in parting the crankcase, owing to the bearing being inclined to stick on the shaft as a result of congealed oil or the like. Bear in mind that the mainshaft must never be hammered as mentioned above, and the parting of the crankcase will be easily accomplished if the case itself in the vicinity of the ball bearing is warmed up for a few moments with a blowlamp. In this case, the aluminium of the crankcase will expand, and thus release the ball bearing which is only pressed into same. The bearing will then come away with the shaft. It should be noted that this does not apply to later 1931 models having a roller bearing on each side.

REPAIR NOTES ON LEVIS ENGINES

Flywheels

It is really not advisable to separate the flywheels if this can possibly be avoided, as this is essentially a job for the works. The special steel nuts which secure the crankpin must be really tightened up deadtight after the flywheels have been taken apart, and in order to verify that the alignment of the flywheels has not suffered, this should be tested with a piece of ½-inch (dead to size) round steel bar, which will just pass through two holes in the flywheels if they are perfectly in line.

Gudgeon Pin

The gudgeon pin is parallel and kept in place by circlips. It may therefore be pushed in or out either way. If it is a trifle tight either to remove or replace, warming the piston will be found effective.

Reassembling

There is no difficulty about the reassembling, and the method will be obvious. See that the copper washer between the cylinder barrel and head is perfectly clean and also both faces. Screw up the head nuts gently, half a turn at a time.

Fig. 19.—TESTING THE FLYWHEELS FOR ALIGNMENT. Use a piece of dead-to-size ½-inch bar. This should just pass through the two holes in the flywheels.

The advantage of the plain copper washer is that no further tightening of the head will be found necessary when the engine has been run, as usually occurs when a C. & A. washer is fitted. When replacing the rocker box and push-rod tube assembly,

REPAIR NOTES ON LEVIS ENGINES

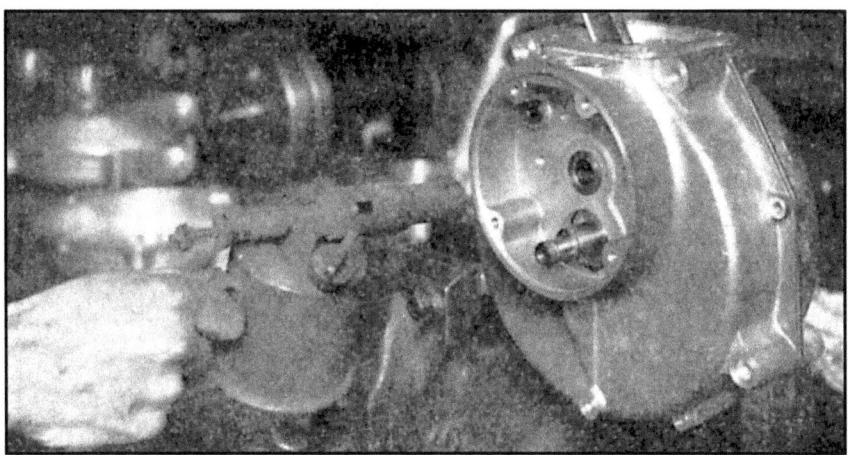

Fig. 20.—A Workshop Tip for Withdrawing the Ballrace.
Use a blowlamp as shown, to warm up the crankcase round about the ballrace.
The expansion of the metal will allow the race to be withdrawn easily.

first of all insert the two push rods in the tube, holding them there with the fingers of the right hand. Then place the parts as nearly as possible into position, carefully noting that the lower ends of the push rods fit into their respective cups on the top of the tappets. Then manipulate the rocker box into position.

Magneto Timing

The magneto timing for all Levis o.h.v. models is as follows: piston on top dead centre, ignition lever fully retarded, platinum points just broken.

Tappet Clearance

The tappet clearance should be infinitesimal, i.e. about ·002 inch when cold. The top rockers are fitted with adjustable ball ends and lock nuts to provide tappet adjustment. The adjustment is easily made with the engine in place in the frame by using the specially cranked screwdriver provided and a spanner.

MATCHLESS MOTOR-CYCLES

By Donald S. Parsons

ALL Matchless motor-cycles, for some years now, have been fitted with engines of Matchless design and manufacture. With but one exception (Model B, 1931) all flywheel-axle bearings are plain on the timing side and roller on the driving side. All crankpin big-end bearings are of the roller type, and all gudgeon-pin and camshaft bearings are of the plain type.

Replacing the Driving-side Main Bearing

The driving-side flywheel-axle bearing consists of the axle, a set of rollers, double row, set in a bronze cage and a hardened steel outer race. The outer race is pressed into the crankcase. If the outside of the crankcase is examined, three holes will be noticed in the boss carrying the outer race. Three metal pins (three stout french nails with the points and heads cut off will serve) must be placed in the three holes, and upon pressure being applied to the pins the race will be removed from its housing. Fig. 1 shows how this may be done. The disk can be of metal or hardwood, and the "pressure" can take the form of steady blows with a mallet. The crankcase half should bear on a level surface. The new race merely requires pressing into the crankcase. This operation can be performed by using a piece of hardwood and a mallet, but care must be taken to see that the race does not tilt when fitting it.

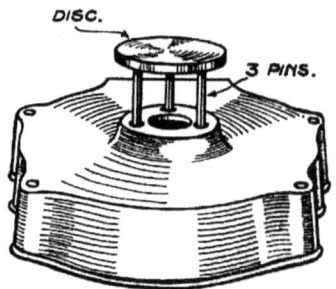

Fig. 1.—Removing the Driving-side Main Bearing.

Place three stout nails with the points cut off in the holes in the crankcase boss. Place a hardwood disk over the nails. The race can then be driven out by steady blows on the disk.

And the Timing Side

The timing-side flywheel-axle bearing is a plain bronze bush, that, in some models, has a flange

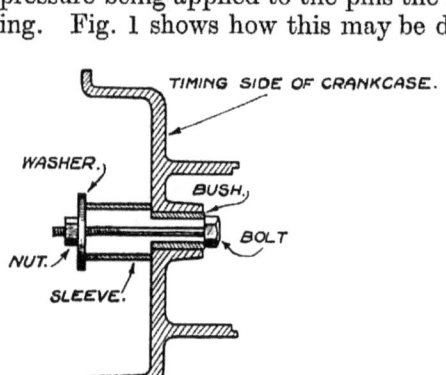

Fig. 2.—Removing the Timing-side Main Bearing.

Use a bolt sleeve washer and nut for this purpose as shown above.

Fig. 3.—Removing S.V. Cylinder Head.

Unscrew the bolts retaining the head to the cylinder. If these bolts show a tendency to stick the engine should be allowed to run till it is warm and then a little paraffin placed around each bolt.

Fig. 4.—Removal of Twin Cylinder.

The induction pipe, carburetter and exhaust pipes must be removed, and each cylinder must be partly rotated before it can be drawn away to clear the piston.

on the "inside" end. The old bush can be removed by using a bolt, sleeve, washer, and nut as shown in Fig. 2. The head of the bolt should be not larger than the outside diameter of the bush, and the sleeve should be a trifle longer than the bush. On tightening the nut on the bolt the bush will be drawn out. It will be readily seen that by rearranging these parts they may be used to draw the new bush into the crankcase.

After Rebushing

On those models that have internal oilways, care must be taken to see that the holes in the bush coincide with those in the crankcase. After a plain bush has been fitted in a crankcase it may be necessary to slightly ease the internal bore of the bush by reamering or scraping until the flywheel-axle is a perfectly free fit in it. Do not tolerate any tightness, but when testing for this see

MATCHLESS MOTOR-CYCLES

that the axle is smeared with engine oil.

The method described above can also be used for removing camshaft bushes, bushes for gudgeon pins and valve guides. Blind camshaft bushes must probably be broken or cut in order to extract them and the new bushes fitted by pressure.

Removing the Engine from Frame

Fig. 5.—A SUBSTITUTE FOR A SPROCKET DRAWER.

Sprockets are best removed with a special withdrawal tool. If one of these is not available, an excellent substitute can be made from two hardwood wedges. First remove the sprocket retaining nut with its locking screw, and then drive the two wedges between the crankcase and the sprocket. Drive fairly hard home, and then "bump" the end of the flywheel axle with a mallet. This jar will release the sprocket.

A complete engine overhaul entails the removal of the engine from the frame. To do this the machine must be raised on both stands, the carburetter, silencer and exhaust pipes taken away, and all oil pipes disconnected. Plug the oil-feed pipe with a piece of wood or rag to prevent oil wastage. Next remove the footrests or footboards, the front chaincase and chain and the magneto chain and case where fitted. The crankcase bolts should then be removed, and this will allow the engine to be taken away from the frame.

DISMANTLING

Cylinder and Valve Tappets

Remove the cylinder as a complete unit. Remove the piston by extracting one of the gudgeon-pin retaining spring rings, and pushing the gudgeon pin out of the piston. This pin is an easy sliding fit, and no tools should be necessary to remove it. Then remove the timing-gear cover. Lift the tappets out of the guides.

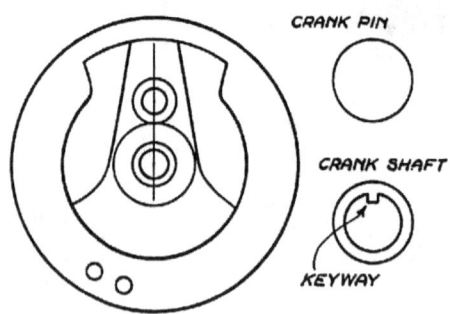

Fig. 6.—SHOWING THE POSITION OF THE KEYWAY IN THE CRANKSHAFT.

Fig. 7.—FLYWHEEL ASSEMBLY.
Make sure that the keyway in the axle is in the position shown in Fig. 6.

Fig. 8.—ADJUSTING THE FLYWHEEL ASSEMBLY.
Note the simple jig used for supporting the crankshaft and the indicator for testing the setting.

Timing Gear

Lift out the timing-gear camshaft and the timing-gear cam levers and spacers. Unscrew the nut that retains the timing-gear small pinion. This has a LEFT-hand thread. The small pinion is a taper fit on the flywheel axle, so if a special withdrawal tool is not available it must be prised off. This is best done by using two tyre levers or similar tools. They should be placed so that the crankcase boss is used as a fulcrum and are opposite to each other; then by placing pressure on each lever at the same time the pinion should be released. In stubborn cases it might be necessary to partly replace the left-hand nut and give this several sharp blows with a lead-faced hammer while maintaining the pressure on the levers.

Main Sprocket

The small screw locking the transmission retaining nut must be removed, followed by the nut. The sprocket can then be removed in a similar manner to that used to remove the timing-gear small pinion.

Crankcase and Flywheel Assembly

Next take away the remaining crankcase bolts, which will enable the two halves of the crankcase to be separated, leaving the complete flywheel assembly. The operation of separating the flywheels should be performed on a clean piece of level paper in order to catch the big-end rollers, otherwise some of these may be lost. Take out the two locking screws that lock the two crankpin nuts. Remove these nuts, and then give the edge of one of the flywheels a good "bump" with a mallet or soft-faced hammer. This will release the flywheel, which should be lifted away, thereby allowing the connecting rod to be removed. Collect the rollers, and then tap out the crankpin from the second flywheel. Unless the flywheel axles are scored or otherwise damaged there is no need to remove them from the flywheels, but if it is desired to do so they may be removed in the same manner as the crankpin. Note that some 1930 and all 1931 crankpins are a parallel fit in the flywheels, and cannot be easily removed unless an "arbor" press is available.

Fig. 9.—Detail of Indicator for testing the Flywheel Assembly.

HOW TO TEST PARTS FOR WEAR

The Bearings

Having cleaned all the parts, the next thing to do is to examine and test them for wear. When doing this all the bearing surfaces should have a thin film of oil on them. The driving-side flywheel axle should fit into the roller cage and rollers, and the rollers, in turn, in the outer race, so that totally there is no appreciable up-and-down play. The timing-side flywheel axle should fit into its bush quite freely, and if any wear has occurred a new bush only will most likely provide the necessary correct fit.

Crankpin and Connecting Rod

Examine the surface of the crankpin, and if in the least way it is pitted a new one should be used. Most connecting rods have the big end hardened and ground so that the rollers bear actually in the connecting rod. If the inner face of the rod is grooved or pitted this entails a new rod. Some models have a detachable hardened outer race that is pressed into the connecting rod. In those cases the renewal is a more simple matter.

MATCHLESS MOTOR-CYCLES

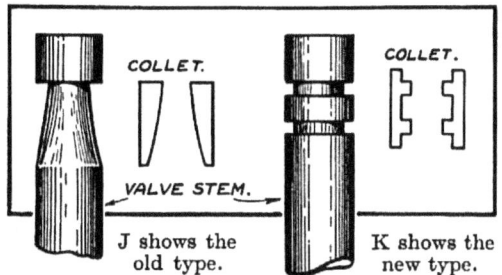

Fig. 10—OLD AND NEW TYPE OVERHEAD VALVE COLLETS. J shows the old type. K shows the new type.

Having decided if a new crankpin and/or a new connecting rod is required, assemble the big-end bearing by placing grease on the pin and "sticking" the rollers round it, afterwards placing the connecting rod over this assembly. The bearing should be free, but there should be no up-and-down play. Rocking the rod sideways on the pin does not indicate that play exists, because there is always a certain amount of movement noticeable. Rollers ·001 inch larger than standard can be obtained for all Matchless engines, and in many cases the fitting of these enables the original connecting rod and crankpin to be used again.

Piston and Gudgeon Pin

The gudgeon pin is intentionally a rather easy fit in both the piston and the bush. If replacements are considered necessary, first of all obtain a new gudgeon pin. Try this in the piston, and if the fit is not too easy and the piston is otherwise in good order, this may be used again. Before replacing a gudgeon-pin bush try the effect of removing the bush from the rod and then refitting it. This action sometimes closes the

Fig. 11.—SETTING THE TIMING GEAR ON THE SILVER ARROW MODEL.

Note the timing marks on two teeth of the worm wheel. The worm thread has a mark on it to indicate the position of these teeth for correct timing. It will have been noticed from the Valve Timing Chart that all single-cylinder machines have the valve timing arranged so that the amount of lead is equivalent to the amount of lag. This renders valve timing a simple matter to set, because it is only necessary to place the piston at the extreme top of its stroke and then insert the timing-gear camshaft so that both of the valves are very slightly lifted for the timing to be correct.

115

MATCHLESS MOTOR-CYCLES

bush so that it is fit for more service. Guard against too tight a fit of the gudgeon pin in the bush, also make sure that the oil hole in the bush registers with the hole in the top of the rod. If the piston is of the split-skirt type, carefully examine the junction of the diagonal split with the horizontal split, and if there is the slightest sign of cracking the piston should be replaced. Remember that these pistons are taper and oval in shape. It will be advisable to fit new piston rings. These s h o u l d h a v e perfectly sharp edges, must be a free fit in the piston grooves, and the gap between each ring should vary from ·004 inch on the small engines to ·007 inch on the larger models.

Fig. 12.—SETTING THE TIMING WHEELS.
Note the timing marks.

Timing Gear

Examine the timing-gear camshaft, and if the cam faces are damaged rubbing with an oilstone slip may make this part fit for another period of service. It is essential that all grooves are removed, otherwise a replacement is merited. The timing-gear cam levers should receive similar attention. These parts are quite cheap, and if serious signs of wear are noticed new parts should be used. Considerable wear on the valve-actuating parts will prevent the correct opening of the valves as regards time and distance, and would thereby reduce the power output to a serious extent. The bushes for the timing-gear camshaft give

Fig. 13.—TIMING THE O.H.C. GEAR.
Note the timing marks.

MATCHLESS MOTOR-CYCLES

a very extended service, and replacements although cheap are rarely needed.

The Cylinder

The cylinder must have all the carbon scraped away and the piston tested in it for fit. To the uninitiated the fit will doubtlessly appear to be very sloppy. This, to a certain extent, is absolutely necessary. The correct clearances are given in the chart below, additional clearances up to two or three thousandths of an inch are of no consequence, and at the worst can only result in piston slap when the engine is cold. This is of no consequence.

TABLE SHOWING CORRECT PISTON CLEARANCES

	BORE OF CYLINDER.				
	54 mm.	62·5 mm.	69 mm.	82·5 mm.	85·5 mm.
Top Land	·019"	·022"	·023 "	·025"	·025"
Second Land . . .	·014"	·018"	·018"	·019"	·019"
Boss	·008"	·005"	·005"	·0055"	·0055"
Skirt	·005"	·003"	·003"	·0035"	·0035"

Valves and Guides

Side-valve engines are fitted with valves marked " IN " and " EX," to indicate inlet and exhaust valves. Inlet valves are made of 3 per cent. nickel steel and exhaust valves of stainless steel. Valve dimensions are identical, and an exhaust valve may be used as an inlet valve without harmful results, but on no account, except as a means of " getting home," must an inlet valve be used as an exhaust valve.

All valve guides are made of chilled cast iron, and are parallel inside and out. They are a press-in fit in the cylinders (or cylinder heads).

REASSEMBLY

Flywheel Assembly

The driving-side flywheel axle is keyed so that it can only be replaced in one position. The retaining nut must be very fully tightened and finally locked with the small screw. Beware of excessive tightening, otherwise the flywheel will crack. The timing-side flywheel axle must be replaced in one position if due consideration is going to be given to the punch marks on the timing wheels. When a straight line is drawn through the axes of the crankpin and the flywheel axle the keyway in the axle should be in a central position on that line. Fig. 6 illustrates this point. This axle must be fixed exactly as the driving-side axle. Next fit the crankpin in

MATCHLESS MOTOR-CYCLES

the driving-side flywheel and fix it with the nut and locking screw. If the pin is drilled with oilway holes these must register with the holes in the flywheels. Assemble the connecting rod and rollers as already described for testing purposes, mount the timing-side flywheel on the crank-pin and reasonably tighten the nut.

Crankcase, Timing Gear and Oil Pump

After truing up the flywheels (Fig. 7 and fig. 8), refit into the crankcase, making the transmission-side rollers and cage go right "home." Smear axle shafts, bearings, etc., with a little oil. Assemble the timing gear, making sure the left-hand nut securing the small pinion is fully tight, but do not overdo or the pinion may burst or crack (see Figs. 11, 12 and 13). On those models fitted with a mechanical pump on the timing cover, the small block threaded on the oil-pump shaft must engage with the jaws on the camshaft.

Piston

Refit the piston, and note the split in the skirt must face forwards. Clean out the gudgeon-pin retaining-ring grooves, and fit new retaining rings if these are at all doubtful.

Before leaving the consideration of a complete engine overhaul it should be noted that economy as to the fitting of new piston rings, valve springs and cylinder-base paper washers is ill advised.

Notes on O.H.V. Engine

The method of dealing with overhead-valve engines is exactly the same as detailed for side-valve models. The overhead-valve gear of course requires special treatment. Nearly every o.h.v. model has double valve springs. These prevent the tendency to valve bounce that might occur at high engine speeds. Most o.h.v. rockers are mounted on roller bearings, and grease should be used to locate the rollers when assembling these. Two types of overhead valves have been used. The earlier type is shown in Fig. 10, J. It will be noted that the split valve collets are plain, while the later type is shown in Fig. 10, K, in which the collets are of a special type. When type J valves are replaced with type K valves, it should be noted that in addition to the special collets it is also necessary to use a different type of valve spring top collar.

TIMING CHART FOR MATCHLESS

MODELS.	INLET.		EXHAUST.		IGNITION MAX. ADV. Before T.D.C.	Tappet Clearance.
	Opens before T.D.C.	Closes after B.D.C.	Opens before B.D.C.	Closes after T.D.C.		
R—1927, RS—1928 R3—1929, RS—1929 R6—1930	15°	52°	58°	14°	40°	·01″
R4—1930, R7—1931	14°	57°	53°	15°	40°	·01″
DS—1931 D—1931	20°	67°	75°	28°	37°	·007″
T2—1927, T—1927 T3—1928 T4—1928 T3—1929 T5—1930 TS—1928-29 TS2—1930	18°	55°	60°	16°	37°	·007″
LR—1927 LR2—1928	20°	68°	68°	25°	40°	·007″
V—1927 V2—1928 V2—1929 V3—1930	23°	64°	74°	22°	40°	·007″
V2S—1928 V2S—1929 V3S—1930	20°	64°	66°	21°	40°	·007″
CS—1931 C—1931	20°	67°	75°	28°	40°	·007″
V5—1929 V6—1930	10½°	46°	52°	10½°	35°	·007″
A—1930 A2—1931	10°	55°	60°	10°	35°	·008″
B—1931	20°	65°	65°	25°	48°	·008″
M3—1927 M3—1928 M3S—1927 M3S—1928	15°	52½°	57½°	12½°	38½°	·01″
X—1929 XR—1929 X2—1930 XR2—1930 X3—1931 XR3—1931	11°	46°	52°	10°	38½°	·01″
M—1927 M—1928	10½°	46°	52°	10½°	40°	·01″

TIMING CHART FOR MATCHLESS

PARTICULARS OF MODELS

MODELS.	YEARS.	CYLS.	BORE.	STROKE.	C.C.	V.
R RS R4 R7	1927 1928 1929 1930 1931	1	62·5	80	246	S.S.
R3 R6 DS	1929 1930 1931	1	62·5	80	246	O.H.V.
T4 T2 D	1928 1929 1927 1931	1	69	93	347	S.S.
TS	1928–29	1	69	93	347	O.H.V.
TS2	1930	1	69	93	347	O.H.V.

MODELS.	YEARS.	CYLS.	BORE.	STROKE.	C.C.	V.
LR LR2	1927 1928	1	69	93	347	O.H.C.
V V2 V3 CS	1927 1928 1929 1930 1931	1	85·5	85·5	495	O.H.V.
V5 V6 C	1929 1930 1931	1	85·5	101·6	586	S.S.
T T3 T5	1927 1928 1929 1930	1	82·5	93	498	S.S.

MODELS.	YEARS.	CYLS.	BORE.	STROKE.	C.C.	V.
M	1927 1928	1	89	95	591	O.H.V.
M3 and M3S X—XR X2, XR2 X3, XR3	1927–8 1929 1930 1931	2	85·5	85·5	990	S.S.
A A2	1930 1931	2	54	86	397	S.S.
B	1931	4	50·8	73·02	593	O.H.C.

NEW HUDSON REPAIR NOTES

By B. Bourke

TO REMOVE ENGINE FROM FRAME

Clean down—remove Accessories

FIRST thoroughly clean down the machine, and clear away the accumulation of mud or dust which has been removed from the motor-cycle. Remove the side shields, front and rear driving chains from the driving side of the machine, then the chain lubricator; next the electrical junction box fitted to the timing side of the engine, just above the mechanical pump, and at the side of the timing chest. (Junction boxes are only fitted to electrically equipped machines.)

Exhaust-lifter Lever

Remove the exhaust-lifter lever, cable and spring by placing the exhaust-lifter lever between the jaws of a movable spanner; then with a little downward pressure on the handle of the spanner the cable can be slipped from the lever. This will also allow the cable and spring to be removed from the cable stop just below the lever.

Magneto Cable

The magneto cable should then be taken away. All that is necessary is to undo the hexagon nut which forms the abutment for the outer casing of the cable. If the cable and plunger, to which it is attached, is drawn upwards to its fullest extent, it will be found that the nipple, into which the end of the cable is soldered, comes above the top of the box on the cam-cage housing. The nipple may now be slipped sideways out of the hole in the plunger in which it fits, thus detaching the cable entirely. Do not lose distance piece.

Engine Fixing Bolts

To remove the engine fixing bolts, which secure the crankcase to the under shield and frame of the machine, remove the nuts from one side of the bolt, place a punch on the end, and then gently tap the bolt out with a hammer, care being taken not to damage the threads.

All engine fixing bolts should be removed, with the exception of the front bottom bolt, which secures the front down tubes, the under shield and crankcase. This bolt should be left until the large hexagon nut,

NEW HUDSON REPAIR NOTES

which secures the top of the front down tube to the head of the machine, is loosened. Now remove the machine off the stand, pack up the under shield until the weight of the engine has been taken from the front engine bolt, then tap out this bolt and swing forward the front down tubes. Now lift the engine slightly, and get someone to remove the packing from under the under shield. This will allow the under shield to swing downwards, and the engine unit may be removed complete with magneto and dynamo *in situ*.

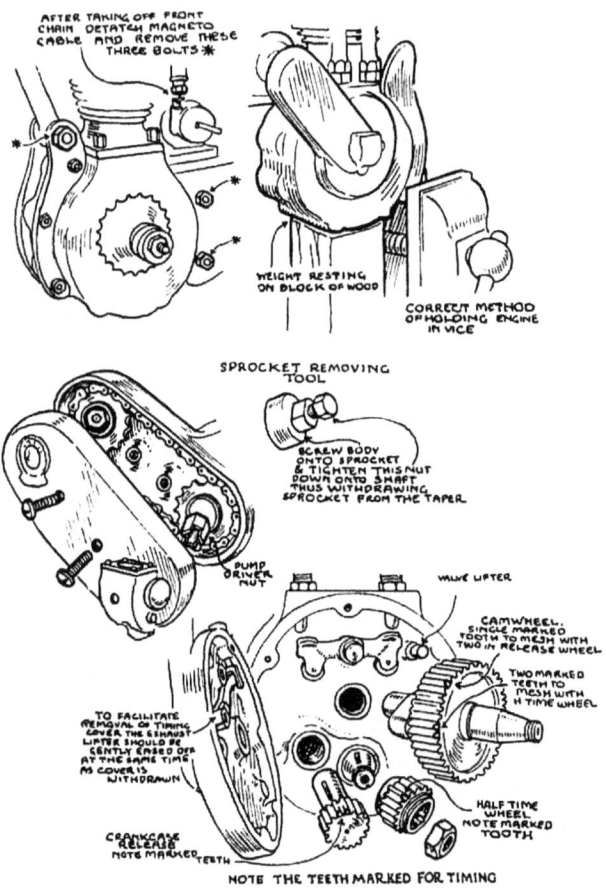

Fig. 1.—PICTORIAL HINTS ON ENGINE DISMANTLING.
Note the special tool for removing the sprocket.

Drain Crankcase

Before removing the engine to the bench drain both crankcase and oil reservoir. To do this place the engine in a position over some receptacle for the oil, then remove both drain plugs, and permit the crankcase and oil reservoir to drain.

A Warning

Care must be taken when placing the engine in a vice, otherwise the crankcase will be seriously damaged. The best plan is to make a wooden cradle to carry the engine. This is easily done by two pieces of strong wood being secured to the bench, parallel with one another, and sufficiently wide enough to permit the crankcase of the engine to rest between them. (Two pieces of 3 × 2-inch wood will be suitable for this purpose.)

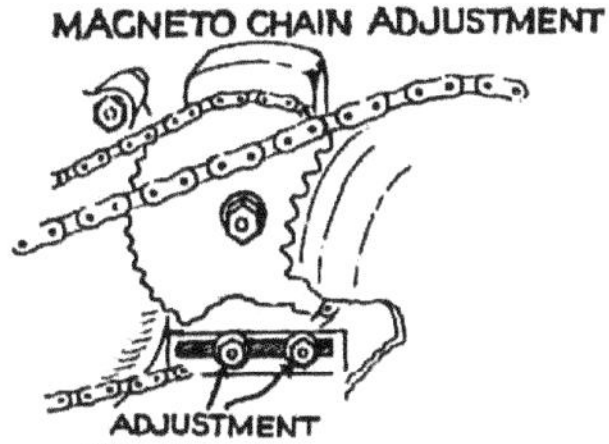

NEW HUDSON REPAIR NOTES

MAGNETO CHAIN ADJUSTMENT

Fig. 2.—Adjusting the Magneto Chain.
The two bolts are slackened allowing the magneto to be shifted.

Magneto and Dynamo Chains

Remove the magneto and dynamo driving chains from the engine. Take away the two magneto fixing bolts, and lift the magneto away from the engine. Now remove the dynamo by unscrewing the large hexagon nut which secures the clamp. By removing the nut the clamp will swing outwards, allowing the dynamo to be withdrawn. Clean both magneto and dynamo, and place in a safe position.

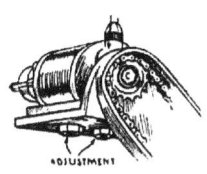

Fig. 3.—Showing another method for adjusting the Magneto Chain.

Shock Absorber and Main Sprocket

Place the engine in the cradle with

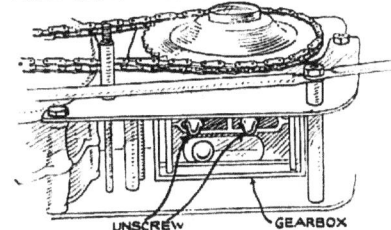

Fig. 4.—Front Chain Adjustment. Showing the position of the adjusting bolts on the underside of the gearbox.

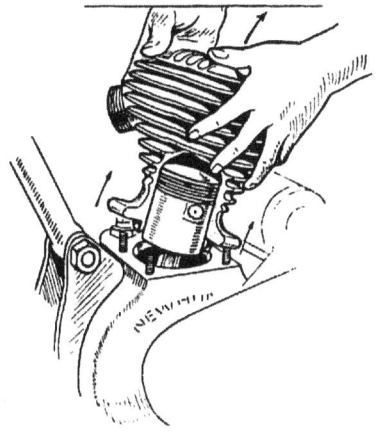

Fig. 5.—Removing the Cylinder. Note that to enable the cylinder to be removed the piston must be at the bottom of its stroke.

the driving side towards the operator. Proceed to remove the shock absorber and driving sprocket, first taking out the split cotter from the castellated nut, and then unscrewing the nut from the shaft; take away the plain washer, which is followed by the abutment plate, or spring thrust plate as it is sometimes called. Remove the shock-absorber spring, and a further abutment plate, which will then leave the driver and sprockets ready to be slipped off the shaft. Refit in the reverse manner.

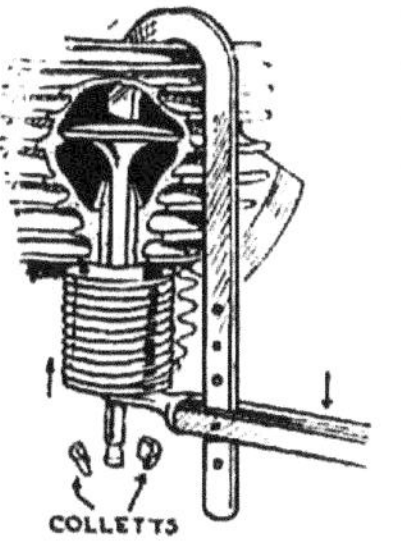

Fig. 6.—A Simple Method of removing the Valve Springs.

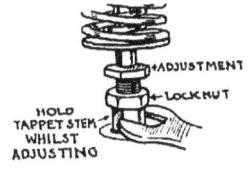

Fig. 7.—Showing how the Tappets are Adjusted.

NEW HUDSON REPAIR NOTES

Valve Gear

Now turn the engine round in the wooden cradle which secures it, with the timing side towards the operator. Proceed to remove the rocker box, tappet rods, cylinder head and cylinder barrel, also piston. When these parts have been removed, and placed in a safe position, then remove the nut securing the exhaust-lifter lever. Place a screwdriver between the timing-case cover and the lever, and gently prise the latter off the shaft.

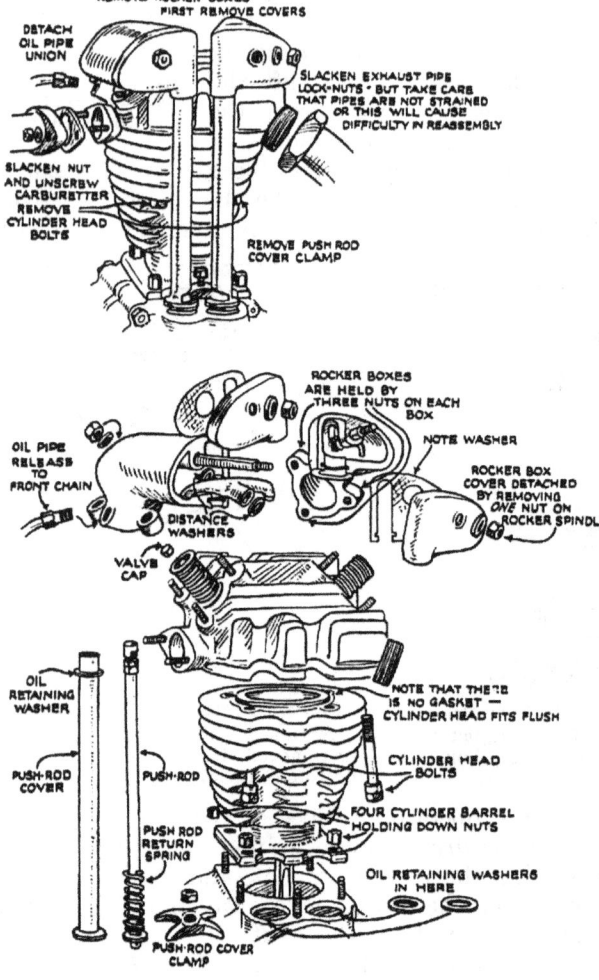

Fig. 8.—DISMANTLING THE OVERHEAD VALVE ENGINE. The preliminary operations are shown in the top sketch. The lower sketch shows the parts dismantled.

Timing Case

Take out the five timing-case cover screws. Should the cover be a little stubborn, gently tap round the edge of it with the handle of a screwdriver or with a small wooden mallet. This will have the necessary effect of loosening the cover, which can then be taken away, leaving the timing gear ready for removal. The screwdriver should not be used to lever off the cover, otherwise the joint will become damaged.

To remove the timing gear, the piston should be at the top of the firing stroke, i.e. with the cam in its highest position. This will then permit the cam to be withdrawn, and the rockers removed, together with the ex-

NEW HUDSON REPAIR NOTES

haust-lift cam. The cam wheel is marked for retiming. The half-time or small timing pinion forms the integral part of the timing-side main-shaft, consequently this is removed with the flywheel assembly. To remove rockers first take away the small distance collar, then the exhaust rocker, which will finally allow the inlet rocker to be taken out.

TO OVERHAUL ENGINE

All engines built between 1927 and 1930, whilst externally different, differ only slightly internally, and for the purpose of dismantling and re-erecting the procedure is practically the same.

The engine, having been removed from the frame, should be thoroughly cleaned externally, then placed in an upright position into a strong vice, with the timing side towards the operator. On no account must it be secured in the vice by other than the lower engine-plate boss. Care must be taken to see that the vice is tightened up securely ; a prop under the other engine-plate boss will assist to carry the weight, and prevent the engine moving in the vice. Proceed to dismantle on the lines already advised.

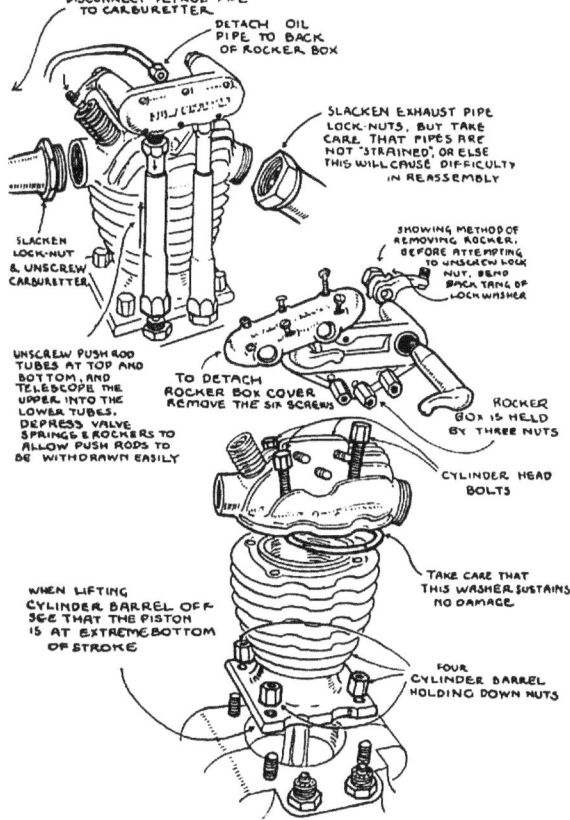

Fig. 9.—DISMANTLING.

Showing, pictorially, the order of dismantling an o.h.v. type cylinder.

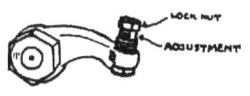

Fig. 10.—ROCKER ADJUSTMENT.

The lock nut is loosened to allow the screw to be adjusted. Tighten nut after setting.

Gudgeon-pin Retainers

With all " O "-type engines, the gudgeon pin is secured by means of gudgeon-pin spring retainers, whilst with the " N "-type, Twin-port and 250-c.c. engines the gudgeon pin is retained by two Duralumin endpads.

NEW HUDSON REPAIR NOTES

Before fitting the retainers see that the small grooves in the gudgeon-pin bosses are free from carbon, then take the spring retainer by the turned-in tail with a pair of round-nosed pliers. Place the head of the spring retainer into the groove and gently twist the pliers until the spring will just slip into place, then release same.

It is recommended that new retainers or pads are fitted each time the piston is removed.

The gudgeon pin of the " O "-type engine is slightly tapered, and is pressed out of the piston towards the timing side of the engine, whilst on all other types of engines the gudgeon pin is of the floating type.

Before removing the piston mark the front of same in order that this component will be refitted in the correct position.

The crankcase is then dismantled in the ordinary manner.

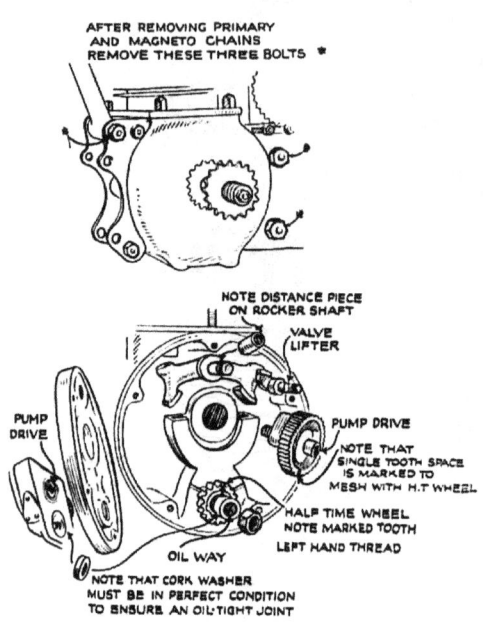

Fig. 11.—CRANKCASE DETAILS (250 c.c.).
The Crankcase should be taken from the frame as shown. Then timing gear should be dismantled.

Taking the Crankcase apart

Should the crankcase spigoted joint be a tight fit, then the effect of tapping round the joint with a mallet or the end of a hammer shaft will loosen the joint. On no account should a screwdriver, or similar tool, be used to force the halves of the crankcase apart, as the use of a screwdriver will damage the joint, which is a most important one, whilst oil leakage will follow.

To facilitate easy and clean handling, thoroughly wash the flywheel assembly to remove the oil. It is necessary that the mainshafts should be carefully examined for signs of wear and tear. Should the shafts be worn, remove them, but not otherwise.

The two mainshafts are fitted to the flywheels by means of a taper into a tapered hole in the flywheel, secured by woodruff keys and right-hand lock nuts, whilst the crankpin is fitted to the flywheels in a similar manner, but keys are not used, nor have they been found necessary.

NEW HUDSON REPAIR NOTES

FLYWHEEL ASSEMBLY

Caution dictates that unless the operator has the necessary technical knowledge in connection with the reassembling and balancing of flywheels, he should not attempt to carry out this operation.

Even with this technical knowledge and without the correct tools the most skilled mechanic cannot be sure of satisfactorily rebalancing the flywheels. It should be remembered that the speed and power developed by the modern motor-cycle engine is such that the slightest tendency for the flywheels to work loose, or run out of truth, would have serious results.

With these facts in mind it is urged that this operation be not undertaken by the unskilled, or without the necessary tools.

To dismantle Flywheel Assembly

To dismantle the flywheel without the necessary works' jigs and tools, the simplest method is to place the flywheels on top of a vice into which has been placed a pair of lead clamps.

Open the vice until the connecting rod will swing down between the jaws to its lowest point, then tighten up the vice, and proceed to remove the crankpin nuts.

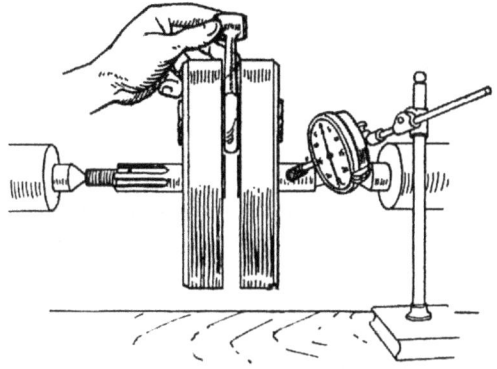

Fig. 12.—FLYWHEELS.
Checking alignment between centres.

If the vice is tightened up securely, no harm will happen to the connecting rod. It is important, however, to see that the rod swings to its lowest point, otherwise there is the possibility that the flywheels will skid away from the connecting rod when an attempt is being made to unlock the crankpin nut; consequently, there be a big chance of twisting the connecting rod.

Should no hand press be available for pressing out the shafts from the flywheels, then a hole through the solid part of the bench, large enough to take a mainshaft, will assist the operator, as on no account must the shaft of an engine be placed between the jaws of a vice, even though lead clamps are used, as the shafts will become bruised, and inefficiency will follow.

To facilitate the splitting of the flywheels, place the flywheel assembly with the mainshaft through the hole in the bench, then take four wooden wedges, place them evenly between the two flywheels and drive home with a mallet, which will have the necessary effect of loosening the tapers of both crankpin and flywheel. The timing-side flywheel, together with its

NEW HUDSON REPAIR NOTES

shaft, should now be removed, leaving the driving side in position on the bench.

It will be noticed that the roller-bearing crankpin assembly is made up of five different parts—two outside distance pieces, double track of rollers (34 in number), a centre hardened partition washer, the big-end steel liner secured in the connecting rod and the crankpin.

Mainshafts

With both mainshafts fitted, now turn attention to the crankpin and double-track roller-bearing assembly.

Big-end Races

Where it is found necessary to fit a new big-end steel race, it cannot be too strongly recommended that this operation should be carried out by the manufacturers. The reason for this is, that the liner is ground after being fitted to the connecting rod; in consequence, no distortion, brought about by pressing the new race into the connecting rod, will be experienced when fitting up the bearing.

Main-bearing Bushes in Crankcase

If new mainshafts are fitted to the flywheel assembly, then it is strongly recommended that new mainshaft bushes should also be fitted to the crankcase.

Do not attempt to fit new bushes to worn shafts, as the end of the shaft will be of a larger diameter than the worn portion; obviously, a new bush will slide over the unworn end of the shaft, but when it reaches the worn part it cannot take up the wear and tear. Always fit new bushes when fitting new shafts.

The bush should be pressed out by a hand press and a tool made from a piece of mild steel bar slightly smaller in diameter than the outside diameter of the bush, about 2 inches long, turned down, in a lathe, $1\frac{1}{2}$ inches from one end to the inside measurement of the bush.

The smaller diameter of the tool is placed into the bush from the outside of the crankcase. Place the half crankcase under the press, packing same up until the bush will just slide out when the arbor of the press is brought into operation. Fit the new bush in the reverse way. Timing-case bushes are removed and fitted in a similar manner.

Correcting Alignment

To assure that the new bushes fitted to the case are in correct alignment, it is necessary to first bolt together the halves of the crankcase, then pass a reamer, the size of the shaft, through the mainshaft bushes. This reamer will correctly line up the bushes.

These bushes must be in line, otherwise the engine will be inefficient when started up; overheating, loss of power and other complications

NEW HUDSON REPAIR NOTES

will follow. Under no consideration should bushes be merely forced into the case, and left to chance that they line up with one another.

Should a reamer, the size of the shaft, not be available, send the crankcase to the manufacturers, together with the flywheel assembly, to have new bushes fitted correctly.

Assuming the operator has the necessary reamer, and has lined up the crankcase bushes, then the fitting of the flywheel assembly can be proceeded with.

Insufficient Endplay

Hold the connecting rod by its small end, and rotate the flywheels to ascertain whether they can be revolved quite freely and without apparent friction. Should the wheels be stiff to rotate, open the crankcase again. In all probability it will be found, upon opening up the case, that the bushes have not been pressed right home. Rectify this, and test once more.

Reducing Endplay

Should there be excessive endplay, this can be taken up by fitting to the mainshaft a thin pen-steel shim washer, or washers, between the flywheel and the bush, until the excessive sideplay has been removed. There should be approximately ·012 inch endplay on the shaft.

Reassembling Timing Gear

Assuming that the crankcase and flywheel assembly are now correct, proceed to fit the timing gear. The cam should be examined, and, if necessary, stoned up. Should the rockers be badly worn, fit new rockers, as worn rockers will prevent the engine from being retimed correctly. This also applies to a badly worn cam wheel.

First fit into position the half-time pinion, one tooth of which is marked with a dot. It will be noticed that the half-time pinion is provided with three keyways, the object of these being to vary the timing if necessary, but it is advisable to fit the pinion with the shaft key in the same keyway in which it was originally fitted.

Next fit in the inlet rocker, the exhaust rocker, exhaust-lifter cam, and finally, with the piston set in its correct position, slip in the cam wheel. The correct timing of the engine is given on a separate chart.

Continue to reassemble the engine in the reverse way to which it was stripped down.

Open up the Crankcase

The crankcase is now ready to be opened. Before doing this, however, lift the case out of the cradle, placing it downwards on to its driving side

NEW HUDSON REPAIR NOTES

until the shaft rests on the bench. Remove the four crankcase bolts, then gently tap the crankcase with a mallet or the end of a hammer shaft round the joint to loosen the two halves of the case from the spigoted joint. The timing-side half of the crankcase should be lifted away, providing the pump spindle has been removed. Care must be taken to assure that none of the small mainshaft rollers become lost. There are 32 rollers in each bearing, also a spacing collar in the driving-side, and a spacing washer in the timing-side, bearings. The steel race should not be removed unless it is necessary to fit a new one. It is then advised that the crankcase and flywheel assembly are returned to the works for rebushing. Thoroughly wash the flywheel assembly, then place with the rest of the components ready for reassembling. On no account should the flywheels be dismantled unless the operator has the necessary technical knowledge and experience for rebalancing them.

NEW IMPERIAL MOTOR-CYCLES

Adjusting Tappets

THE method is similar on both o.h.v. and s.v. models. The tappet-rod tubes in the former and the valve-spring covers in the latter are telescopic, and are screwed on the tappet guides. The lower half of the cover must be unscrewed and pushed up until the tappets are exposed (see Fig. 1). These are adjusted in the usual way by loosening the lock nut, and screwing up the tappet head to take up any clearance. Whilst there should be ·005 inch in the side valve, there should be no perceptible clearance in the o.h.v. model, but just sufficient to allow the steel cap on the valve stem to be revolved. Lock the tappet head and screw down the covers.

Removing Cylinder

The side-valve models are so simple that very little comment is necessary. On some of the larger engines there is insufficient clearance to allow the cylinder to be removed independently of the piston, in which case the gudgeon pin should be pushed out as soon as this is exposed, and the cylinder with the piston removed together. In the case of the o.h.v. model, assuming the obvious fittings have been taken off, the tappet-rod covers should be unscrewed at the bottom and the top; where screwed into the cylinder head, slide over each other until the push-rod ends can be seen (Fig. 1). Rotate the engine so that the piston is at the bottom of the stroke. If a screwdriver is now placed under the rocker-shaft nut and used as a lever to depress the valve, the tappet rods with the covers can be taken away. The exhaust-lifter wire can also be disconnected. Now unscrew the four head holding-down bolts, slacken off each in turn, and the head can then be lifted off. *Note.*—The bolts on the left-hand side are somewhat recessed owing to the deep finning. It is advisable to have a short box spanner to deal with these. The valves are fitted with two springs each, and retained by the usual split cotters. Take the hardened steel caps from the valve stem and carefully examine these. If there are any signs of wear they should be replaced owing to the difficulty of getting accurate tappet clearance. This is all the dismantling that is necessary for decarbonising and grinding in valves, etc.

Rocker Gear

The rockers can be taken out by undoing the rocker-shaft castellated nut and unscrewing the shaft or spindle. Test the bearing for play, and rebush if necessary ; also examine the shaft for signs of wear. Should it be necessary, the rocker box can be detached by undoing the two nuts inside the box.

NEW IMPERIAL MOTOR-CYCLES

Removing the Complete Unit from Frame

Having dismantled thus far, the cylinder barrel and piston may be removed, the former by undoing the four loose nuts. The gudgeon pin is a "push-in" fit in the piston, and may be retained by spring circlips or fitted with end pads. Should the crankcase need attention, the whole unit, consisting of engine, gearbox and magneto, should be taken out of the frame. The New Imperial design renders this a comparatively simple matter.

Timing Gear

It is advisable at this stage to strip the timing gear. Take off the timing cover and withdraw the cam wheels, oil-pump spindle and gear wheel. Now take off the mainshaft pinion nut. This has a *left-hand* thread, and should be turned in a clockwise direction to unscrew. This should necessarily be very tight, and requires a good-fitting box spanner and a long tommy-bar to undo it. To prevent the flywheels turning, the chain should be jammed on the other side of the engine, or the sprockets prevented from turning. For this reason it is recommended to remove this nut before taking the unit from the frame.

Fig. 1.—ADJUSTING TAPPETS.

The right-hand tube is telescoped over the top half to enable the tappets to be adjusted. The left-hand tube top half is unscrewed to enable the tube and tappet rod to be removed.

NEW IMPERIAL MOTOR-CYCLES

Having disconnected the various fittings, such as cables, footrests, exhaust pipes and rear chain, etc., and the front- and rear-frame bolts, the unit can be lifted out. Now remove the magneto by taking off the chain-cover, the chain and sprockets, the back half of the chain-case, and the two bolts and nuts holding the magneto platform to the engine p l a t e s.

Fig. 2.—ADJUSTING THE ENGINE CHAIN.
Showing the adjusting bolt which draws the gearbox to the rear when the chain requires tightening. This also shows the speedometer drive and lock nut.

It will be noticed that the engine plates are slotted to allow the chain to be adjusted. The gearbox can now be taken away with the two rear engine plates by withdrawing the bolts holding the latter to the engine. It may be necessary to slacken the two shouldered bolts clamping the plates through the top of the gearbox.

Engine-chain Adjustment

Note.—These bolts should also be slackened off when the front chain is being adjusted. This is done by screwing the adjusting bolt fitted to the plate, bridging the two side plates at the rear of the gearbox (Fig. 2). Always remember to tighten the two shouldered bolts after adjusting the chain, and also to readjust the rear chain.

Engine-sprocket Shock Absorber

The crankcase assembly is now separated from the other sub-assemblies, and dismantling can be continued by removing the engine sprocket. Remove the split pin and unscrew the locking nut, which will release the spring. Then free the locking plate where this is pressed into the slots in the adapter, and unscrew the extended nut by the slots at the end

NEW IMPERIAL MOTOR-CYCLES

(Fig. 3). The sleeve and the sprocket can then be taken off, leaving the adapter in position. This is keyed on the engine mainshaft, and may be a little obstinate to remove. If this is " jarred " by smartly tapping on the splines with a copper hammer, at the same time turning the shaft to another position, the tapers should be freed. The reader will appreciate the care necessary to avoid straining the mainshaft itself.

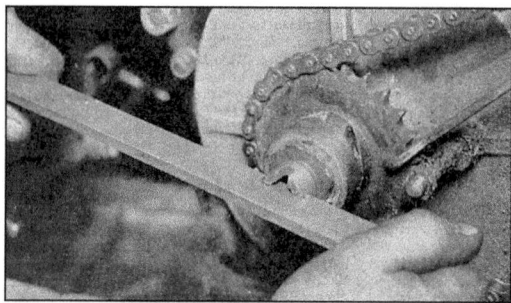

Fig. 3.—Dismantling the Sprocket Shock Absorber.
The locking-plate tongue is shown lifted out of the splines, and the extended nut is being unscrewed. Note how the sprocket is prevented from turning.

Crankcase Assembly

This can be stripped, and the flywheels taken apart. The big end has a roller bearing with a detachable liner to the connecting rod. All lighter models are fitted with bushes to both main bearings, and the other types are fitted with a journal bearing on the driving side. Both taper and parallel mainshafts are fitted to the flywheels. The tappet guides are screwed into the crankcase. Model " 2 " engines are fitted with the Pilgrim type mechanical oil pump. This is a wet-sump system. The dry-sump system is used with the other models. This is carried out by a double-acting plunger pump driven by a direct gear from the mainshaft pinion. This seldom gives trouble, and failure of the oil supply, indicated when the plunger does not protrude, is usually due either to no oil in tank or " choked " filter.

NEW IMPERIAL TIMING CHART

MODELS.	INLET.		EXHAUST.		IGNI-TION. MAX. ADV. Before T.D.C.	Tappet Clearance.	
	Opens before T.D.C.	Closes after B.D.C.	Opens before B.D.C.	Closes after T.D.C.		Inlet.	Ex-haust.
500 c.c. O.H.V., 1928–31 .	15°	45°	60°	20°	12°	nil when	nil cold
500 c.c. S.V., 1928–31. .	10°	45°	60°	20°	8°	·005″	·005″
350 c.c. O.H.V., 1927–31 .	15°	45°	60°	20°	12°	nil	nil
350 c.c. S.V., 1926–31. .	10°	45°	60°	20°	8°	·005″	·005″

SPECIAL HINTS ON NORTON ENGINES

By W. C. HAYCRAFT

ENGINE DISMANTLING AND REASSEMBLING

Stripping S.V. Engines for Decarbonisation

WHERE a top overhaul only is contemplated, it is simply necessary, in the case of the 1931 s.v. engines, to remove the plug, unscrew the fixing bolts and gently prise off the detachable head with a suitable tool, being careful not to damage the copper gasket. Afterwards the cylinder barrel may be withdrawn if it is desired to inspect the piston. Once the head has been removed, and the carburetter, exhaust valve lifter and exhaust pipe disconnected, the barrel itself may be drawn off almost vertically with the piston practically on bottom dead centre. On all s.v. engines the valves are most readily removed with the cylinder or cylinder barrel in position, using either the special extractor supplied by Norton Motors Ltd., or a proprietary tool such as the Terry. A sharp tap on each valve spring when compressed will allow the split collets to be removed with the fingers. Should the valve caps, provided on s.v. engines where the head is non-detachable, be very stiff, apply paraffin. If this is ineffective warm up the engine, insert cold water in each valve-cap hollow, and use a spanner immediately.

Non-detachable Head Cylinders

In the case of 1930 and previous s.v. engines no detachable head is fitted, and the cylinder must be removed. To do this it will be found necessary, after removing the carburetter, exhaust pipe, valve cover and valve-lifter cable, to put the piston almost on bottom dead centre with the connecting rod slightly to the rear, and before drawing the cylinder off the truncated cast-iron piston to rotate it bodily through 180°, so that the integral valve chest faces the near side and the stub induction pipe faces towards the front, when the cylinder may be gently drawn off the piston until the lower scraper ring emerges from its mouth. This procedure is required owing to the comparatively long piston stroke and consequently somewhat tall cylinder.

Stripping O.H.V. Engines for Decarbonisation

All o.h.v. engines have, of course, detachable heads, and decarbonisation is readily effected after first removing the push rods and rocker box,

SPECIAL HINTS ON NORTON ENGINES

and prising the head off the barrel, as on the s.v. engines. When breaking the joint and removing the cylinder head, great care must be taken to avoid damaging the ground faces. Any deep scratches are likely to cause gas leakage, and in this event the two faces will have to be ground in similarly to the valves. As in the case of the 1931 s.v. models, removal of the cylinder barrel presents no difficulty once the head has been removed.

Stripping O.H.C. Engines for Decarbonisation

On these engines removal of the petrol tank is advised before decarbonisation. Rocker-box removal is unnecessary, owing to the special design enabling this to be swung clear of the detachable cylinder head on its vertical shaft pivot. The head and barrel are then readily removed. As on the o.h.v. engines great care must be taken to avoid damaging the ground faces.

Withdrawal of Petrol Tank

This has a four-bolt fixing. When withdrawing, preparatory to decarbonising an o.h.c. engine or removing an engine from the frame, raise tank at saddle end and draw gently back until bulbous nose clears handlebar clips.

Fig. 1.—Removal of Norton Push Rods and Covers.

SPECIAL HINTS ON NORTON ENGINES

REMOVING OVERHEAD VALVE GEAR

Push-rod Removal

The push-rods on Norton o.h.v. engines of 1930 and subsequent pattern are enclosed in tubular covers sealed at each end. To remove proceed as follows. Unscrew the union nut fitting over crankcase adapter and remove rocker-box panel cover. Now apply a fairly heavy open-ended spanner to rocker-shaft nuts at rear of rocker box, and rotate nuts clockwise (Fig. 1). This will compress valve springs and free push rods from the rocker-arm ball ends, enabling both push rods and covers to be pulled away and raised clear of the crankcase.

On engines of earlier than 1930 design, where the rockers are not mounted in a self-contained rocker box but on special carrier standards, and no covers are provided, a somewhat different method of removal is called for. In the case of o.h.v. engines having straight-pattern rockers, rest a screwdriver on each rocker-standard distance-piece tube and lever inside end of rocker arm upwards until push rod is clear. Where arched-pattern rockers are used, the push rods may be removed by similar application of a lever or cranked tommy bar, taking care not to use excessive force when extracting the push rods, or the cupped ends and tappet heads may suffer injury. Force the push-rod return spring downwards so as to release the spring from the recess in the push-rod return spring stop, and then pull upwards to extract the rod.

To remove push rods on early E.S.2 engines having enclosed return springs, unscrew the spring covers and slide them up the push rods, which may be removed in the manner just described. On replacement do not forget to recharge the rubber oil retainers, otherwise quick wear and need for further valve-clearance adjustment will be necessitated. If rubber shows signs of perishing, renew. There are several excellent proprietary push-rod end lubricators now marketed.

O.H.V. Rocker-box Removal

Nineteen-thirty and subsequent Nortons have a cast aluminium box without any kind of platform, and its removal simply entails the unscrewing of the bolts securing it to the four cylinder-head retaining sleeves after first disconnecting the exhaust valve lifter.

Removal of O.H.V. Rocker Carrier Standards

On 1929 and earlier push-rod engines having no actual rocker box, removal of the rockers simply involves the removal of the four rocker-standard retaining bolts with a suitable box spanner, when the standards, tie rods and rockers may be withdrawn as a complete assembly and subsequently dismantled if necessary.

SPECIAL HINTS ON NORTON ENGINES

Fig. 2.—SHOWING ROCKER BOX SWUNG ASIDE ON O.H.C. ENGINE FOR CYLINDER-HEAD REMOVAL.

Swinging aside O.H.C. Rocker Box

As already mentioned, decarbonising and the removal of the cylinder head or cylinder on the o.h.c. engines does not necessitate the actual *removal* of the rocker box, an operation probably involving some difficulty and upsetting of the valve timing on this type of power unit, but swinging it to one side as shown at Fig. 2.

In the Case of 1930 and subsequent O.H.C. Engines

Proceed as follows : remove the rocker-box holding-down bolts and the distance pieces between the cylinder-head bolts and rocker box. Then slightly loosen the vertical-shaft cover-tube gland nuts and unscrew the nuts retaining the cylinder head, after which the joint may be carefully broken. Having done this, stand by the near side of the machine and tilt the rocker box away about $\frac{1}{4}$ inch, so that the valve-clearance adjusters are almost clear of the spring cups. The cylinder head can then be raised about $\frac{3}{8}$ inch to allow it just to clear the barrel spigot. It should be lifted off sideways away from the rocker box. If removal of the cylinder barrel is intended, the rocker box should be rotated through 180°.

Earlier Patterns

When dealing with o.h.c. engines of earlier pattern than 1930, proceed thus : first remove the inspection cover at the top bevels in order to ascertain their relative positions, and rotate the engine until the single

SPECIAL HINTS ON NORTON ENGINES

punch mark on the vertical-shaft bevel coincides with the two marks on the camshaft bevel. This will enable the correct timing to be checked when finally positioning and retightening the rocker box. To avoid the risk of straining the bottom of the vertical shaft tube, loosen the lower bevel-panel cover by partially unscrewing the cheese-headed screws. The rocker box, complete with vertical shaft and housing, should be raised about ½ inch to clear the rocker-box platform nuts, and rotated through 180°, so that the upper bevel inspection cover faces the near side. Be most careful not to raise the rocker box excessively, or the splined vertical shaft will be withdrawn from the lower bevel, necessitating retiming. After removing the four rocker-box platform set-screws the head may be detached, followed by the cylinder barrel if necessary.

Removal of Overhead Valves

This presents no special difficulty once the cylinder head has been removed, but owing to the employment of duplex coil springs, considerable pressure is required to compress them sufficiently to enable the split collets to be removed with the fingers. The use of a valve-spring compressor is therefore advised.

PISTON REMOVAL

Two types of pistons are used on Norton engines—a truncated cast-iron type on most s.v. models, and an aluminium slipper type on all o.h.v. and o.h.c. models. On some s.v. models it will be found that their owners have substituted a high-compression aluminium piston for the standard cast-iron type, which is quite permissible on these engines.

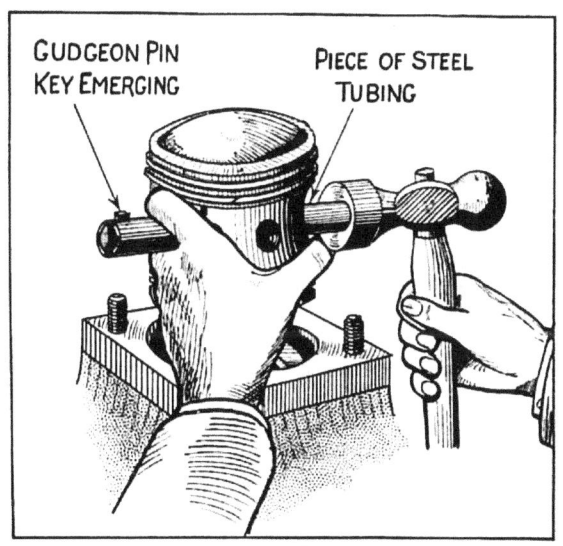

Fig. 3.—Removing Gudgeon Pin.

First remove the cotter pin, and from the same side drive out the gudgeon pin as shown above, using a piece of steel tubing. This applies to cast-iron pistons only.

Standard Cast-iron Piston

Assuming a standard cast-iron piston is fitted, it will be found that the gudgeon pin is of the non-floating pattern, and no attempt should be made to drive

SPECIAL HINTS ON NORTON ENGINES

it out before removing the cotter pin on the near side locking it in position. To remove the gudgeon pin proceed as follows : close the ends of the cotter pin with a small pair of pliers and withdraw it. Then, after obtaining a soft round drift, or preferably a piece of tubing a trifle smaller in diameter than the gudgeon pin, gently tap the gudgeon pin out with a light hammer *from the side whence the split pin has been removed* until the key on the opposite end of the pin emerges from the key slot cut on the piston. Only a few additional taps will be required to remove the gudgeon pin entirely. While doing this it is extremely important not to allow the hammer thrust to be transmitted to the connecting rod. The piston should therefore be held firmly in the palm of the left hand, the rod itself being held between the left forefinger and thumb. The piston may now be withdrawn and decarbonised if necessary. Careful note should be made, having regard to reassembly, of the exact position of the piston relative to the connecting rod.

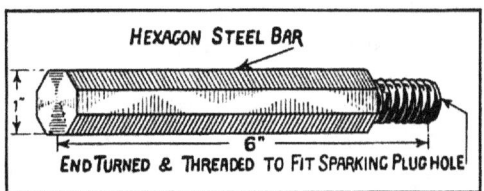

Fig. 4.—TO AID DECARBONISING.

Hexagon steel bar which may be clamped in vice. Cylinder head to be decarbonised is fitted to threaded end by the sparking-plug hole, thus providing a rigid mounting for the work to be done.

Aluminium Piston

In the case of the aluminium type piston it will be found that the gudgeon pin is fully floating, and it may readily be pushed out after first removing with a small pair of pliers the two spring circlips (fitted unless brass end caps are used).

Piston-ring Slot Gap

It should be noted that with the cast-iron pistons Norton Motors Ltd. recommend a slot gap of ·005 inch. With aluminium pistons the gap should be approximately three times as great.

Holding Cylinder Head when Decarbonising

In order to prevent the ground face of an o.h.v. or o.h.c. cylinder head sustaining damage during the process of removing the carbon, and to render decarbonising easier, it is the best course, if much decarbonising is done, to obtain a suitable length of mild hexagon steel bar, screw a sparking-plug thread on one end as shown at Fig. 4, and clamp the bar in a vice. If the cylinder head be now fitted a very accessible and rigid mounting will be provided and the carbon may be chipped off, the ports polished and valves ground in if necessary. An alternative method is to make use of an old sparking plug, although for obvious reasons this is less satisfactory than that just described.

SPECIAL HINTS ON NORTON ENGINES

Removing Carbon

All carbon deposits on the piston crown and combustion chamber may be removed with a screwdriver. In the case of an aluminium piston, be very careful not to press hard, or the surface will be damaged, and on no account immerse in a caustic soda solution.

Grinding-in Valves

On the s.v. engines the valve heads are slotted in the usual way to receive the blade of a screwdriver. On other engines a small hand vice or other implement is necessary to pull the valves up against their seats. A simple but efficient tool can be made by cutting several inches off a piece of suitable diameter steel tubing, fitting at one end a small set-screw for holding the valve stem, and drilling the other end to receive a tommy bar or steel rod.

Grinding-in Cylinder Barrel and Head Faces

In the event of either face having sustained injury, grind-in as in the case of a valve after first removing the cylinder barrel studs. To remove these screw two nuts on each stud and use each nut as a lock nut against the other. Before applying the grinding paste fill up the stud holes with grease to avoid the abrasive getting on the threads.

Valve Springs

If an o.h.v. or o.h.c. engine is being prepared for competition work involving exceptionally high speeds, it is desirable to replace the standard valve springs with extra powerful ones, obtainable from the manufacturers. Always renew springs if there is any indication of weakness, for on Norton engines the condition of the valve springs is very important.

Raising Compression Ratio

Raising of the compression ratio with a view to obtaining an increase of maximum speed can be advantageously effected on many Norton engines, but it should be pointed out that the fitting of special high-compression pistons will avoid the necessity for removing any metal from the cylinder base or cylinder head. In the case of o.h.c. engines removal of metal must not be attempted, as this will inevitably interfere with the camshaft drive.

REASSEMBLY AND ADJUSTMENT

Reassembly after Decarbonising

This is quite straightforward, except that the points mentioned previously must be borne in mind ; that is to say, when refitting a cast-iron piston, which must be replaced on the connecting rod exactly as removed, the gudgeon pin must be inserted from the near side and gently

SPECIAL HINTS ON NORTON ENGINES

tapped in until its key re-engages the key slot in the piston and the split pin can be replaced through the drilled hole in the gudgeon pin on the opposite side. Similarly, when refitting the cylinder to the piston itself after replacing the valves, the cylinder should be held with the valve chest facing the near side. Although the cylinder base on all engines is deeply spigoted, a paper washer should be inserted between the cylinder and crankcase. A suitable washer can be made in the usual way by running a mallet round a piece of stout paper held over the spigot, but it is preferable to use a ready-made washer as supplied by Norton Motors Ltd.

In the case of the o.h.v. engines the rocker box may be completely

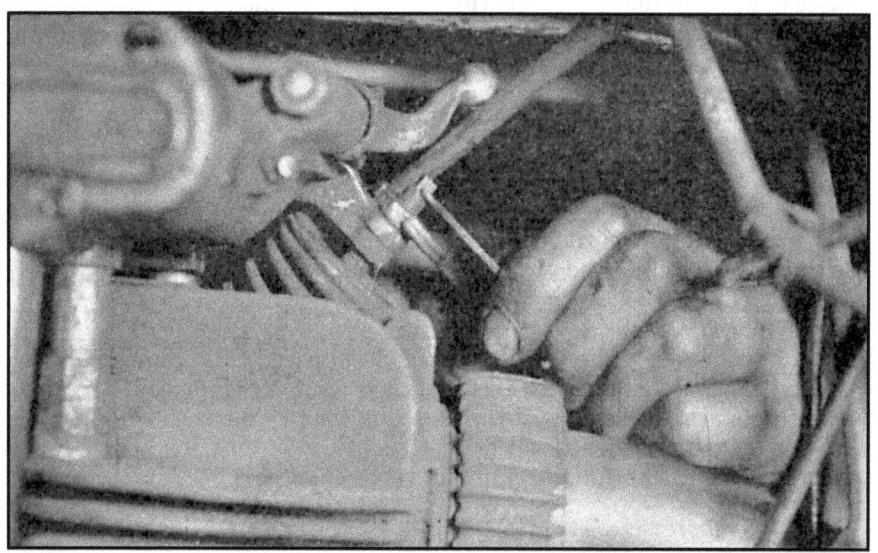

Fig. 5.—ADJUSTING THE VALVE CLEARANCES ON O.H.V. MODEL.

reassembled and refitted to the cylinder head. It is important, when replacing the valve springs, to see that the inner springs are correctly located on the washers at the valve guide bases, and when replacing the cylinder head on the barrel to see that the joint faces are scrupulously clean and that the retaining nuts are uniformly tightened.

When reassembling an o.h.c. engine, the compression plug must be refitted prior to rocker-box and vertical-shaft adjustment.

Sparking Plugs

In the event of the plug electrodes being found badly burnt or "whiskered," or the plug insulation being found defective, replace in the case of s.v. engines with a short-reach K.L.G. H.S.3, or the latest

SPECIAL HINTS ON NORTON ENGINES

K.1, or a Lodge H.1 plug. In the case of o.h.v. engines fit a K.L.G. H.S.3, or the latest K.S.5, or a Lodge H.45 plug. Afterwards test gap with the usual twenty-thousandth feeler gauge. K.L.G. type 246 plugs should be used on the o.h.c. engines except for running-in, when a K.L.G. H.S.3 is preferable. For racing fit a K.L.G. 348 plug, as this will stand enormous heat. If it oils up badly, try a K.L.G. 341 or 396 plug.

In connection with the removal of refractory plugs and their refitting, it is of interest to note that the Robinhood Engineering Works now market a most useful garage tool with worm-gear operation.

Valve Clearances

Norton engines, in common with most high-efficiency power units possessing considerable valve-timing overlap, are very sensitive in regard to valve clearances.

In the case of the s.v. engines, the inlet and exhaust tappet clearances should be with a *cold* engine ·003 and ·005 inch, respectively. Adjustment is effected in the usual way, by holding with one spanner the adjustable tappet head and with another loosening the lock nut.

With the push-rod o.h.v. engines the clearances between the valve stems and rocker adjusters should be—for touring ·002 and ·004 inch, respectively; while for racing they should be ·005 and ·008 inch, respectively. In both cases the square-headed grub screws and lock nuts should be adjusted with the engine *cold*.

The valve clearances on the o.h.c. Nortons are adjusted similarly to the o.h.v. models, but in this case the inlet and exhaust clearances with a *cold* engine should be—for touring ·010 and ·015 inch, respectively; for racing they should be ·012 and ·020 inch, respectively.

Valve-lifter Adjustment

When testing on a s.v. engine the clearance at the exhaust tappet, be quite sure that the exhaust valve lifter sleeve fitting over the tappet guide is not raised by the centrally pivoted lever, due to absence of backlash at the handlebar control, sufficiently to prevent the tappet base seating on the cam rocker. There should be $\frac{1}{32}$ to $\frac{1}{16}$ inch backlash in order to ensure the exhaust valve always fully closing and full engine compression being maintained at all temperatures with the tappet adjustment correctly set.

Similarly, when testing the clearance between the valve stem and rocker adjuster on an o.h.v. or o.h.c. engine, be sure there is sufficient exhaust valve lifter play. It is unnecessary to be extremely cautious when making the adjustment, for excessive valve lift cannot cause the inlet and exhaust valves to clash, as is the case with a few engines of the overhead valve type.

SPECIAL HINTS ON NORTON ENGINES

GENERAL OVERHAULING NOTES

Dismantling O.H.V. Rockers

On 1930 and later engines dismantling simply involves removal of the rocker-box front cover, the rocker-shaft nuts at the opposite side and the exhaust valve lifter bolt, when the duplex rockers may be withdrawn from their plain bearings. Endplay exceeding ·003 inch should be eliminated by means of the nuts on the near side, and if there is any marked play between the bushes and rockers, the bushes should be pressed out and new ones fitted. Renew also the ball ends of the rocker-arm adjuster screws if these are much worn. When reassembling on no account overlook the small semicircular keys retaining the valve rockers to the inner rockers.

On engines of earlier design than 1930 roller bearings house the rockers. To dismantle proceed as follows: remove rocker-pin lock nuts, unscrew pins and lift rockers upwards. Be most careful not to lose any of the rollers, which are retained in each phosphor-bronze cage by two washers. It should be noted that endplay exceeding ·003 inch can be taken up by adjustment of the centre bolt. To adjust, slack off the dome lock nut at the end of centre bolt, unscrew the bolt, say a quarter of a revolution, and while holding bolt retighten the lock nut. Repeat the operation if necessary, but see that the rocker does not move stiffly.

Dismantling O.H.C. Rocker Box

First remove lock nuts securing the rocker arms to the tapered ends of the cam-rocker shafts; remove rocker-box cover, exhaust valve lifter lever and bolt and withdraw rockers from their bushes.

Removal of the camshaft involves detaching the top bevel pinion, which is keyed to the shaft and secured by a lock nut. Removal of this lock nut will allow of the pinion being withdrawn. Three keyways will be found cut on the pinion, and it is very important to observe on dismantling which keyway is used and to reassemble similarly. On some engines a distance washer may be found behind the pinions. Be careful to refit this. The cams themselves are a sliding fit on the cam-shaft and can readily be replaced.

Removing Engine from Frame (1930 Models)

Whenever a very thorough overhaul is undertaken, necessitating parting the crankcase for bearing inspection and perhaps rebushing, it is, of course, necessary to remove the engine from the frame prior to complete dismantling on the bench.

On the cradle-frame models it is possible, and indeed the best plan, to remove the entire power unit complete with magneto and carburetter after first removing the petrol tank, exhaust pipe, primary chaincase,

SPECIAL HINTS ON NORTON ENGINES

chain, and disconnecting the carburetter, ignition and exhaust valve lifter control cables. To remove engine, first withdraw the footrest support rod, when the footrest hangers with distance pieces will become detachable. Now remove the three bolts securing the front engine plates to the frame and crankcase. Three bolts now secure the engine to the frame, two in the cradle and one passing through the combined magneto platform and rear plates. Withdraw these three bolts from the transmission side, after which the power unit may be gently lowered to the ground by gripping it firmly and tilting it in a forward direction until the magneto platform clears the frame lugs, enabling the engine to be pulled clear from the transmission side.

In the case of the diamond-frame models, in addition to disconnecting the usual control cables, front chain and exhaust system, it is necessary to remove the carburetter. Then detach the magneto support rod from the eye in the frame lug, and remove nuts from the front engine lug and gear-bracket bolts on the transmission side, and gently hammer out bolts, using a suitable rod or tommy bar. The engine can now be gently lowered to the ground and placed on the bench. It is often a good plan to place some wood packing beneath the crankcase before withdrawing the last securing bolts in case the engine should accidentally drop out.

Fig. 6.—Prising off Magneto Sprocket with a Screwdriver.

Although a screwdriver used as a lever may sometimes prove effective, a sprocket drawer is preferable.

With engines dating prior to 1923, camshaft sprockets should be removed with the aid of a flat-nosed punch and hammer.

Timing Gear Dismantling (S.V. and O.H.V.)

The first preliminary is to remove the magneto driving sprocket from the tapered and keyed end of the exhaust camshaft in the case of all 1930 engines except the cradle-frame types, or from the tapered and keyed end of the inlet camshaft in the case of the 1931 engines. To do this, remove the lock nut (right-hand thread) with chain still in place, and then use a sprocket drawer to remove the sprocket.

Should it be necessary to remove the camshaft sprocket on an engine of earlier design than 1923, special care must be taken, or considerable damage may be done. Instead of the sprocket fitting on a taper, it is screwed with a right-hand thread to the camshaft and secured by a lock nut. After this nut has been removed the sprocket can be un-

SPECIAL HINTS ON NORTON ENGINES

screwed with the aid of a flat-nosed punch and hammer. Two suitable holes are provided for this purpose.

To expose the timing gear it is now simply necessary to remove the timing-case cover (complete with mechanical pump in the case of 1930 engines) by prising it off with a screwdriver after taking out the securing bolts (great care should be used with a screwdriver, or the joint will be damaged). It should be first eased off, say ¼ inch, and to prevent premature extraction of the cam wheels the screwdriver should be inserted between the cover and case. The rockers and cam wheels may then be removed by hand and inspected for wear. Before doing this, however, see that the cam wheels are marked to ensure correct replacement without having to retime. It is best to make light scratches or pencil marks, and then to punch-mark them properly on the bench afterwards. The main reason why Norton Motors Ltd. do not themselves mark the cam wheels is that they use detachable cams of very high-grade steel, and it is sometimes found that, when screwing on new cams to the camshafts, small thread variations result in a slight alteration of the cam positions relative to the wheels, thus rendering retiming or at least checking necessary. Thus, if on removal of the cam wheels and camshafts of a Norton that has done a big mileage a close inspection reveals that wear has occurred sufficient to retard seriously the inlet valve opening and exhaust valve closing (the symptom

Fig. 7.—How to loosen the Engine Sprocket Key.

of which is usually a marked impairment of performance especially as regards speed), new cams should be obtained and fitted, and the engine must later be retimed. If the timing gear is very noisy it may be advisable to fit new cam wheels also. Care must be taken to see that correct replacements are made. Cams suitable for 1926 and subsequent Norton engines are stamped "W.7," while cams designed for most 1924–5 engines are stamped "90." As a general rule Norton cams are very durable, and only when engines are very worn or it is intended to tune for speed work is it necessary to fit new cams. Do not interfere with the small engine pinion except when it is necessary to part the crankcase halves for removal of the crankshaft. On reassembly the nut securing the pinion must be tightened up deadtight.[1] When reassembling timing gear and

[1] Left-hand thread.

SPECIAL HINTS ON NORTON ENGINES

replacing the cover do not omit to replace the paper washer, for on practically all 1930 engines the whole oil supply is first fed to the timing case.

Removing O.H.C. Vertical Shaft

Cylinder-head removal has already been referred to, and it was mentioned that for decarbonising the lower end of the vertical shaft need not be withdrawn. This should now be done, and the crankcase panel cover should be removed, taking care not to remove the large screw in its centre or the oil-level adjuster. It is then possible to remove the lower vertical shaft bevel and self-aligning bearing, together with their aluminium housing after withdrawing the pins which retain this to the crankcase. Do not dismantle bearing unless essential, as its locking ring requires very skilful fitting.

Crankshaft Removal

Separation of the crankcase halves and removal of the crankshaft and flywheels can readily be effected after the cylinder, piston and timing gear have been removed. The crankshaft itself, however, which is of the usual built-up type, should not be dismantled unless the facilities and necessary skill are available for the subsequent truing up and accurate alignment of the flywheels. This should, however, be within the scope of most well-equipped garages and repair shops.

The first essential preliminary to separation of the crankcase halves is to remove, in the case of all D.S. lubricated engines, the entire oil-pump driving worm and worm wheel, where fitted. In the case of an o.h.c. engine, the mainshaft bevel pinion, which is keyed, must also be removed by withdrawing it off its taper with a suitable tool. The engine pinion and engine sprocket should now be taken off. It should be mentioned that the pinion nut has a left-hand thread. Both fit on tapers and are keyed and held in place by lock nuts. Generally the engine pinion (which is never under severe loading) can be readily levered off. The engine sprocket, however, is often found somewhat refractory.

To remove the engine sprocket take off the nut and lock nut, and after locating the exact position of its keyway, direct several light hammer blows, using a flat-nosed punch or tommy bar held vertically over the keyway behind the sprocket, as shown at Fig. 7. This should loosen the key and enable the sprocket to be levered or tapped off. If very obstinate use a sprocket drawer.

To separate the crankcase halves, if difficulty is experienced after removing all nuts and bolts, grip one half of the crankcase in each hand and bump the crankcase gently on the bench, at the same time pulling the halves away from each other, when they should come apart. Make a note of the condition of the mainshaft ball bearings, especially that on the driving side, which on the o.h.c. engines is fitted together with a roller

SPECIAL HINTS ON NORTON ENGINES

bearing. Very little sideplay of the crankshaft is permissible, and end-play exceeding $\frac{1}{32}$ inch should be taken up. When reassembling, the crankcase joint should be made with seccotine or preferably goldsize.

Dismantling Crankshaft

As already mentioned, this should not be done unless the means are at hand (i.e. a lathe is available) for proper realignment of the flywheels. To separate the flywheels it is, of course, only necessary to remove the crankpin complete with the connecting rod and big-end roller bearing. To do this the nuts and locking plates securing the tapered crankpin ends to the flywheels must be removed, and the crankpin driven out from each flywheel with a few sharp hammer blows. It is unlikely that the mainshafts will require to be removed, but if so, it should be noted that both are friction fits and keyed to the flywheel bosses, and are best changed by Norton Motors Ltd.

Big-end Bearing

The big-end roller bearing consists of the hardened steel crankpin, 16 pairs of rollers running between two turned flanges on the crank-pin and a bush pressed into the connecting rod. To dismantle the bearing after flywheel removal it is only necessary to take off the two steel washers next to the flanges and slide the connecting rod big-end off the rollers. The connecting-rod bush may then be pressed out and renewed if necessary. If there is any serious big-end play it is advisable to renew the crankpin bush and rollers. When reassembling be careful to see that all the 32 rollers are replaced, and do not forget the two crankpin washers. The simplest method of replacing the rollers is to coat the centre of the crankpin with thick grease, to which the rollers will adhere. Having assembled, tie a piece of string diagonally across the two washers till ready to fit flywheels.

The Small-end Bearing

A plain phosphor-bronze bush is pressed into the small end of the connecting rod, and to remove the bush requires the application of a piece of steel tubing in diameter slightly larger than the bush and a suitable nut and bolt for exerting screw pressure against one end of the bush. See that an oil groove is provided on the new bush. If the small-end play is considerable, it will probably be necessary to fit a new gudgeon pin as well as a bush.

TIMING CHART FOR NORTON ENGINES

MODELS.	INLET.		EXHAUST.		IGNITION. MAX. ADV. Before T.D.C.	Tappet Clearance.	
	Opens before T.D.C.	Closes after B.D.C.	Opens before B.D.C.	Closes after T.D.C.		Ex.	In.
1924							
Big 4 S.V.	20°–25°	50°–55°	55°–60°	20°–25°	20°–25°	·005″	·003″
3½ h.p. S.V.	20°–25°	50°–55°	55°–60°	20°–25°	20°–25°	·005″	·003″
1925							
Big 4 S.V.	20°–25°	50°–55°	55°–60°	20°–25°	20°–25°	·005″	·003″
3½ h.p. S.V.	20°–25°	50°–55°	60°–65°	20°–25°	20°–25°	·005″	·003″
1926							
490 c.c. O.H.V.	25°–30°	40°–45°	55°–60°	25°–30°	35°–40°	·003″	·003″
490 c.c. S.V.	25°–30°	40°–45°	55°–60°	25°–30°	20°–25°	·005″	·003″
Big 4 S.V.	25°–30°	40°–45°	55°–60°	25°–30°	20°–25°	·005″	·003″
588 c.c. O.H.V.	25°–30°	40°–45°	55°–60°	25°–30°	35°–40°	·003″	·003″
1927							
490 c.c. O.H.V.	25°–30°	40°–45°	55°–60°	25°–30°	35°–40°	·003″	·003″
490 c.c. S.V.	25°–30°	40°–45°	55°–60°	25°–30°	20°–25°	·005″	·003″
Big 4 S.V.	25°–30°	40°–45°	55°–60°	25°–30°	20°–25°	·005″	·003″
588 c.c. O.H.V.	25°–30°	40°–45°	55°–60°	25°–30°	35°–40°	·003″	·003″
1928 and 1929							
490 c.c. O.H.V.	25°–30°	40°–45°	55°–60°	25°–30°	35°–40°	·003″	·003″
490 c.c. S.V.	25°–30°	40°–45°	55°–60°	25°–30°	20°–25°	·005″	·003″
Big 4 S.V.	25°–30°	40°–45°	55°–60°	25°–30°	20°–25°	·005″	·003″
588 O.H.V.	25°–30°	40°–45°	55°–60°	25°–30°	20°–25°	·003″	·003″
490 c.c. O.H.C.	35°	—	—	40°	—	·010″	·006″
1930							
490 c.c. O.H.C., CS 1	35°	—	—	40°	50°–55°	·010″	·006″
348 c.c. O.H.C., CJ	35°	—	—	40°	50°	·010″	·006″
348 c.c. O.H.V., JE	35°	—	—	40°	42°	·004″	·002″
490 c.c. O.H.V., 490 c.c. S.V., Big 4 .	As for 1928 and 1929.						
1931							
490 c.c. O.H.V. (Models 18, 20, ES. II)	25°–30°	43°–48°	60°–65°	25°–30°	42°	·004″	·002″
490 c.c. S.V. (Model 16 H)	25°–30°	43°–48°	60°–65°	25°–30°	25°	·006″	·004″
Big 4 S.V. (Model 1)	25°–30°	43°–48°	60°–65°	25°–30°	20°	·006″	·004″
588 c.c. O.H.V. (Model 19)	25°–30°	43°–48°	60°–65°	25°–30°	42°	·004″	·002″
490 c.c. O.H.C. (Model CS 1)	35°	—	—	40°	50°	·010″	·006″
348 c.c. O.H.C. (Model CJ)	35°	—	—	40°	50°	·010″	·006″
348 c.c. O.H.V. Model JE)	25°–30°	43°–48°	60°–65°	25°–30°	42°	·004″	·002″

MAINTENANCE, REPAIR AND OVERHAUL OF P. & M. (PANTHER) ENGINES

By E. F. Chidley

THE outstanding features of P. & M. (Panther) machines remain practically unchanged from 1924 to 1931, but detail improvements have been incorporated each season, and where a part or parts have altered in design, which affect the instructions referring to such parts, a modification is made.

DISMANTLING ENGINE

Preliminaries

Remove exhaust system complete by unscrewing union nuts and bolt fixing silencer to frame. No special spanner is required for the former, as these can generally be loosened by inserting a piece of $\frac{1}{2}$-inch flat wood between the fins so that it fits well down into the corner, and giving this a sharp blow with a hammer. Punch to left to unscrew (right-hand thread). In the case of all models earlier than 1930 Redwing, the pipes are simply a push fit into the ports. Take off front and rear chain guards (after removing footpads 1930 and 1931 models). The chains should be disconnected by the spring clip joint and laid aside for attention later. Remove magneto control wire at magneto end, also sparking-plug wire from plug. This high-tension lead should now be pulled through from under the tank and wound in a coil. Take off petrol pipe complete, and in doing so make sure that the tank union does not unscrew when disconnecting at the tank end (the former should be held by an adjusting spanner).

The Carburetter

The carburetter can now be removed complete by taking out the two $\frac{1}{4}$-inch bolts which hold this to the inlet port. Unscrew the milled ring on the top of the main body and withdraw the throttle and air slides. The latter, complete with the control wires, should now be tied up to the tank rail to avoid damage to the tapered needle attached to the throttle slide (on models 1926 upwards the wires and slide can be slipped over the pipe connecting saddle tanks). The exhaust valve lifter is uncoupled in the following manner.

MAINTENANCE, ETC., OF P. & M. (PANTHER) ENGINES

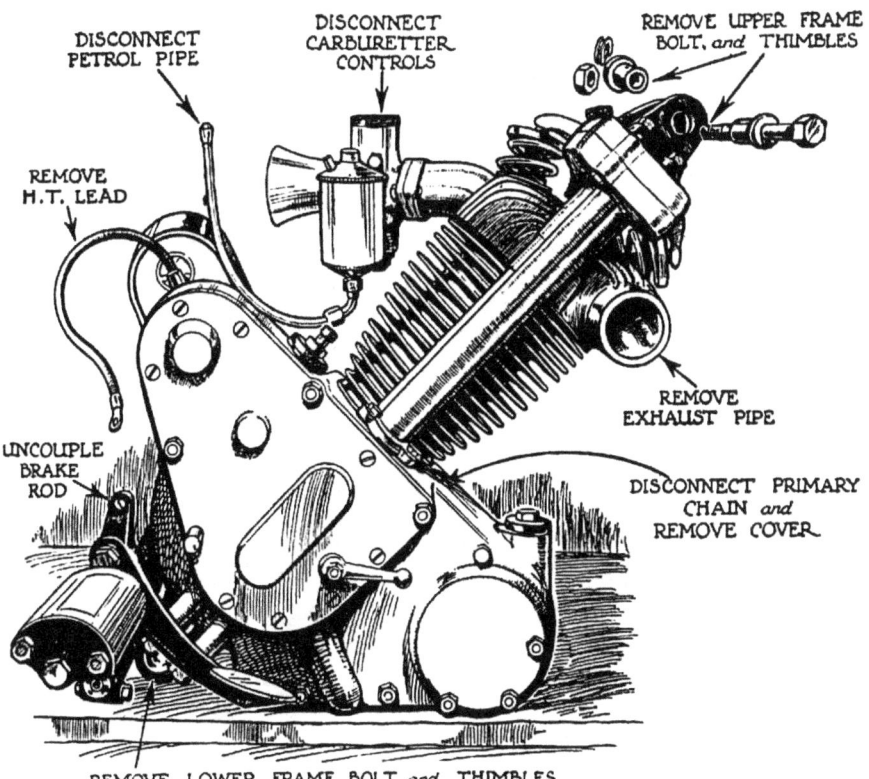

Fig. 1.—How to remove the Complete Panther Unit from the Frame.

Disconnect Controls

Turn engine until the exhaust valve is open. Pull control wire on top of rocker box upwards (see Fig. 3), and with the left hand slide downwards the small barrel (221). This will allow removal of the horseshoe-shaped collar (222). The barrel piece will now slip upwards over the wire adjuster (220), and permit of the wire nipple being released from the internal valve lifter (40). The back brake should now be disconnected at the pedal end, after which the engine is free from all connections.

Removing Engine from the Frame

The engine is held in the frame both top and bottom in the same manner. Remove both top and bottom engine bolts (both of which are fitted with split pins). The bolts hold in position a pair of parallel cones (see Fig. 1). Punch the bottom cones out first (the second cone being punched out by a piece of round steel or similar article to prevent the engine dropping forward and thereby denting the front mudguard). The

MAINTENANCE, ETC., OF P. & M. (PANTHER) ENGINES

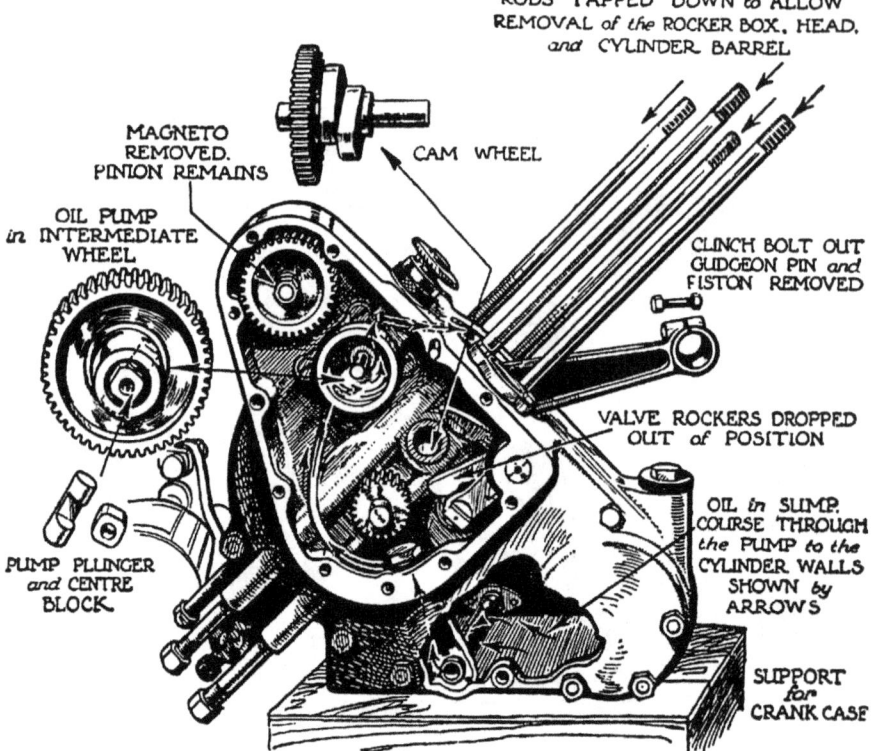

Fig. 2.—How the Panther Engine is dismantled without Removal from Frame.

front wheel should now be turned sideways so that the engine can swing forward, pivoting on the top cones. Place a piece of wood or similar packing under the engine to support it, and then punch out the top two cones, after which the engine can be lifted away to the bench for further attention.

Not Necessary when Decarbonising only

In order to dismantle the engine for decarbonising, valve grinding, etc., it is *not* necessary to remove the engine from the frame or to disconnect front chain, chain guard or brakes (see Fig. 2). Place a petrol tin or similar support under the sump and remove high-tension lead, exhaust pipes, valve-lifter wire, carburetter, top engine bolt and cones and slide upwards the bottom half of the telescopic push-rod tube. The push rods will then be exposed at the bottom end where they fit into the tappet cups. The four nuts at the top end of the long rods passing through the engine must be removed, when the top lugs (201, Fig. 4) will lift off. The long rods should now be tapped downwards.

MAINTENANCE, ETC., OF P. & M. (PANTHER) ENGINES

Removing Rockers

Take hold of rocker box in right hand, and with the left hand on push rods lift bodily until the push rods are clear of the tappet cups (59, Fig. 4). The distance washers (206, Fig. 4) will now lift off, and the engine rods push downwards through the cylinder head.

Take Care to check Distance Pieces

Note that on all models previous to 1931 there are three pairs of distance pieces of different length. Take a note of these when dismantling, otherwise you may get fogged when reassembling. The longest pair go under rocker box on *timing* side; the next size go *under* rocker box on driving side, and the shortest pair on *top* of rocker box, driving side.

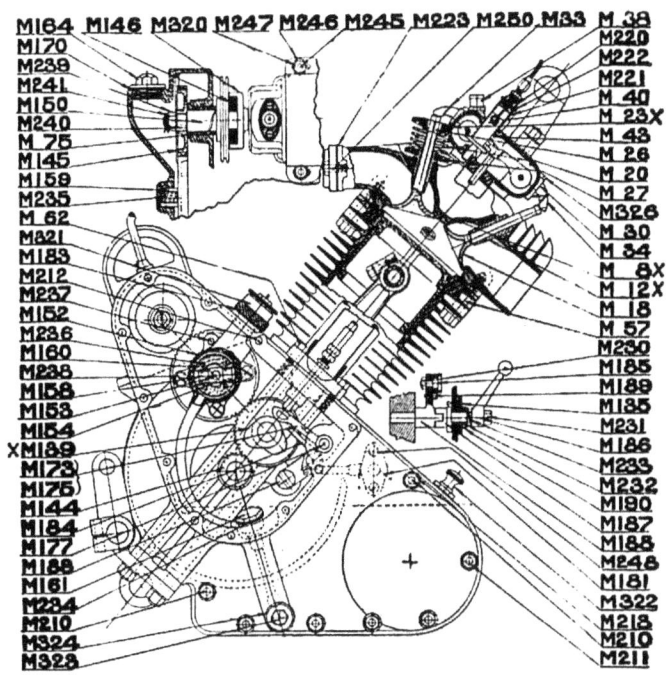

Fig. 3.—PARTS OF THE P. & M. (PANTHER) AND WHERE PLACED.

This diagram will be useful for locating the various parts mentioned in the text when dismantling the engine.

Remove Cylinder and Head

To remove the head, two more ⅜-inch nuts must be removed between cylinder fins front and back, except on models earlier than 1926. The long engine rods should now be pushed down as far as they will go, and after removing cylinder, unless being completely dismantled, place a clean rag in the mouth of the crankcase to prevent any foreign matter from finding its way in.

Gudgeon-pin Fixing

By pushing through the gudgeon pin on models up to 1927 or removing the gudgeon-pin clinch bolt (171) on models 1928–30, the piston can

MAINTENANCE, ETC., OF P. & M. (PANTHER) ENGINES

be taken in hand for cleaning and polishing. It is a wise policy to mark the piston before removing, so that it can be assembled in the same way. Distance washers on 1931 models are cast with the head (see Figs. 3 and 4).

Further dismantling of Engine—Crankcase

Commence to dismantle in the order set out above, and proceed as follows. The three ¼-inch nuts and nine screws secure the timing-case cover, and when removing the latter, a cap and spring (159, Fig. 3) will be found in a recess close to the magneto-wheel recess. The purpose of this cap and spring is to keep the oil-pump wheel (238) pressed home in the pump housing (152) to avoid any possibility of air leak.

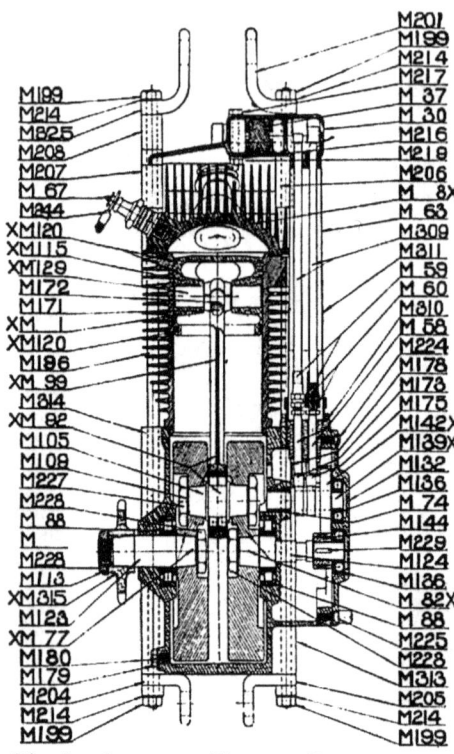

Fig. 4.—ANOTHER USEFUL DIAGRAM FOR LOCATING THE PARTS.

The numbers of the parts are referred to in the text.

Carefully examine Timing Gear

The intermediate pinion (238) will lift out (oil suction tends to hold it). It will be found that all timing wheels are marked with a spot, and it is therefore a simple matter to reset to correct timing. On modern motor-cycles cams do not wear until they have run very many thousands of miles, but any wear which may have taken place will be shown by ridges on the cam (139). A more frequent point of wear is the tappet levers (173), and if these show any signs of "flats" they should be replaced. Do not attempt to regrind the surface of these cam levers, as by so doing you will probably get a different radius, which will considerably affect the valve timing. The writer has known of cases where the valve timing was as much as 15° out, and this was traced to the cam levers having been ground to remove the flats.

A Very Useful Tip

The shaft (177) carrying these levers is a push fit in the timing case, but is easily removed in the following manner. The shaft is provided

MAINTENANCE, ETC., OF P. & M. (PANTHER) ENGINES

with an internal thread of ¼ inch × 26. Take one of the crankcase bolts from which you remove the nut to take off timing cover. Screw the nut on to the bolt for a few threads and then screw the bolt into the cam-lever shaft (177). By lightly tapping outwards the nut on the other end of this bolt, the shaft will be found to pull outwards.

Very Important

Remember the small distance washer *behind these cam levers*, and do *not forget this when reassembling*; also, when reassembling, do not drive the shaft in too far or the cam levers will bind. The end of the shaft should be *just flush* with the timing case. The big-end bearing of the connecting rod (92, Fig. 4) should permit of a small amount of side play, and if there is any up-and-down play the bearing must be renewed. Always dismantle the crankcase from the driving side first.

How the Sprocket is Fitted

The engine sprocket (315, Fig. 4) is not keyed on, and after taking off lock nut and washer the sprocket will usually come off easily if a stout short piece of solid brass is placed between the teeth on the rear side and given a good sharp blow with a heavy hammer. Do not attempt to separate the crankcase with a screwdriver. If a piece of wood is used as a punch, the case will generally separate without force.

The Magneto

Remove magneto by taking off the two ¼-inch nuts (247, Fig. 3) which hold the base plate to crankcase, and disengage driving dog (146) by pulling magneto outwards. There is no need to dismantle driving wheel in timing gear (145), as the dog coupling is marked with a centre spot for retiming. A sprocket draw tool is necessary to draw the main pinion (144) from shaft, as this is fitted on a fairly long key (229). After removing the long engine rods by pulling them through bottom engine lugs and remaining bolts, passing through crankcase, the timing side half will lift away.

Taking apart Flywheels

The flywheel assembly should be held in a vice. The crankpin nuts (227) must be removed (note locking washers). A piece of round ⅜-inch steel inserted in one of the holes in the rim of the flywheel will give leverage. Single-row Hoffman bearings are fitted on all models up to 1926. From 1927 onwards, a double-row bearing is fitted (see Fig. 5).

If Big-end Bearing is Badly Worn

Oversize rollers cannot be satisfactorily fitted unless the crankpin (105, Fig. 4) is ground true. Such work can be dealt with best by the manufacturer of the bearings, but if excessive wear has taken place, both

MAINTENANCE, ETC., OF P. & M. (PANTHER) ENGINES

the crankpin and outer sleeve may have to be ground out to such an extent that special rollers would be required.

More Economical Too!

Unless the reader has facilities for getting such regrinding done locally at a moderate cost, he will find it more satisfactory for the connecting rod to be returned to the makers for a complete bearing to be fitted.

The Difficulty that Arises

I advise the return of the connecting rod, as when the bearing is pressed into the rod it must be fitted without undue force. The "pressing-in" process causes a certain contraction or shrinkage of the outer race, and the reader will therefore realise that a bearing which is perfectly free *out* of the connecting rod might be binding badly when *in* the connecting rod. Many a new big-end bearing has been ruined in 100 miles through being fitted too tightly. It is for this reason that many manufacturers will not supply these bearings unless the connecting rod is returned for fitting.

If you decide to fit the Big-end Bearing

If the reader has the necessary tools for pressing out the outer sleeve and decides to fit a new bearing, he must first mark the rod so that the new ring is pressed in from the reverse side to that from which the old ring is punched out. The new ring (or outer race) should enter the connecting rod for about half its width without force, and if it will not press fully home with medium pressure the race should be removed and a fraction ground out of the connecting rod until it is possible to press in the race without considerable force.

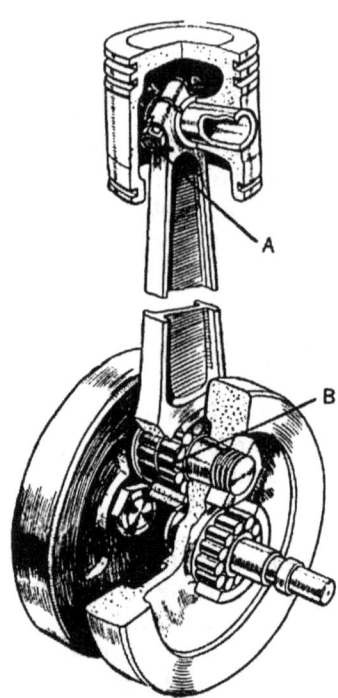

Fig. 5.—DETAILS OF CRANKSHAFT, CONNECTING ROD AND PISTON.

A indicates the clinch bolt. When tightening this up see that it is in line with the recess in the gudgeon pin. B indicates the big-end bearing. This should permit of a little sideplay, but no up-and-down movement. If the latter is present the bearing should be removed.

Assembling the Flywheels

Remember that the crankpin must revolve *quite freely* when *fitted*. When assembling the flywheels, the crankpin should be fitted to the

MAINTENANCE, ETC., OF P. & M. (PANTHER) ENGINES

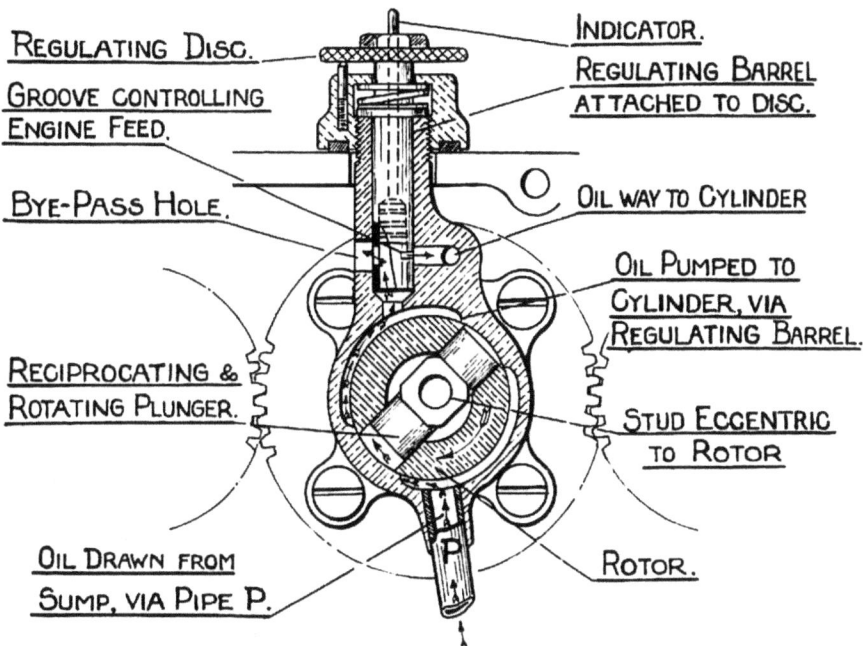

Fig. 6.—Details of the Oil Pump.

driving side first and the lock nut screwed well home, but do not turn down the lip of the lock washer until both nuts are fully home.

A Point regarding Small-end Bushes

The gudgeon-pin bushes on models 1924–6 are of phosphor bronze which are pressed in to the rod in the usual way, and call for no great skill in fitting, but here again the writer would emphasise the importance of the gudgeon pin being perfectly free *after* the bush is fitted. A tight gudgeon-pin bearing will cause piston knock and rattle. The reader will appreciate that when the piston is about halfway up or down the stroke, the angularity of the connecting rod will tend to " rock " the piston if it is binding on the gudgeon-pin bearing. On models 1927–30 the gudgeon pin is clamped in connecting rod and floats in piston. Always fit new lock washer and nip up clinch bolt with a good box spanner, taking care that the clinch bolt is in line with recess in gudgeon pin.

Mainshaft Bearing

The remaining point for attention is now the main engine shaft bearing (88, Fig. 4).

MAINTENANCE, ETC., OF P. & M. (PANTHER) ENGINES

It will be observed that all Panther engines have, strictly speaking, a three-bearing mainshaft, viz. one roller bearing in *each* half-crankcase, and a self-aligning ball bearing in the timing-case cover (136). These bearings should be tested for up-and-down play and replaced if necessary. Models 1924–5 were fitted with ball bearings which should be replaced by roller bearings of 1926–30 types if required. One-thirty-second inch in end-play is advisable, but any excess can usually be taken up by fitting a new bronze supporting bush on the driving side (in the case of early models).

Oil Pump

Reference to Figs. 6 and 6A will probably make it clear that as the plunger is of such large dimensions and is always running *in* oil, it is almost impossible for wear to take place in any part of this pump. If any slackness is noticeable between the plunger and its housing, the former should be replaced. The union nut at the bottom end of delivery pipe (161, Fig. 3) should be checked, as any looseness at this point would permit of air being drawn in, and so affect the operation of the pump. Oil leaking from the regulator usually points to a slightly worn indicator rod or defective gland washer (183).

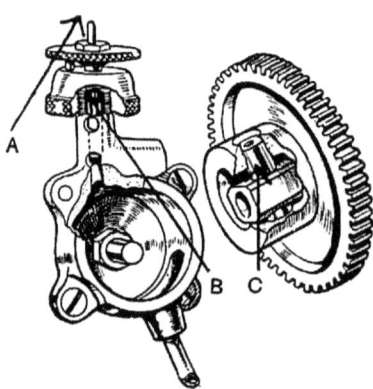

Fig. 6A.—WHERE THE OIL PUMP MAY DEVELOP FAULTS.

Oil leaking from the regulator may be caused by a worn indicator A, or defective gland washer B. The plunger C may become slack in its housing, in which case it should be replaced.

Tappets

By the use of cam levers (173, Fig. 4) side thrust on the tappets (58, Fig. 4) is practically eliminated. If wear has taken place in the guides (310) it is cheaper to fit oversize tappets unless the guides have worn oval. The latter, as will be observed, also form the base for push-rod tubes, and to remove these the two bolts (62, Fig. 3) which secure same should be removed and the guides knocked out from the underside.

Decompressor

Before reassembling the timing gear examine the small tongue piece (184, Fig. 3) attached to the operating shaft (188), and replace if this shows signs of wear. The smallest amount of wear at this point will make the decompressor inoperative owing to the small lift required.

If New Ballraces are Necessary

The self-aligning ballraces (136, Fig. 4) are sometimes loath to leave their housings, and a good plan for the removal of these is to hold the cover

MAINTENANCE, ETC., OF P. & M. (PANTHER) ENGINES

plate over a small gasjet in such a manner as to warm the aluminium around the bearings. Lightly tapping the cover plate will then usually cause the bearings to drop out. If the bearings revolve freely without any feel of catching, there is no need to replace them.

Reassembling Crankcase and Timing Gear

Assuming that all timing wheels have now been replaced, according to the marks, the faces of timing case and cover should be scraped perfectly clean. An even coat of Hermetite or L'Hermitical should now be applied to the cover plate, and in refitting this *do not forget the spring plunger* (159, Fig. 3) which presses against the intermediate pinion (spring in timing cover). Replace the oil filter in crankcase (323) if this is damaged at all, and after fitting magneto the complete crankcase assembly can be placed on one side, with a rag in the mouth of crankcase to prevent dirt entering.

If New Guides are Required

The guides knock out from the inside, and can usually be removed quite easily in the following manner.

On models 1930 and 1931 a $\frac{3}{8}$-inch bolt should be passed through the guide with the head on the inside. A stout punch or piece of solid brass should then be placed on the bolt head and given one or two sharp blows with a fairly heavy hammer. In fitting the new guide, however, these must be treated with more respect, and the bolt head should only be tapped lightly in this case, otherwise the end of the guide may become "burred over." It is safer to take a piece of brass or copper $\frac{1}{2}$ or $\frac{9}{16}$ inch in diameter, 4 inches long, and get this turned down for 2 inches to $\frac{3}{8}$ inch diameter, so that it is a nice fit in the guide, and leaves a shoulder on the outside; now carefully drive home the guide.

The same remarks apply to models 1924–9, except that a $\frac{5}{16}$-inch mandrel should be used instead of $\frac{3}{8}$-inch.

A Point to observe with 1930-1 Models

When fitting inlet guides on 1930–1 models, see that the oil hole in guide coincides with the oil lead in the cylinder head. When new valves are fitted to new guides, make sure that the former is perfectly free, especially the inlet, which so often tends to run dry on the early models. The writer once lost a first-class award at Brooklands as a result of fitting a new guide and valve which was too good a fit.

The Rocker Box

The rocker box on all models up to 1930 is composed of a very hard alloy similar to that used for railway locomotives, and the rocker shafts take their bearing direct in this metal (see Fig. 7). Owing to the exceptional length of the shafts and the fact that they are lubricated by a

MAINTENANCE, ETC., OF P. & M. (PANTHER) ENGINES

felt pad, it is very seldom found that any wear has taken place in these bearings. A certain amount of endplay is permissible, but if any direct up-and-down play is found the wear can be taken up in a like manner to the split big ends on car engines. It will be observed that the box is made in two halves. After separating, the surfaces can be reduced slightly and the shaft bearing reamered out to the correct size. This, however, is not a job which can be carried out without the necessary tools, and the writer recommends that the box be sent to the manufacturers for this work. If the rocker ends show signs of wear they should be replaced. Do not attempt to grind out indentations, as unless the same radius or curve is left on the rocker ends, it will cause rapid wear to both push rods and valves.

1930 and 1931 models have a one-piece rocker box of different alloy, and in this case the rockers are separate from the shafts, the latter running through a phosphor-bronze bush which is pressed into the box.

On reassembly of head and rocker box, adjust tappets to give 2/1000ths clearance on inlet and 3/1000ths on exhaust.

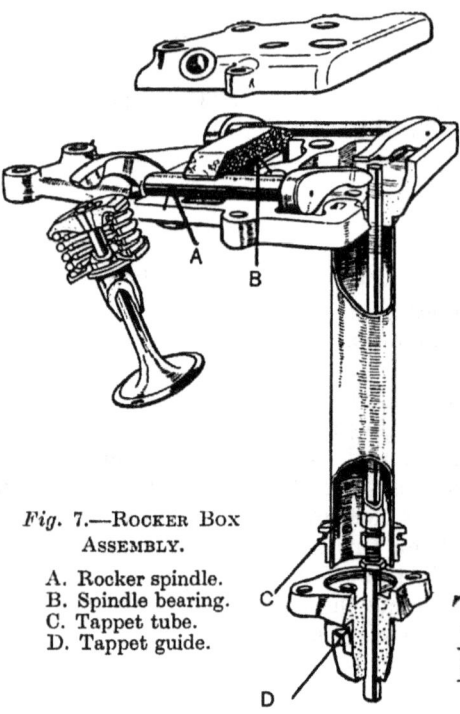

Fig. 7.—Rocker Box Assembly.

A. Rocker spindle.
B. Spindle bearing.
C. Tappet tube.
D. Tappet guide.

TIMING CHART FOR "P. & M." ENGINES

MODELS.	INLET.		EXHAUST.		IGNITION. MAX. ADV. Before T.D.C.	Tappet Clearance.	
	Opens before T.D.C.	Closes after B.D.C.	Opens before B.D.C.	Closes after T.D.C.		Inlet.	Exhaust.
500 c.c. and 600 c.c. 1924–31	10°	45°	65°	15°	47°	·002″	·003″
500 c.c. T.T. Panther 1926–28	10°	45°	65°	15°	47°	·002″	·003″
4¼ h.p. 1922–23	—5°*	32°	55°	5°	30°	·002″	·003″
4¼ h.p. 1920–21	—11°*	26°	50°	11°	30°	·002″	·003″

* *After* T.D.C.

REPAIRS AND ADJUSTMENTS TO THE RALEIGH ENGINE

By T. L. WILLIAMS and B. F. C. FELLOWES

TO REMOVE ENGINE FROM FRAME

Dismantling

The machine should be stood on its rear stand, and the front wheel wedged by a block to prevent any possibility of the machine moving in a forward direction. Removal of all extraneous fittings, such as petrol pipes and carburetter, exhaust pipe or pipes in the case of the twin port machine, magneto driving chain, engine chain, chaincase, footrests, and sparking plug, etc., is a simple matter, and the valve lifter mechanism should then be removed. This latter is quite simple in all cases, needing no explanation.

Removing Outside Type Flywheel

Most of the earlier Raleigh models were fitted with an outside flywheel, and this must be removed before the engine plate bolts can be withdrawn. On $2\frac{3}{4}$-h.p. models a flywheel cap is fitted, having a left-hand thread. This should be unscrewed, when will be seen the crankshaft or flywheel nut lock plate. Unbend this, and then unscrew the nut until it protrudes a short distance over the end of the shaft. Then replace the cap, which should be screwed up against the flywheel nut by means of the special "Cee" spanner provided in the standard Raleigh tool kit. A few light taps with a wooden mallet will suffice to cause the flywheel to come adrift from the taper shaft. It should here be noted that a key is not fitted, the two perfectly ground tapers being quite sufficient to firmly hold the flywheel.

The Lightweight Model Flywheel

The procedure for $2\frac{1}{4}$-h.p. models is a little different. No flywheel cap is fitted, and after bending back the lock washer as described for $2\frac{3}{4}$-h.p. models, remove the nut and then pack suitable wedges (wood for preference) between the back of the flywheel rim and engine plates. A few taps on the end of the shaft, again with a wooden mallet, will then free the wheel.

How to remove the Sprocket

Before actual removal of the flywheel it would be as well to inspect the engine sprocket. If worn, the teeth will be hook shaped, and replace-

THE RALEIGH ENGINE

Fig. 1.—Binding back the Flywheel Nut Lock Plate.

THE RALEIGH ENGINE

ment necessary. The sprocket is screwed to a boss on the flywheel by a right-hand thread. Lightly tap the sprocket round, by means of a hammer and a copper drift if available, otherwise a short piece of hardwood will serve.

Dealing with Cylinder Trouble

The flywheel, in the case of this type of engine, having been taken off, the bolts can next be removed, and the engine dropped out of the frame. Hold the engine in the vice by means of the crankcase bosses, and remove the cylinder. It may be that slight score marks will be felt rather than seen. If these are only slight, "lapping" out will most probably suffice to effect their removal. The best method of doing this is to make a wooden "connecting rod" with a hole in the "small end" to take the gudgeon pin. Hold the cylinder firmly in the vice by means of the flange, and then smear the rings and cylinder bore with a mixture of metal polish and paraffin. If available, an old piston should be used for this job, though not absolutely necessary. Work the piston up and down in the cylinder bore, at the same time imparting a twisting motion (Fig. 3). The

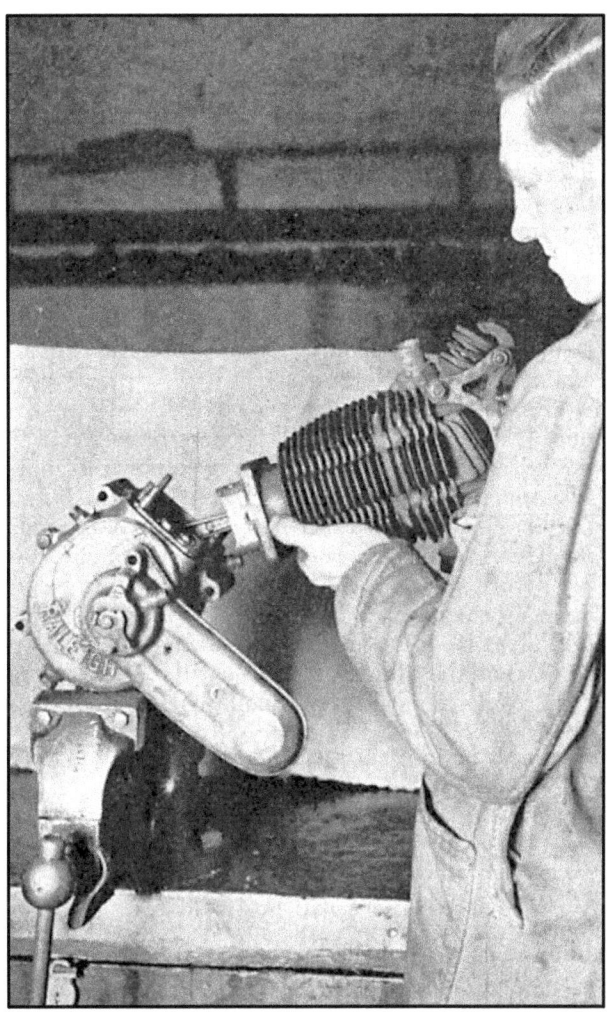

Fig. 2.—HOLD THE ENGINE IN THE VICE BY MEANS OF THE CRANKCASE BOSSES AND REMOVE THE CYLINDER.

process should be continued until the marks can be felt to have disappeared, and a set of new rings should then be fitted. For Raleigh machines, the correct gap is, on standard machines ·005 inch, and on sports ·015 inch. When the new rings have been fitted the piston should again be "lapped in" for a few minutes. Incidentally, this same process should always be followed when fitting an entirely new piston.

Valve Guides

The valves and valve guides should next receive treatment, the inlet valve guide in particular being examined for, and replaced in the event of, wear, because otherwise this will cause a bad air leakage, making starting extremely difficult.

Timing Gear

Before removing the timing cover, test the timing gear for "back lash," bearing the result in mind when the cam and rocker gear are under examination at a later stage.

Next remove the timing cover, held by cheese-headed screws, and note whether the cam and rockers have worn. This is not likely until many thousands of miles have been covered, but if so will be obvious by the appearance of "flats." Should these "flats" be only slight, they may be "rubbed" down by means of an oilstone. Grinding should not be attempted, as the rockers are case hardened.

Before splitting the crankcase, difficulty may be experienced in withdrawing the crankshaft pinion. A lock washer is used to secure the nut, and after its removal a pulley drawer, if available, should be employed to extract the pinion. If not available, two tyre levers will be found as good a means as any for accomplishing this (Fig. 5).

Examine Main Bearings

Before actually splitting the crankcase test the mainshaft for side-play by pulling on the engine sprocket. No up-and-down play is permissible, but slight endplay, not exceeding $\frac{1}{32}$ inch, may be allowed. The races themselves should also be examined, and if worn, replaced. Wear on these races will be felt if they are moved by the two thumbs while the case is on the bench.

Fitting New Main Bearings

Removal of the races sometimes presents difficulty to the amateur. Immerse, for a few moments, the half case from which it is desired to remove the race in water which has nearly reached boiling-point. This will cause the case to expand, and a light tap of the case on to the wooden bench will allow the bearing to drop out. The same process may be followed when fitting a new race.

The difficulty likely to arise in connection with the stripping down

THE RALEIGH ENGINE

and rebuilding of the big-end bearing is the removal, and later the tightening up, of the crankpin nut. Of the two, the timing side nut will offer the least resistance.

Fitting Big-end Bearings

On removal of the nut, gently tap the shaft with a rawhide mallet, which will cause the shaft to then spring off the crankpin taper. The connecting rod can then be withdrawn, and the work of fitting new rollers, if required, proceeded with. The method of doing this is to pack the

Fig. 3.—WORK THE PISTON UP AND DOWN IN THE CYLINDER BORE.

crankpin with grease, setting the rollers round the pin in the same way as the balls are set in an ordinary hub bearing.

Factory Method

At the Raleigh Works the flywheels are assembled on " Vee " blocks, and the use of an " Ames " dial gauge, recording to an accuracy of half a thousandth part of an inch, ensures them running absolutely true (Fig. 8). Also, for finally locking up, a special box spanner and long tommy bar is used, and for these two reasons the amateur at least will be well advised to despatch the complete crankshaft assembly to works for overhaul when required.

An Alternative

The alternative method of lining up the flywheels is to first tighten up the crankpin nut until the flywheels are tightly held, and then place

THE RALEIGH ENGINE

the shafts between lathe centres. They can then be rotated by means of the connecting rod, and any eccentricity will be observed from the way in which they run. At each sight, they must be removed from the lathe and tapped in the correct direction and then again tested. This must be repeated until perfect alignment is achieved. It will be seen that absolute truth is essential on this particular job, and the greatest care must be

Fig. 4.—How to detect Bad Alignment of the Connecting Rod.

Lay a steel straightedge across the crankcase cylinder faces as shown above, then rotate the engine until on the down stroke the piston skirt meets the straightedge. If the connecting rod is not in line the edge of the piston will not coincide with the straightedge. If this is the case the connecting rod must be carefully aligned, using a cranking iron.

taken when finally tightening up the crankpin nut that alignment is not altered.

An Important Reminder

The method of heating the crankcase by immersion in hot water for the purpose of fitting new mainshaft races has already been dealt with, but it would perhaps be as well to give here a reminder of the importance of not omitting to fit the bearing retaining ring or rings which fit in grooves cut in the shafts. On some Raleigh models there is a retaining ring for both races, on others for the timing side race only, and in the case of the " MJ " and " MO " models neither race is so fitted, but this is obvious by the absence of the grooves.

THE RALEIGH ENGINE

If it should be necessary to fit a new bush to the little-end bearing of the connecting rod the old bush should be drawn out and the replacement pressed in. Any attempt to knock out the old bush will almost be certain to cause the new bearing to be out of line, and may even result in bending the connecting rod.

To withdraw the bush, obtain an ordinary hexagon-headed bolt and nut, say ½ inch in diameter and about 4 inches long, a washer just slightly less than the outside diameter of the bush, and a sleeve or short length of tubing just slightly larger than the bush. The washer should then be slipped over the bolt, and the latter inserted through the bush. Next fit the sleeve along the remainder of the bolt, and by tightening up the nut against a second washer the bush will be withdrawn from the rod through the sleeve. Obviously a reversal of the operation will allow the new bush to be pressed into place in exactly the same way. Incidentally, when this has been done, do not forget to drill the oil hole in the bush, in line with the hole in the connecting rod itself. (See also Fig. 9).

Fig. 5.—Two Tyre Levers may be used to withdraw the Crankshaft Pinion.

Check the Connecting Rod

A frequent cause of excessive piston wear and seizure is connecting rod mal-alignment, which can easily be checked. With the cylinder removed, lay a steel straightedge across the crankcase cylinder faces, and

THE RALEIGH ENGINE

then rotate the engine until on the down stroke the piston skirt meets the straightedge. If the connecting rod is not in line, this will be immediately apparent. A cranking iron can be used to bend the rod in the desired direction; naturally, great care must be exercised. (See Fig. 4, p. 108.)

Valve Thimbles

On the earlier types of Raleigh 348-c.c. and 496-c.c. twin-port o.h.v. engines, case-hardened steel thimbles were fitted to the ends of the valve stems to prevent wear. Later, this was discontinued and a slightly different design of overhead rocker employed. It will be seen, therefore, that where engines have left works with the new type rocker without the thimbles, these must not afterwards be fitted.

SEEKING THOSE EXTRA M.P.H.—SPECIAL TUNING HINTS

As is well known, the Raleigh Company list a very fast racing machine known as the 350-c.c. T.T. Replica. As the name implies, this machine is in all respects an exact replica of those which have competed so successfully in numerous important races during the last two years or more. To many, however, the original cost of such a machine is prohibitive, but consolation may be taken in the fact that owners of any of the o.h.v. types can obtain a few miles per hour more from their machines by following carefully the hints here given.

Attention to the Ports

First of all, the cylinder head and valve ports must be carefully polished, the inlet valve and around the plug hole in particular. This is rather a tedious operation except where facilities exist for the job to be done by means of a small emery wheel attached to a flexible shaft, which of course is the method adopted by the makers. A 6-inch half-round file should be obtained, and after softening bent to a shape which will permit of easy working through the valve ports and inside the head. Before rehardening make sure that the bend is sufficient or, on the other hand, not too steep to permit of easy handling.

Factory Assistance

The head must be carefully held in the vice and the job can then be commenced in earnest. Take the greatest care not to damage the valve seatings, and when sufficient material has been removed finish off with emery paper. This is a job which can be very efficiently carried out by the Raleigh Cycle Co., Ltd., at the modest cost of 7s. 6d. only, and for this reason it is doubtful whether the trouble to the private owner is really worth while.

Now the Piston

The piston should next be dealt with. Any high spots should be very carefully removed by means of a fine Swiss file—note, not emery

THE RALEIGH ENGINE

paper. These spots, if present, will be found as bright areas standing out quite boldly from the usual greyness of the piston. Make sure also that the piston has sufficient clearance, especially on the four sharp edges and just above the rings. The rings themselves should be lapped into the cylinder as previously described, and of course correctly gapped. In this connection, do not remove one of the rings unless the event in which the machine is competing is a sprint race of a few hundred yards only. Naturally, the valves must be given special attention and make perfect contact on their seatings, and, moreover, the stems must be quite free in their guides. A really good plug is essential for high-speed work, the Lodge type H.45 being particularly suitable.

If the Compression Plate is Removed

The compression plate underneath the cylinder flange should be removed, and the engine must then be run on a petrol-benzol mixture and a larger jet fitted to the carburetter to suit the changed conditions.

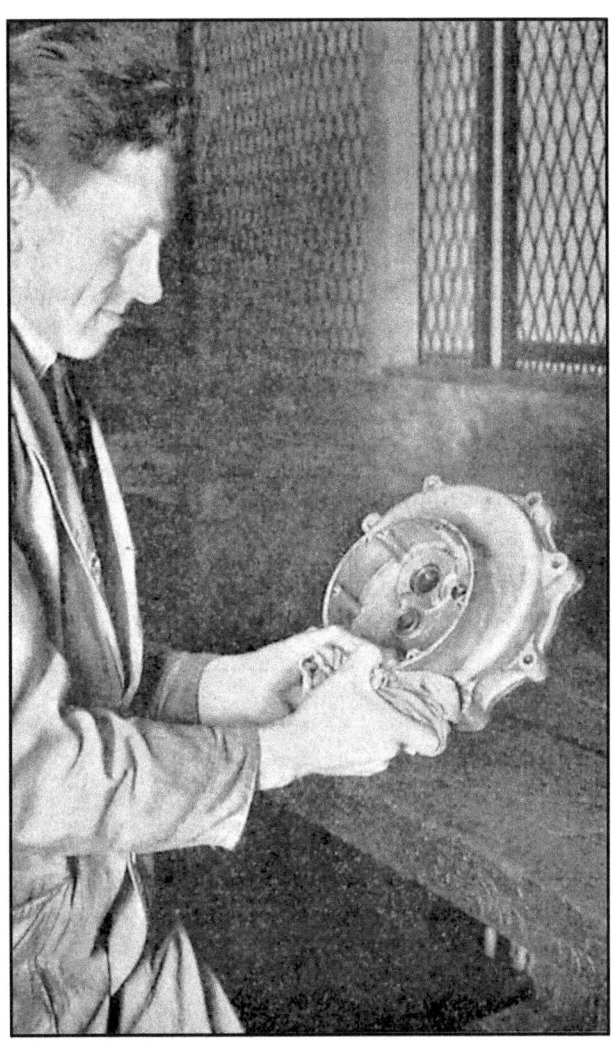

Fig. 6.—A LIGHT TAP OF THE CASE ON TO THE BENCH WILL ALLOW THE BEARING TO DROP OUT.

THE RALEIGH ENGINE

Do not Forget

It should here be noted that when the plate is removed the piston will travel farther up the cylinder barrel. A ridge of hard carbon will most likely have formed at the extreme top of the barrel, where the piston crown originally came to, and this must be removed, as otherwise the piston, travelling higher, will strike this hard ridge, and broken piston rings will result.

H.C. Pistons

Should a still higher compression ratio be needed, the manufacturers will supply a special piston and rings, which will raise the compression ratio, from, in the case of the 500-c.c. machine, 5·75 to 1 to 8 to 1, and the 350-c.c. machine from 5·7 to 1 to 7·75 to 1. For the 500-c.c. machine the piston in question is known as MR. 208 and piston rings MR. 209, and for the 350-c.c. machine piston MS. 345 and piston rings MS. 348. With either of these pistons fitted it is necessary to employ an alcohol fuel such as P.M.S. 2 or R.D. 1, and the carburetter must be tuned to suit. Fit a ·113 needle jet when either of the above fuels are used, and for P.M.S. 2 a size 300–325 jet, and with R.D. 1 a size 350–375 jet. Owing to alcohol fuels showing a great variation, the correct jet size can only be determined by trial and error.

Special Springs

A most important point to bear in mind when the sports piston is fitted is that stronger valve springs will be required, and in fact they

Fig. 7.—PACK THE CRANKPIN WITH GREASE.

THE RALEIGH ENGINE

Fig. 8.—Testing the Flywheel Assembly by Means of a Dial Gauge.
An interesting workshop process, but not a job for the amateur.

should be changed fairly frequently, as they lose their tension after a time. When ordering, the numbers of these springs are MS. 373 and MS. 374 inner and outer respectively.

More Advance

The ignition timing will require a different setting, which again will best be found by experiment on the road. This, however, will be somewhere in the region of 40° of advance before top dead centre. After arriving at, and making the final setting, see that the adjustment of the magneto driving chain is normal, because if this is allowed to slacken off it will retard the ignition and, in addition, cause the engine to run hot.

General Hints

Do not make the mistake of giving all the attention to the engine only. The front forks and fork shock-absorber adjustment must be just right for the rider's weight. Tyre pressures must be as recommended by the manufacturers, and in order to obtain perfect steering the wheels must be in absolute alignment. This can be checked by laying a long straightedge, or even a piece of tightly stretched string, alongside both wheels, and then adjusting until contact is made by the rims at the four points.

Chains which are too tight will not only cause excessive wear on the sprockets and impose an unfair strain on the engine and gearbox bearings, but will definitely cause a decrease in the maximum speed of the machine. Therefore, err on the side of slackness. The wheel bearings themselves

THE RALEIGH ENGINE

must be absolutely free, and both brakes should be adjusted so that there is no possibility of them binding.

Particularly if the event to be entered is over a long distance, adjust the handlebars, footrests and saddle, so that the rider feels really "at home." This is most important, as besides minimising physical fatigue, a correct riding position will cause the machine to be faster, due to lessened wind resistance, and even more important, will give the rider a sense of perfect security and control.

For normal fast road work the standard gear ratios are best. Even when running downhill a higher gear is of no advantage, but in stripped condition, and when fitted with lighter tyres and wheels, the engine will undoubtedly pull a higher gear, which can be brought about by fitting a one-, or perhaps two-tooth larger engine sprocket.

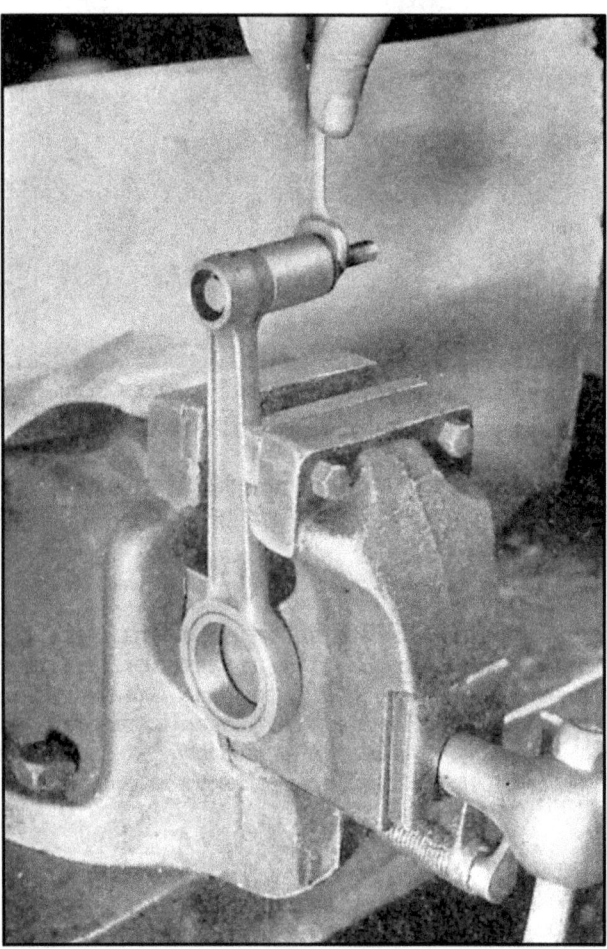

Fig. 9.—THE BUSH BEING WITHDRAWN FROM THE ROD THROUGH THE SLEEVE.

For touring work a mineral oil will be found most suitable, but for racing use a castor base lubricant, although this will necessitate more frequent decarbonisation.

TIMING CHART FOR "RALEIGH"

MODELS.	INLET.		EXHAUST.		IGNITION MAX. ADV. Before T.D.C.	Tappet Clearance.	
	Opens before T.D.C.	Closes after B.D.C.	Opens before B.D.C.	Closes after T.D.C.		Inlet.	Exhaust.
2¾ h.p. Light Weight. Prior to 1925 . .	0°	40°	55°	12°	35°	·004″	·006″
3·48 h.p. S.V., 1925–9.	5°	50°	60°	20°	35°	·004″	·006″
3·48 h.p. O.H.V. T.T. Replica . . .	15°	60°	65°	30°	38°	·003″	·003″
7·98 h.p. S.V. Vee Twin	0°	40°	55°	12°	35°	·004″	·006″
198 c.c. S.V., 1930–1 .	0°	40°	55°	12°	30°	·004″	·006″
248 c.c. S.V., 1930–1 .	0°	40°	55°	12°	25°	·004″	·006″
298 c.c. S.V., 1930–1 .	0°	40°	55°	12°	25°	·004″	·006″
348 c.c. S.V., 1930–1 .	15°	60°	50°	23°	30°	·004″	·006″
496 c.c. S.V., 1930–1 .	15°	60°	50°	23°	30°	·004″	·006″
598 c.c. S.V., 1930–1 .	15°	60°	50°	23°	30°	·004″	·006″
348 c.c. O.H.V., 1930–1	15°	60°	50°	23°	38°	·003″	·003″
496 c.c. O.H.V., 1930–1	15°	60°	50°	23°	35°	·003″	·003″
598 c.c. O.H.V., 1930–1	15°	60°	50°	23°	32°	·003″	·003″

ROYAL ENFIELD ENGINES

By W. C. HAYCRAFT

THE SIDE-VALVE ENGINES

A TOP overhaul requires, in the case of all 1931 s.v. models except two (3·46-h.p. and 4·88-h.p.), removal of the detachable cylinder head only. With these two models and all 1930 s.v. engines without detachable heads, the entire cylinder must be removed. This procedure is in any case necessary if the piston is to be examined.

Where no Detachable Head is Provided

Proceed, except with the dry-sump lubricated engines, as follows: firstly, remove the petrol and oil pipes, the sparking plug, carburetter and exhaust pipe. Do not detach the carburetter slides, but remove the entire assembly. Now take off the four nuts holding the cylinder to the crankcase, loosening them diagonally to avoid straining the cylinder. Then lift the cylinder clear of the crankcase studs and rotate the engine until the piston is at the bottom of its stroke. By raising the cylinder a trifle it will be found possible to push out by hand the fully floating gudgeon pin, when the cylinder and piston can be removed *together*. (After cylinder removal be careful not to damage the surfaces of either the cylinder or crankcase, otherwise after reassembling trouble will be experienced with oil leaking from the joint. Also see that the paper washer is not damaged.)

With the 9·76-h.p. Engine

The above operation must, of course, be repeated—once for each cylinder. Be very careful not to interchange the pistons after removal. They should therefore be marked " F." and " R." (front and rear). Note that when removing the two cylinders the induction manifold can be removed complete with the carburetter after undoing the two union nuts at the inlet ports.

If the Valve Caps are of Aluminium

It is best to allow the engine to cool before attempting removal of the caps, for aluminium contracts more than cast iron, and any stiffness when warm will probably disappear automatically.

ROYAL ENFIELD ENGINES

On the 1930 3·46-h.p. Engine

Removal of the petrol tank will allow of the cylinder being drawn straight off the piston instead of being removed with it as described above.

To remove the Cylinder on the 1930 2·25-h.p. Engine

It is advisable to remove the long induction pipe as well as the carburetter before attempting cylinder removal. In this case the cylinder and piston can be removed separately.

To remove the Cylinder on the 1930 and 1931 4·88-h.p. Engine

It will be found necessary before lifting the cylinder and piston off to withdraw both tappets and then to rotate the cylinder until the valves face the front down tube.

With the 1930 D.S. Lubricated Engine

The cylinder and piston may be removed separately after placing the piston at the bottom of its stroke and tilting the cylinder forwards slightly. When removing the cylinder, be careful not to strain the connecting rod.

Fig. 1.—CYLINDER HEADS ARE READILY DETACHABLE.

Each head is held on to its barrel by nine studs and nuts. After removal of the nuts the head can be easily lifted off as shown, leaving the carburetter, exhaust pipes, etc., undisturbed.

To remove the Detachable Cylinder Head

Take off the nine nuts holding the head to the cylinder barrel and gently lift the head off as shown in Fig. 1. Be sure to loosen the nuts

ROYAL ENFIELD ENGINES

uniformly and do not prise the head off with a sharp tool, as this is apt to damage the copper cylinder-head washer. The carburetter and exhaust pipe need not be interfered with.

To remove the Cylinder Barrel

After lifting off the cylinder head it is first necessary to detach the flange-fitting carburetter (complete with induction pipe in the case of the twin-cylinder models) and control cables. It is also necessary to remove the exhaust pipe by loosening the nut contracting the locking ring. Then place the piston at the bottom of its stroke after removing the four cylinder-barrel base nuts and lift the barrel off by drawing it upwards and slightly forwards, as shown in Fig. 2, until it clears the top of the piston.

Fig. 2.—To REMOVE THE CYLINDER BARREL.

First detach the induction pipe complete with carburetter. Then remove the exhaust pipe from the cylinder, undo the four cylinder-base nuts, place the piston at the bottom of its stroke and lift the barrel away as shown.

To remove the Piston

Where fully floating gudgeon pins with brass endcaps are used (see Fig. 11) the pins can be immediately pushed or gently tapped out of the piston bosses. On recent engines gudgeon-pin retaining springs are fitted on each side of the pin, and it is necessary to remove *one* of these spring circlips to enable the gudgeon pin to be pushed out from the

ROYAL ENFIELD ENGINES

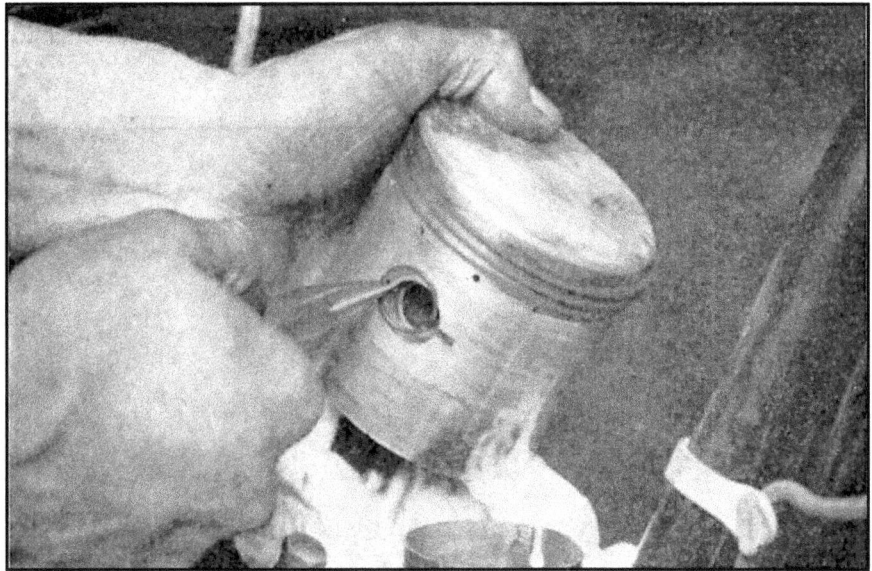

Fig. 3.—Removing Gudgeon-pin Spring Circlip.

The gudgeon pins are of the fully floating type and are prevented from scoring the cylinder walls by means of wire circlips. These are easily removed by means of a pair of thin-nosed pliers or with the tang end of a file inserted in the saw cut formed at one side of the piston.

opposite side. Fig. 3 shows how to remove a spring circlip with a small pair of thin-nosed pliers. It can also be done by inserting the tang end of a file in the saw-cut seen on the right side of the gudgeon-pin hole. Usually it can be pushed out by hand (Fig. 4) and the piston can then be lifted off the connecting rod. After removing the piston and marking it to ensure correct replacement (i.e. the right way round in the right cylinder), wrap a rag around the connecting rod to prevent foreign articles entering the crankcase.

Valve Removal

To remove the valves with the cylinder barrels or cylinder in position, it is necessary to compress each valve spring with a proprietary spring compressor, such as the Terry, and then to withdraw the flat cotter or split collar, whichever is used. If the cylinder barrel or cylinder has been removed, the valves may be extracted by placing it upside down on the bench with packing under the valve heads, and pressing on each spring cap with a suitable implement until the cotters or collars can be removed and the valves themselves drawn out.

In the case of the 1930 3·46-h.p. engine the collars lodge against wire retaining clips, and these must first be taken off.

ROYAL ENFIELD ENGINES

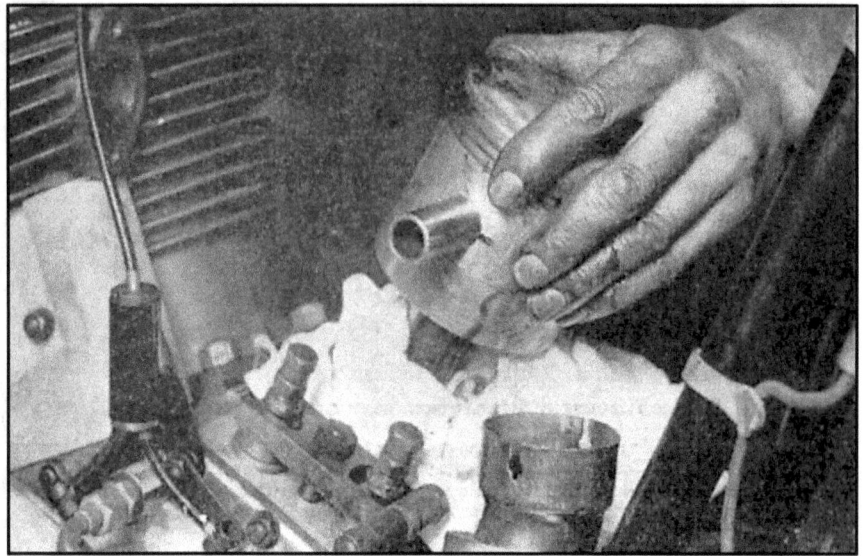

Fig. 4.—REMOVING THE GUDGEON PIN.

Having removed one circlip, the gudgeon pin can be pushed or lightly tapped out from the other end, and the piston lifted away. Clean rag should be packed round the connecting rod to prevent anything falling into the crankcase. The pistons should be marked and reassembled the same way round in the correct cylinders.

Reassembly

This is quite straightforward. It is simply necessary to replace the parts in the reverse order in which they were dismantled. All parts should be scrupulously cleaned, and the cylinder barrel or cylinder walls should be well oiled before inserting the piston. Tighten up all nuts finger-tight first, and then give each nut a successive turn when finally tightening to ensure the joint surfaces bedding down properly. Be careful not to omit any washers.

When reassembling valves and valve springs fitted with wire-retaining clips for the collars, make sure that the clips lodge properly, both in the valve-stem grooves and in the split-collar recesses.

Important Note

On the Big Twin it is of vital importance that the oilway in the cylinder base of the front cylinder (see Fig. 5) registers with the corresponding hole in the base washer.

To test the Valve Seatings

After valve grinding and reassembly, but before refitting the cylinder barrel or cylinder, it is a good plan to test the valve seats by pouring

ROYAL ENFIELD ENGINES

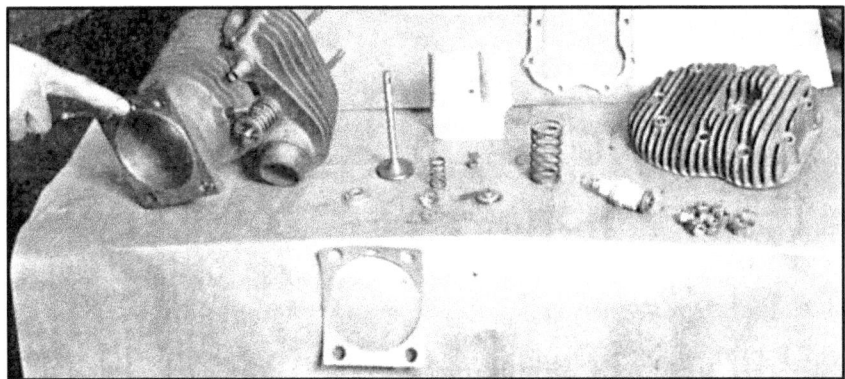

Fig. 5.—An Important Precaution with the Big Twin Engine.

The valves are readily removed from the cylinder by compressing the spring and drawing out the valve cotter. Note the oilway in the base of the front cylinder through which is taken the feed from the mechanical pump. Care must be taken that the hole in the cylinder-base washer registers with this when reassembling.

petrol into the ports and watching for leakage past the valves. Only the slightest amount of moisture should escape.

Removing Tappet Guides (S.V. and O.H.V.)

The tappets can be removed together with their guides without any special tools. Take off the nut holding the tappet guide clamp to the

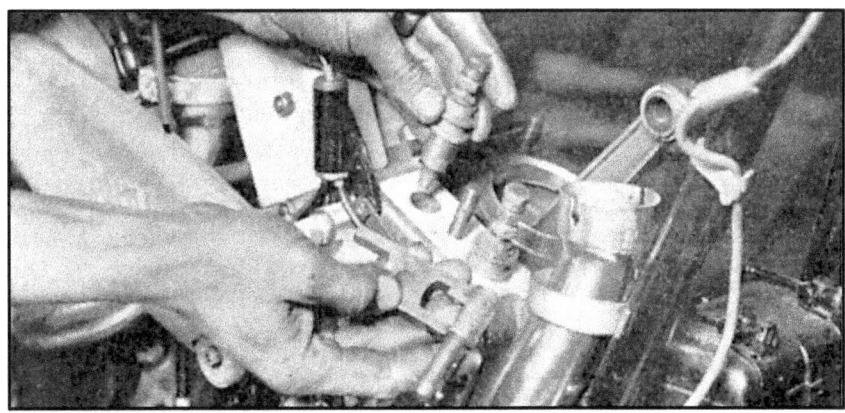

Fig. 6.—To remove the Tappets and Guides.

First take away the tappet clamp, which is held with a single stud and nut. The tappets and guides can then be drawn out as can be seen. The exhaust-lifter lever comes away with tappet clamp and need not be detached from it.

ROYAL ENFIELD ENGINES

crankcase, and remove the clamp without detaching the exhaust valve-lifter lever. It is usually necessary to remove the tappet heads and lock nuts before removing the guides from the crankcase, as the tappet feet on some models are too large to pass through the holes in which the guides fit. Should the guides be stiff, tap gently upwards with a hammer, using a brass or aluminium drift.

Tappet Clearances

On reassembly, the tappet heads and lock nuts should be adjusted until there is with the engine *cold* a clearance of ·004 inch at the inlet-valve stem and ·006 inch at the exhaust-valve stem.

Fig. 7.—Dismantling Timing Gear.

The timing gear shown is the type used from 1927–30. Two inlet cams and one exhaust are mounted on a single shaft, and operate the tappets through rockers. The 1931 cam gear is similar, but gives a higher lift to the inlet cams. The exhaust-lifter mechanism is now placed outside the timing case. On single cylinder engines two cams only are used.

When retiming the Magneto

On a twin-cylinder engine note that the contact-breaker cam corresponding to the rear (firing) cylinder is the one followed by the longer distance between the two cams. The brass segment on the slip ring also corresponds with the lead to the rear cylinder.

When removing the Engine

In the case of 1930 models equipped with electric lighting, it is necessary to remove the timing cover, as the projecting screw thread on the armature shaft fouls the back of the magneto chaincase.

ROYAL ENFIELD ENGINES

Dismantling Timing Gear

In order to prevent the cams coming away with the cover, first place the engine so that the exhaust valve is lifted. The pressure on the exhaust cam is sufficient to keep it in place, while the inlet can be held with the thumb on the extension projecting through the cover. As two-cam engines have marked timing it is not really important to keep the cams in place in these engines.

To remove the Small Timing Pinion and Engine Sprocket (S.V. and O.H.V.)

Insert a ⅜-inch rod through the hole in the cam-wheel bush. This will prevent the crankpin boss and flywheels from moving. Then remove the timing pinion and engine sprocket nuts (that for the timing pinion has a left-hand thread) except on the Big Twin. The pinion and sprocket can now be drawn off

Fig. 8.—BEFORE DISMANTLING AN O.H.V. ENGINE THE TANK SHOULD BE REMOVED.

To do this disconnect the petrol pipe and gear-control rod and remove the four tank-support pins from under the side of the tank, which can then be lifted off as shown. The whole engine is then very readily accessible.

with a sprocket drawer. If one is not handy, use a screwdriver or tapered implement as a wedge, but be careful not to damage the shaft.

ROYAL ENFIELD ENGINES

Fig. 9.— 346-c.c. O.H.V. Cylinder Head being lifted from the Barrel.

On some o.h.v. models the barrel and cylinder head are both lifted together and turned on their axes through 90°. The detachable cylinder head may then be removed from the barrel.

Fig. 10.—Lifting away Cylinder Barrel.

By placing the piston at the bottom of its stroke the cylinder barrel can be lifted away as shown. Take care not to damage the piston by allowing it to fall against the connecting rod or cylinder-base studs.

ROYAL ENFIELD ENGINES

Play in Big-end Bearings (S.V. and O.H.V.)

It should be noted that on all engines fitted with roller bearings for the big ends and mainshafts a certain amount of play is necessary, and some "rock" in the connecting rod may be felt with the bearings in good order. Where there is an appreciable amount of up-and-down play the crankshaft assembly should be removed by undoing the crankcase bolts. It should be sent to the works or to a competent repairer for new bearings to be fitted. With regard to the small-end bearing, the gudgeon pin should be a free working fit in the bush and a push fit in the bosses.

Remaking Joints

When remaking the timing cover, magneto chaincase and crankcase joints, shellac, seccotine or a similar substance should be applied to the metal surfaces. Use this sparingly, and not so thin that it fills any oil passages.

THE OVERHEAD VALVE ENGINES

Firstly remove the Petrol Tank

This is strongly advocated prior to engine dismantling. Disconnect the petrol pipe and gear control rod, and remove the four tank support pins from the underside of the tank and lift off as shown in Fig. 8. The entire engine is then very accessible. Where a steering damper is fitted, this must, of course, also be disconnected, except on the 1931 models, where it has a frame anchorage.

Fig. 11.—Removing Gudgeon Pin.

The gudgeon pin can be pushed out or lightly tapped, using a piece of wood as a drift. The illustration shows a gudgeon pin with copper end pads, but in some cases wire circlips are fitted, one of which must be removed before the pin is pushed out. Mark the piston to ensure reassembling the same way round.

ROYAL ENFIELD ENGINES

Then to prepare for Decarbonisation

Proceed thus: detach the sparking plug, carburetter, petrol and oil pipes, exhaust pipes and silencers (on the single-port engine there is, of course, only one pipe). Also disconnect the exhaust-valve lifter cable. The rocker box and cylinder head can now be removed.

To remove the Rocker Box

Firstly, unscrew the top and bottom telescopic push-rod sleeves, and take out the four pins holding down the overhead rocker box, which

Fig. 12.—ARE THE OIL PUMPS WORKING CORRECTLY?

This can be readily verified. If the oil-feed plug (shown partly withdrawn) be unscrewed one or two turns, the oil from the feed pump will be seen escaping past the washer. The oil from the return pump can be seen, after removal of the filler cap, issuing from the hole indicated by the pencil above. When carrying out these tests the engine must, of course, be running.

can now be lifted to one side after disconnecting the exhaust-valve lifter cable. The new four-valve engine has no rocker box, and the side plates have to be removed.

To remove the Cylinder Head

Unscrew the rocker box support posts, and lift the head off as shown in Fig. 9. It is best not to prise the head off, as this is apt to damage the copper washer.

With the 3·46-h.p. and Four-valve Engines

It is necessary to remove the four cylinder-barrel base nuts, and then to rotate both the cylinder barrel and head through 90°,

ROYAL ENFIELD ENGINES

when the head can be lifted clear of the studs permanently fixed to the barrel after first removing the securing nuts.

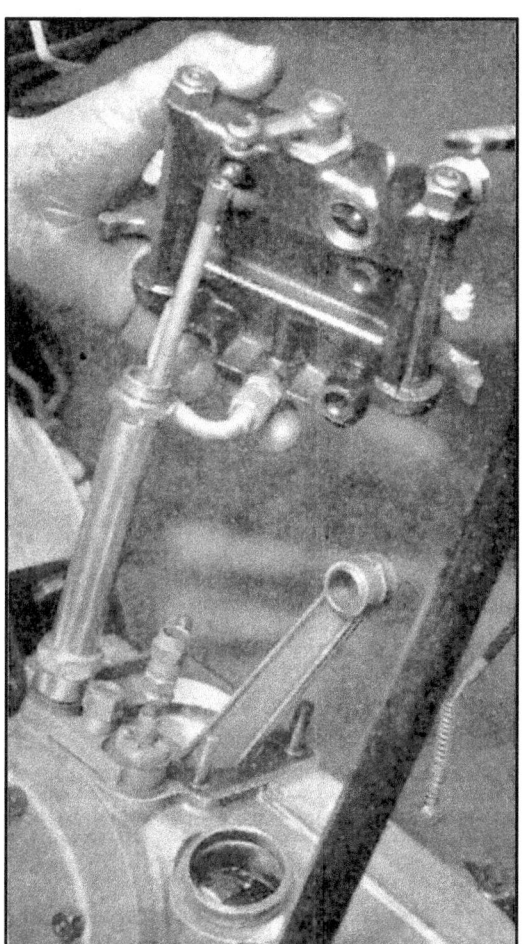

Fig. 13.—How the Rocker Box is Lubricated.

When the engine is running, oil mist is blown up the holes surrounding the tappet guides and up the telescopic push-rod cover tubes to the rocker box. The push-rod ends and rocker bearings are thus adequately lubricated under all normal conditions, but grease nipples are fitted to the rockers so that additional lubrication can be given when exceptional circumstances demand it.

To remove the Cylinder Barrel

Proceed as with the s.v. engines. Place the piston at the bottom of its stroke and draw the barrel straight off the piston as shown in Fig. 10. Take care not to allow the piston skirt to fall sharply against the connecting rod or crankcase studs.

Removing the Piston

Where spring circlips are used, take out one of them and press out the gudgeon pin as with the s.v. engines. The gudgeon pin can be pushed straight out or tapped out (using a piece of wood as a drift) where end-caps are used. Now take off the piston.

Valve Removal

To remove the powerful valve springs on the o.h.v. engines requires the use of a spring compressor, when the split collars can be taken off and the valves drawn out. Avoid interchanging the valves, as there are differences in stem diameters and composition of valves.

In the case of the 1930 4·88-h.p. engine, wire retaining springs are used as a ledge for the split collars and these must be removed, together with the hardened end caps, which should be tapped out.

ROYAL ENFIELD ENGINES

Reassembly

Replace all parts in the reverse order of dismantling, and pay due regard to the points already mentioned in the case of the s.v. engines. See that the rocker box beds down properly on the cylinder head, the valves in which may be tested for proper seating as described for the s.v. engines. When replacing the o.h.v. cylinder barrel, the compression plate may be omitted, if desired. This will give slightly more power, but there may be an increased tendency for knocking unless a percentage of benzol is used.

When removing the Timing Pinion

With all single camshaft engines, but not the 1930 D.S. models or any two-camshaft machines except 1929 model 505, note which of the three keyways was in use and reassemble accordingly.

Valve Clearances

On the 1931 4·99-h.p. o.h.v., adjustment is in the o.h. rocker over the push-rod. On the four-valve model separate adjustment is provided in the o.h. rockers over each valve. Use thin paper as a feeler gauge to adjust each valve. One thickness only of thin paper should just pass between the adjusting screw and the valve end cap.

Fig. 14.—Removing Two-stroke Cylinder.

After removing the exhaust pipes, silencer and release-valve cover, the engine can be dropped slightly in front. This will permit the cylinder being lifted clear of the piston.

ROYAL ENFIELD ENGINES

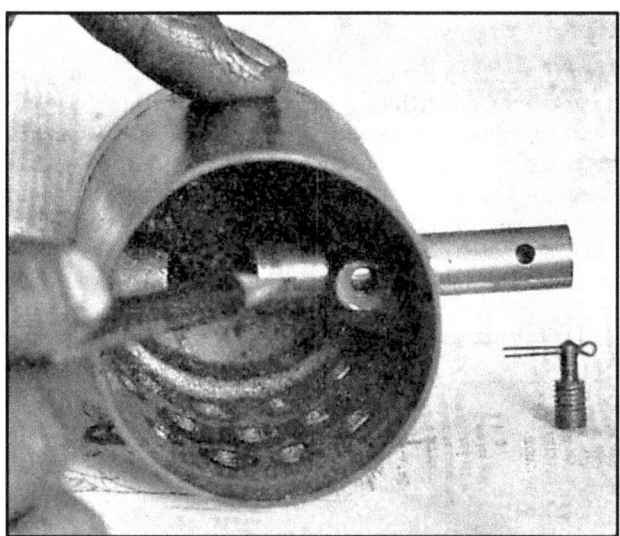

Fig. 15.—ANOTHER METHOD FOR SECURING GUDGEON PIN.

The gudgeon pin is secured in the piston by a grub screw, which is locked by a special spring split pin. On later models a floating gudgeon pin is used.

Raising Compression Ratio

As already mentioned, the compression plate (where fitted) may be removed. Special high-compression pistons are also obtainable from the manufacturers, and if used in conjunction with the extra powerful springs enable engine speeds of approximately 6,000 r.p.m. to be attained.

Is the D.S. Lubrication System Functioning?

This can be immediately verified by unscrewing the oil-feed plug (shown partly withdrawn, Fig. 12) one or two turns, when the oil from the feed pump will be noticed escaping past the washer with the engine running. The oil from the return pump can be seen, after removal of the filler cap, issuing from the hole indicated by the pointer in Fig. 12.

Rocker-box Lubrication

For all normal conditions the rocker-box is amply lubricated by the engine. Oil mist is blown up the holes surrounding the tappet guides and reaches the rocker box via the telescopic push-rod sleeves (Fig. 13). Grease-gun nipples are provided to meet extreme circumstances. The four-valve, which has roller bearings to rockers, has not got oil mist lubrication. Here occasional grease-gun lubrication is necessary.

THE TWO-STROKE ENGINES

The following notes apply to the 2·25-h.p. engines manufactured up to the end of 1930, since when the model has been introduced in an improved form.

ROYAL ENFIELD ENGINES

To Decarbonise the Sports Engine

The cylinder complete must be removed first, and the head can then be removed to facilitate decarbonisation.

Disconnect the pressure-release valve control and remove the sparking plug. Disconnect the petrol pipe, take off the carburetter, exhaust pipes and silencer. Then remove the four cylinder-base nuts and after placing the piston at B.D.C. draw the barrel gently off. Do not let the piston fall sharply against the connecting rod.

Then unscrew the four bolts holding the aluminium cylinder head to the cylinder barrel, carefully break the joint and lift off the head. On this engine no copper washer is interposed between the cylinder head and barrel, and special care must be taken to avoid damaging the metal-to-metal surfaces, otherwise gas leakage may occur.

Where no Detachable Head is Provided

After removing the carburetter, exhaust pipes, silencer and pressure-release valve cover, withdraw the bolt connecting the front engine plates to the frame lug and allow the engine to drop slightly in front. The cylinder can then be lifted clear of the piston, as shown in Fig. 14, after first placing the piston at the bottom of its stroke.

Fig. 16.—Assemble the Piston Correctly.

The sloping face of the top should be to the front and the steep face to the rear. This is essential to the correct working of the engine. On the later models the piston hits the cylinder head if assembled incorrectly.

ROYAL ENFIELD ENGINES

Piston Removal

On recent engines having a fully floating gudgeon pin, it is only necessary to push or tap this out. On earlier models a grub screw and split pin, as shown in Fig. 15, are used for securing the gudgeon pin in the piston. To remove the piston it is necessary to take out the split pin, remove the grub screw and push out the gudgeon pin, when the piston can be lifted off.

Piston Rings

Should one of the small pegs, which prevent the rings from rotating in their groves, become damaged or shear off, it should be seen to ; otherwise the end of the ring may foul one of the cylinder ports and cause considerable damage.

Reassembly

This is straightforward but it is *imperative* to reassemble the piston the correct way round, i.e. with the long sloping deflector face to the front and the short steep one to the rear (see Fig. 16.). Unless this is done the engine will not function properly, and on late designs the piston may foul the cylinder head with disastrous consequences.

To dismantle Pressure Release Valve of Detachable Head Model

Take off the three nuts holding the valve body to the cylinder head and withdraw the complete valve, which is a taper fit and may require tapping to free. Compress the spring and withdraw the cotter. This releases the collar and spring and frees the valve.

Parting Crankcase

This should not be done unless essential, and exceptional care must be taken when refitting to make an absolutely gastight joint, for, remember, the charge is compressed in the crankcase of a two-stroke.

ROYAL ENFIELD TIMING CHART

MODELS.	INLET. Opens before T.D.C.	INLET. Closes after B.D.C.	EXHAUST. Opens before B.D.C.	EXHAUST. Closes after T.D.C.	IGNITION MAX. ADV. before T.D.C.
Z50. 225 c.c. S.V., 1928–9	10°	50°	65°	25°	33°
B30. 225 c.c. S.V., 1930	10°	50°	65°	25°	33°
350. 346 c.c. S.V., 1927–9	0°	65°	40°	30°	32°
C30. 346 c.c. S.V., 1930	5°	75°	55°	30°	32°
F30. 346 c.c. S.V. Dry Sump, 1930	20°	80°	60°	55°	32°
C31. 346 c.c. S.V., 1931	5°	75°	55°	30°	32°
F31. 346 c.c. S.V. Dry Sump, 1931	20°	80°	60°	55°	32°
351. 346 c.c. O.H.V., 1927–8	0°	65°	40°	30°	38°
351. 346 c.c. O.H.V., 1928–9	22°	60°	60°	22°	38°
355. 346 c.c. O.H.V., 1928–9	22°	60°	60°	22°	38°
CO30, 31. 346 c.c. O.H.V., 1930–1	22°	60°	60°	22°	38°
CS31. 346 c.c. O.H.V., 1931	22°	60°	60°	22°	38°
G30. 346 c.c. O.H.V. Dry Sump, early 1930	35°	75°	75°	35°	38°
G30. 346 c.c. O.H.V. Dry Sump, late 1930	35°	85°	65°	55°	38°
G31. 346 c.c. O.H.V. Dry Sump, 1931	35°	85°	65°	55°	38°
500. 488 c.c. S.V., 1927–8	0°	65°	40°	30°	35°
501. 488 c.c. S.V., 1929	5°	75°	55°	30°	35°
502. 488 c.c. S.V., 1929	5°	75°	55°	30°	35°
D30. 488 c.c. S.V., 1930	5°	75°	55°	30°	35°
H30. 488 c.c. S.V. Dry Sump, 1930	20°	80°	60°	55°	35°
HA31. 488 c.c. S.V. Dry Sump, 1931	20°	80°	60°	55°	35°
H31. 570 c.c. S.V. Dry Sump, 1931	15°	80°	55°	40°	33°
505. 488 c.c. O.H.V., 1929	30°	65°	65°	30°	40°
E30. 488 c.c. O.H.V., 1930	30°	65°	65°	30°	40°
J30. 488 c.c. O.H.V. Dry Sump, 1930	35°	85°	65°	55°	40°
JA31. 488 c.c. O.H.V. Dry Sump, 1931	35°	85°	65°	55°	40°
JF31. 488 c.c. 4-valve Dry Sump, 1931	40°	70°	70°	40°	40°
J31. 499 c.c. O.H.V. Dry Sump, 1931	40°	80°	80°	40°	38°
180. 976 c.c. Twin, 1927–9	0°	45°	60°	15°	35°
182. 976 c.c. Twin, 1927–9	0°	45°	60°	15°	35°
K30. 976 c.c. Twin, 1930	0°	45°	60°	15°	35°
K31. 976 c.c. Twin, 1931	0°	70°	60°	30°	35°

TAPPET CLEARANCES – Valve Timings are given at ·005″ clearance.
Correct Running Clearance for O.H.V. engines is zero when cold.
Correct Running Clearance for S.V. engines is ·004″ inlet, ·006″ exhaust when cold.

REPAIR AND MAINTENANCE OF RUDGE ENGINES

By B. P. RANSOM (*Rudge Whitworth, Ltd.*)

Fig. 1.—ADJUSTING TAPPETS (1931 ULSTER).
Note the tappet-rod cover is lifted clear after the nut, which secures this by the slotted lug, has been slackened off.

OVERHAUL AND ADJUSTMENT OF POWER UNIT

Inspect your Tappets Regularly

COMMENCING with the engine, very regular inspection of tappet adjustments is desirable. These should be adjusted when the engine is cold, and should be so set that the push rod rotates freely between the fingers, but has no perceptible up-and-down movement. If a tight spot is felt when the rod is rotated, it means that either tappet or push rod is bent, and if it is not found practicable to straighten them they should be replaced.

The inlet should be run thus—the exhaust should be adjusted back to give ·002 inch clearance (Fig. 1). If the clearance is allowed to become excessive, hammering results, and wear on the overhead rockers may be expected.

REPAIR AND MAINTENANCE OF RUDGE ENGINES

Fig. 2.—Tightening Cylinder Head Bolts.
Give each bolt half a turn at a time. Note the front right-hand bolt partly screwed up.

REPAIR AND MAINTENANCE OF RUDGE ENGINES

Types of Rockers

The 1928 and 1929 special overhead rockers were of the barrel type, with internal rollers. If it is found necessary to remove these from the head, when replacing them the rollers should be secured in place with thick grease, and the spindle introduced before fitting to the head.

The 1930 and 1931 heads have rocker-bearing supports cast integral with them, and the previous arrangement of rollers is reversed, as in this case they run on the rockers and in races pressed into the supports. A small amount of endplay in the overhead rockers is unimportant, but undue lift makes tappet adjustment difficult, and should be eliminated by the replacement of rollers, which will usually be sufficient to correct matters.

Fig. 3.—DETACHING HEAD, FIRST STAGE.

Note the rocker-box cover is removed. The exhaust lifter adjuster, which also secures the tappet-rod cover, is disconnected. The cylinder head bolts are unscrewed so that the head may be raised (1930 Rudge Special).

Points to Note on Cylinder Head Joints

The joint between the cylinder head and barrel is made with a copper asbestos washer, prior to 1930, when the plain copper gasket was introduced. Great care is needed in tightening the head bolts (Fig. 2). If one is pulled up first, it will be hopeless to expect to make a gastight joint. It is better to go round the head, giving each bolt half a turn at a time. The tapped holes in the head are blind, therefore it is as well to make sure the bolts are the correct length, as if one bottoms, it is quite possible to twist it off. Do not forget that these bolts are too long to enter their respective holes after the cylinder has been bolted to the crankcase, and consequently should be put in place before the cylinder is replaced.

The Cylinder Head

The cylinder head should be carefully examined. It is important to note the positions of the four valves, and to replace each one in its original seating. If the engine has run any length of time, it is possible that the valve guides, or at any rate the inlet guides, will need replacing. In this

REPAIR AND MAINTENANCE OF RUDGE ENGINES

case, the seatings should be recut—and in any case if a cutter is available, this will reduce the labour of grinding in to a minimum.

Cutting Valve Seatings

One should take great care not to remove more metal than is necessary to just clean up the seat, for if the cutter goes too deep the opening of the valve will be masked, with consequent loss of performance. If, when the valves are ground in and refitted, it is found that one rocker arm touches a little before the other, this should be rectified by filing a little from the end of the longer valve stem.

This does not apply to the radial valve 350-c.c. and 250-c.c. models of 1931, in which case the matter can be rectified by independent adjustment of the rocker pillars.

Polished Ports

The Ulster and all racing engines are turned out with the interior of the cylinder head polished, and the ports streamlined. The firm are prepared to carry out this work on other models for a reasonable charge.

The condition of the valve springs should be noted. The correct poundage for Ulster and racing 500-c.c. engines is 80, while the most suitable spring for the special is 60 lb. at half of lift of valve.

Fig. 4.—Removing Head of 1930 Special.

Special Clearances are Allowed

It will be noted, on removing the cylinder barrel, that the piston clearance is considerable. This is quite in order. The Rudge engine has been developed from racing experience, and it has been found advisable to allow quite a perceptible amount of play at vital points.

Another of these points is the big-end bearing. This " slop " is one of the factors which allow the Rudge engine to be driven so hard and for such long periods without showing symptoms of tiredness.

Reducing Endplay on Early Models

The 1928 engines and all 1929 engines except the Ulster had a two-bearing crankshaft. These bearings were merely pressed into the crank-

REPAIR AND MAINTENANCE OF RUDGE ENGINES

case. After long usage occasionally it is found that a little endplay develops on the crankshaft. This is taken up by fitting extra washers between the flywheels and the bearings. The first washer should be put on the driving side, the second on the timing, and so on. A range of suitable washers of various thicknesses can be obtained from the firm.

Fig. 5.—ADJUSTING EXHAUST LIFTER ON 1931 ULSTER MODEL.

Notes on Flywheels

It is not possible for the amateur to dismantle and satisfactorily re-erect his flywheels, and if attention to the big end is necessary the whole flywheel assembly should be returned to the works. The four tapers are there pulled up by special tackle very considerably more securely than is possible outside.

The 1929 Ulster engine and all subsequent models have a three-bearing crankshaft. There is one ball and one roller bearing on the drive side, and a roller bearing on the timing side. The ball bearing is outside and is pressed into the crankshaft first. This is locked into place with a screwed ring, the removal of which may present difficulties, unless a length of hexagon steel 5 or 6 inches long and $1\frac{6}{16}$ inches across the flats be available. One end can be introduced into the hexagon hole in the locking ring, and the other gripped by a large adjustable spanner, when the ring can be unscrewed without difficulty. There is a short tubular distance piece between the two bearings on the left-hand side. It is

REPAIR AND MAINTENANCE OF RUDGE ENGINES

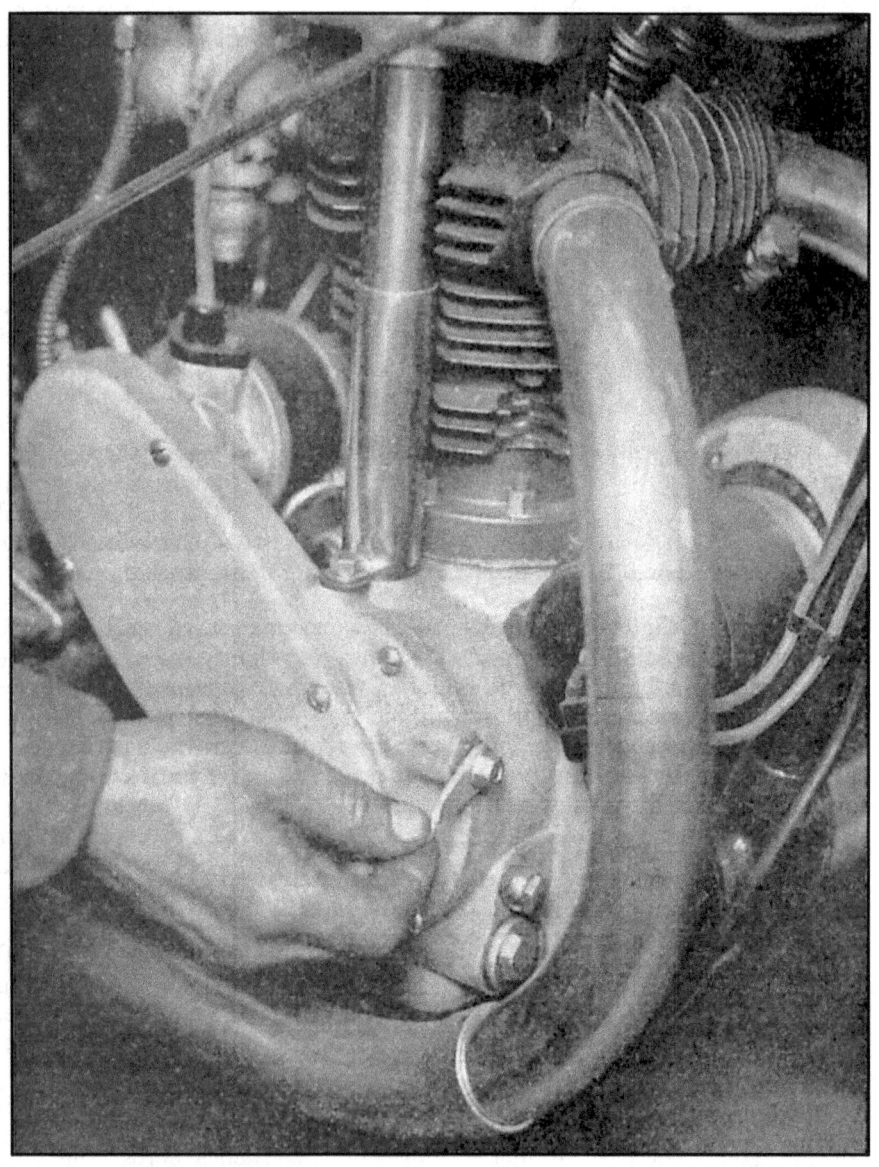

Fig. 6.—Setting the Decompressor Lever of 1931 Ulster.
This fitting affords easing starting. The lever is fitted to a serrated shaft.

REPAIR AND MAINTENANCE OF RUDGE ENGINES

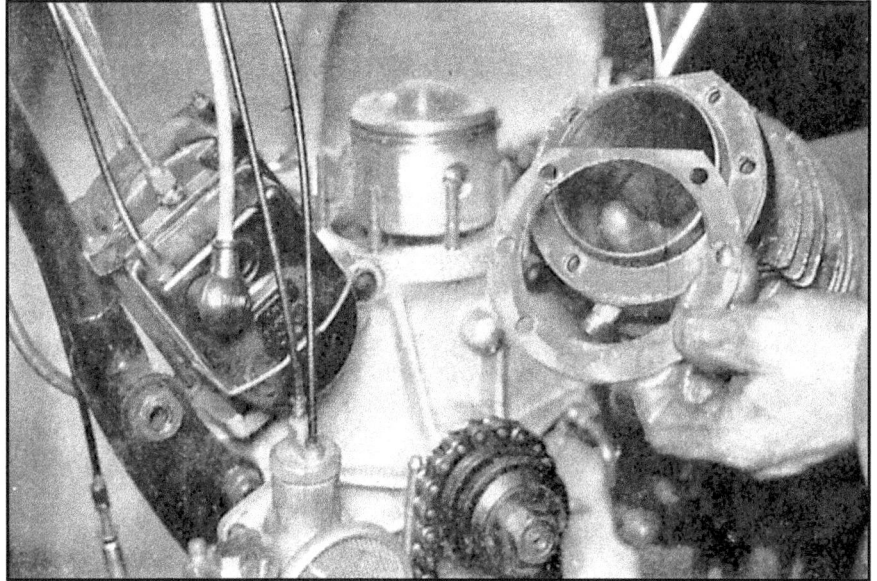

Fig. 7.—Cylinder Barrel removed, showing the Compression Plate.

most important that this be replaced—the consequences of omission are disastrous. The small timing pinion is secured to the right-hand axle by a taper and right-hand nut. It is not advisable to attempt to remove this pinion unless an extractor is available.

The shock absorber on the left-hand axle requires but little attention. It is lubricated by an oilway drilled up the axle. The end nut should, however, be locked up very securely indeed.

Compression Ratios—a Warning *re* Compression Plates

The majority of Rudge engines are provided with one or more compression plates under the cylinder base (Fig. 7). In some cases these may be removed for tuning purposes, and in others this is not possible.

The 1929 Ulster engine is a case in point. This engine has a compression ratio of 6·5 with the plate in position, and the clearance between piston and valves is so small that if the plate be removed there is grave danger of them fouling each other, with consequent risk of a wrecked piston and bent valves. This danger would of course be accentuated by the inadvertent use of the exhaust valve lifter while the engine was revving, or the possibility of a sticking valve.

A Useful Tip for checking Clearance between Piston and Valves

In any case, when removing a plate, it is advisable to check the clearances carefully. This may be done by sticking a piece of plasticine to the piston top and slowly rotating the engine by hand. The thickness

REPAIR AND MAINTENANCE OF RUDGE ENGINES

of plasticine at the greatest depth of the indentation made by the valves of course then represents the clearance. It may also be necessary to obtain shorter push rods if more than one plate is to be removed.

How to measure the Compression Ratio of an Engine

A compression ratio of 7·25 should not be exceeded for use with petrol-benzole mixture, while 8·25 is about the maximum possible. This can of course only be employed with alcohol fuels. The compression ratio is most conveniently measured by pouring oil from a graduated measuring glass into the central plug hole while the piston is at the top of the stroke. Allow time for the oil on the inside of the glass to drain back, and note the amount required to fill the cylinder head. With a 500-c.c. engine, 80 c.c. would represent a ratio of approximately 7·25, while 69 c.c. would be about 8·25. A compression plate ·1 inch in thickness represents 14 c.c. with an 85-mm. bore. Do not forget that to obtain the full advantage of an increased compression ratio, it will be necessary to readjust the carburetter and to increase the jet sizes.

Ignition Timing

The most suitable ignition timing for all touring 500-c.c. engines is for the points to break between 35° and 39° before top dead centre when the control is fully advanced. In the case of Ulster and racing engines, this may be increased to 45°. The 350-c.c. engines should be timed to break from 39° to 42° before top.

Valve Timing Details

The tappets should be set to a clearance of ·020 inch, and the exhaust valve should then open 54° before bottom dead centre, and close 17° after top. The inlet should open 2° before top, and close 41° after bottom. The timing having been set as nearly as above as is practicable, the tappets should then be readjusted, allowing no perceptible clearance on the inlet, and ·002 inch clearance on the exhaust.

All 350-c.c. touring engines from 1929 to 1931 are timed as follows :

Set the tappets to a clearance of ·015 inch, and time the exhaust valve to open 70° before bottom, and to close on top dead centre. The inlet should then open 22° before top, and close 24° after bottom.

The Ulster engines from 1929 to 1931, all dirt-track engines, and the 1931 T.T. Replica are timed thus :

The tappets are set to a clearance of ·010 inch and the exhaust should open 56° before bottom, and close 36° after top. The inlet should open 36° before top and close 56° after bottom.

In all cases it will be found more convenient to time from the bottom of the stroke—that is to say, if the exhaust opening is correct the others will follow.

TIMING CHART FOR "RUDGE"

MODELS.	INLET.		EXHAUST.		IGNITION MAX. ADV.	Tappet Clearance when Timing.
	Opens before T.D.C.	Closes after B.D.C.	Opens before B.D.C.	Closes after T.D.C.	Before T.D.C.	
500 c.c., Four Valve, 1924–6	−8°*	37°	50°	10°	35–39°	·01″
350 c.c., 1924–5	−8°*	36°	50°	10°	35°	·01″
500 c.c., 1927	−8°*	49°	54°	10°	35–39°	·01″
Special Models, 1928–31, and 1928 Sports, 1929–31	5°	41°	54°	17°	39–42°	·02″

* These settings are *after* T.D.C.

MODELS.	INLET.		EXHAUST.		IGNITION MAX. ADV.	Tappet Clearance when Timing.
	Opens before T.D.C.	Closes after B.D.C.	Opens before B.D.C.	Closes after T.D.C.	Before T.D.C.	
350 c.c., 1929–30	21°	25°	70°	1°	39–42°	·017″
350 c.c., 1931	5°	41°	54°	17°	39–42°	·017″
"Ulster" Models: 1929–30 1931	36° 30°	56° 50°	56° 58°	36° 30°	45–48°	·02″
250 c.c., 1931	5°	41°	54°	17°	41–44°	·015″

When the timing operations are completed, the tappets should be adjusted until there is only just perceptible clearance between the overhead rockers and the valve stems with the engine cold.

SPECIAL HINTS ON SCOTT ENGINES

By J. H. KELLY (*Scott Motors Ltd.*)

Fig. 1.—REMOVING THE CRANKPIN SCREW.
Note how the crankcase door flange is machined away to allow for crankpin screw removal.

TAKING DOWN A SCOTT ENGINE

FIRST, a timely warning: DON'T TAKE OFF THE WATERCOOLED HEAD FOR DECARBONISING—this is only a water jacket, and is distinct from the cylinder itself.

Removing the Cylinders

Drain water from radiator, take out plugs, radiator (gently please !), remove silencer, transfer covers, cylinder holding-down bolts, carburetter on Supers only (not essential, but allows more room), and on Supers right-hand exhaust port cover. Then lift off the cylinders.

If these are tight, replace plugs, engage gear, open throttle and turn

SPECIAL HINTS ON SCOTT ENGINES

Fig. 2.—REMOVING PISTON AND ROD COMPLETE FROM CRANKCASE.
Note the right hand tilts the rod and the left hand turns flywheel backwards, thus drawing crankpin bush away from con rod.

back wheel *slowly*, until block moves up from the crankcase against compression.

Crankcase Doors

Having removed crankcase doors (on late Flyers and Replicas these must be removed *before* cylinder bolts can be taken out), remove crankpin screws, stamped right- and left-hand respectively, by using door strap as screwdriver. If these are tight, tap end of strap whilst in screw slot; failing that, tap gently with hammer and light punch. (On Supers and Flyers it will be noted that the crankcase door flange is machined away at one point to allow for removal of screw: it will only come away at this point—don't force.)

Pistons and Con Rods—Removal

Take out big-end rollers (COUNT THEM IN YOUR HAND—12 EACH SIDE), then turn flywheel to top of stroke—tilt con rod sideways, turn flywheel back slightly—i.e. taking crankpin bush "out of the con rod," piston and con rod come out together nicely.

All gudgeons (except very old type, split-pinned or lock ringed) tap out from the inside (i.e. flywheel side), and if piston bosses are at all worn, oversize gudgeons *must* be fitted, otherwise the old gudgeons will

SPECIAL HINTS ON SCOTT ENGINES

eventually float out, with unhappy results to the cylinder walls. (*Note.*—Oversize gudgeons, $\tfrac{1\cdot 2}{1000}$ in oversize, are supplied by works and depot.)

Pistons and Con Rods—Adjustment and Repairs

If pistons show signs of having seized, ease off *lightly* with a very fine file, and if cylinders are marked, lap out with crocus powder and oil, but extreme care must be taken to ensure that the cylinders are washed perfectly free of powder afterwards. Don't use your own pistons for this job—beg, borrow, or steal an old one.

When trying pistons and rings in cylinders, put a small wad of paper in the head first, as in some cases it is possible to jam the piston rings if the piston is pushed too far up into the head.

If the rings show more than $\tfrac{10}{1000}$ gap, fit new ones (using only genuine Scott rings for the job: cheap rings mean loss of efficiency, and are false economy, anyhow).

Fig. 3.—Removing Right-hand Crank.

Note centre bolt is slackened off a few turns, and a sharp blow drives out crank. Warning: support crankcase on a block of wood first, and see that the crankpin bush on the under side registers with the crankcase cut away—otherwise the flange may get broken when the crank drops out.

Genuine Scott rings are supplied slightly oversize (circumference), and it may be necessary to file slightly to fit (incidentally, radial depth and width are dead right on these rings) inspect your gaps through the ports ;

SPECIAL HINTS ON SCOTT ENGINES

Fig. 4.—GRINDING IN PACKING GLANDS ON SCOTT ENGINE BEFORE REASSEMBLY.

Fig. 5.—UNDOING LEFT-HAND THREADED NUT OF CRANKSHAFT BOLT.
Lay a tyre lever or strip of metal (NOT SHARP EDGES, PLEASE ! !) in crankcase as shown, and the crank pin bush will rest on it whilst nut is being slackened off.

SPECIAL HINTS ON SCOTT ENGINES

and remember that old engines wear more at the middle than at the bottom of the stroke, and a ring tight at the bottom may be just right at the top; make due allowance for this, and fit each ring separately.

Clean ring grooves thoroughly, and roll rings round piston; don't have any "sticky" spots (a free ring is very necessary for a two-stroke and one tight ring spoils the whole performance), and if an old ring has been badly seized in, chamfer the piston ring groove edge very slightly.

Refitting Rings for Fast Work

For "fast" work rings should be fitted with a very small gap and lapped in with jewellers' rouge and oil. The same warning *re* cleaning your pistons and cylinders applies here.

Engines should be run carefully for fifty miles (a little oil in the petrol is advisable), and if fitted for fast work, one hundred miles.

Use an ordinary penknife or a Woolworth's scout-knife for removing carbon, clean all ports thoroughly, polish your pistons vigorously *on the top only* with metal polish (this will render your next decoke easier), and clean out the oil grooves, but do not polish the sides of the pistons.

Fig. 6.—BUILDING UP CRANKSHAFT.

After the crank bolt has been screwed up, each crank should be driven into the flywheel, using a hammer and tubular punch.

Reassembling Pistons and Con Rods

When replacing con rods, put these back correctly. It is generally assumed that, as long as the small-end bush fixing screw is uppermost, all is well, but it isn't.

A small centre-punch mark will be seen on the side of the rod, at the

SPECIAL HINTS ON SCOTT ENGINES

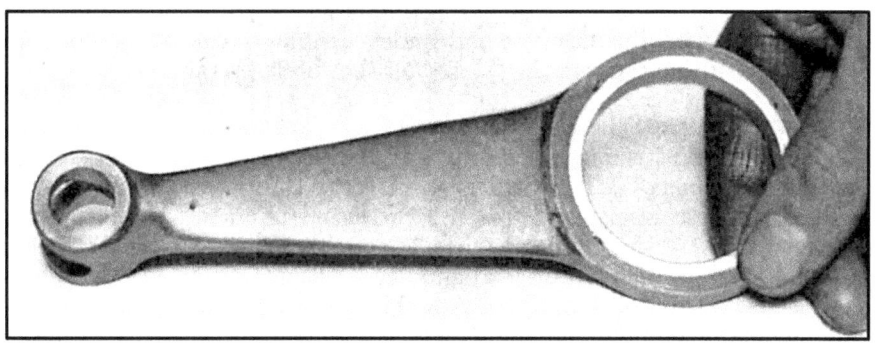

Fig. 7.—SHOWING CENTRE-PUNCH MARK ON CON ROD.
This side faces flywheel.

top, near the small end, and this should face the flywheel; keep each rod to its own side of the engine, as they come out.

Watercooled Head

If this leaks badly, remove two locking rings and lift off the head; clean the surfaces carefully, fit new rubber and c/a washers; use Hermetite or Metalastine, allow to get tacky before putting on the head, tighten the head down evenly and *gently* (remember the head is very thin), and allow to stand for a few hours before filling with water.

It will be found that the head can be tightened a little more after a day or so's running.

Did you know this?

The London Depot of Scott Motors, Ltd., will be pleased to lend a special spanner for these head nuts against a deposit of 10s.; no charge is made for use and deposit is returned in full. The same facility is given in the case of a half-compression locking-ring tool, the deposit here being 5s.

Joints

Always use new packings, these are quite cheap.

All joints should be fitted dry, except base linen rings, on which you may use either seccotine or oil. Trim up transfer and induction washers to the ports, to ensure an even flow of gas.

Gauzes

These are fitted to most 596 engines and the early 486 and 532 models, but a little more speed and acceleration may be gained by their removal. If the engine spits badly with the gauzes out, replace them immediately.

SPECIAL HINTS ON SCOTT ENGINES

Cylinder Bolts

When tightening down the cylinder holding-down bolts, do these diagonally; this relieves the " last bolt " of undue strain.

A Warning—leave the Skirts alone

Many Scott owners, no doubt intrigued by the usual press photos and descriptions of T.T. Scotts, or inspired by those weird and wonderful tuning hints so freely broadcast, have rushed blindly into the practice of cutting away the cylinder skirts below the cylinder transfer ports in order to gain a little more speed and acceleration.

Whilst it is more than likely that this end has been attained, the slow running has been practically destroyed—a little thought will explain why!

Now the T.T. Replica, of course, *is* cut away, BUT *the inlet and exhaust ports are altered accordingly* to balance up for the slow running. This part of the business is never mentioned by the " tuning expert."

Never meddle with these dangerous experiments; remember the Scott Works and the Depot are always only too willing to give advice on such points: they will be delighted to help you get the best out of your Scott.

HOW TO TAKE SCOTT ENGINE OUT OF FRAME

Having attended to the cylinders and pistons, it now remains to get the balance of the engine out of the frame, as follows:

Remove engine chains, (engine and/or magneto), four bottom ⅜-inch engine bolts and large top bolt, and lift assembly from frame.

In the Case of " Flyer " Models

Support crankcase with box or petrol can, remove chains, take out carburetter slides, disconnect clutch wire, remove three main engine bolts, taking out the *top* one last.

For 1928–31 Flyers take out *front* bolt first and

Fig. 8.—CORRECT WAY TO REPLACE FLYWHEEL.
Note fingers rest naturally in deep rim of flywheel.

SPECIAL HINTS ON SCOTT ENGINES

remove front stand; when reassembling, put this bolt back first, *without* stand and washers, and after replacing other two bolts, take out front one again and replace stand and washers at your ease. This saves a lot of " juggling " with front stand.

REPLACING ENGINES (COMPLETE) IN FRAME

Super will go back into frame quite comfortably if the right-hand exhaust port cover is left off.

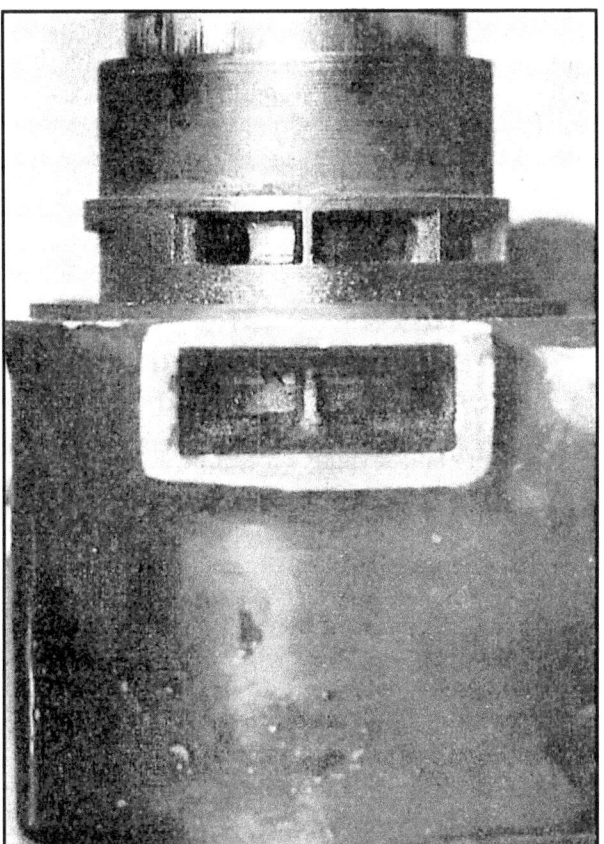

Fig. 9.—IT IS POSSIBLE TO EXAMINE THE PISTON RING GAP THROUGH TRANSFER PORT.

" Flyer " Models

These should be put in upside down and swung up into position (see Fig. 10), fitting front bolt (only) first (see note *re* 1928–31 Flyers above).

Incidentally, it is worth while taking out the gearbox at the same time on these models, as on removal of two gear tray bolts and nuts, sprocket housing complete, two underneath nuts to gearbox studs, the tray can be swung downwards and the whole gearbox dropped through the frame—an extra five minutes' work! This will also save disconnecting the gear chain, which will come out with the engine.

A Note on the Threespeed Super

In this particular job it is far simpler and easier to remove engine and gearbox on the undertray in one unit—but don't forget to remove the clutch wire first—so easily forgotten!

SPECIAL HINTS ON SCOTT ENGINES

DISMANTLING CRANKSHAFT

A delicate job, but quite straightforward. Proceed as follows : unscrew LEFT-hand nut in centre of right-hand crank, undo bolt on left-hand side a few turns (right-hand thread), a smart blow on the bolt head will dislodge crank ; bolt can then be unscrewed, releasing right-hand crank and rollers. (COUNT THEM—SUPERS 13, and FLYERS 15.)

The left-hand crank can then be removed by a steel bar passed through the flywheel, giving it a smart blow.

Take great care in replacing cranks ; a little grease (vaseline) will hold the rollers in position (bed these down on the bearing by passing a piece of string round the outside of rollers, when in position, and tighten), replace packing gland (after grinding this in with a little *fine* valve-grinding paste or knife-powder, see Fig. 4) and be sure that the tongue of this engages with the keyway in the flywheel.

After the crank bolt is screwed up, each crank should be driven into the flywheel, using a hammer and tubular punch (three sharp blows only).

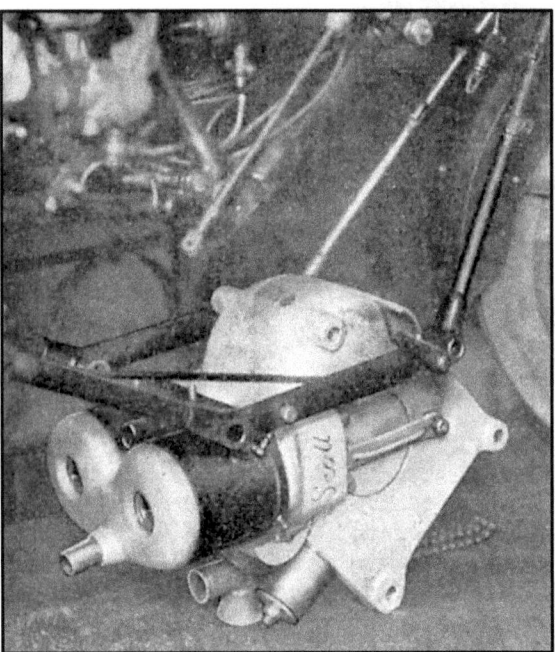

Fig. 10.—FLYER ENGINE READY TO SWING UP INTO FRAME.

Warning

Whenever hammering up a crank, the other one *must* be in position first and a solid mass brought to bear up against it, so that the force of the blow is not transferred to the crankcase cup.

Each crank must be knocked up in turn and crank bolt tightened a little, and cranks MUST be driven up solid to flywheel, otherwise the flywheel key may shear.

Always use a new crankshaft bolt and nut, as these tend to " stretch," and left-hand thread is invariably damaged.

When tightening up bolt and nut, don't overdo it ; the left-hand nut may need to be thinned down to clear the large hole roller plate. See

SPECIAL HINTS ON SCOTT ENGINES

that the latter seats firmly on the crank, then check that it really clears the nut ; rivet the nut over lightly to prevent working loose.

When replacing flywheel, see that this is put back right, i.e. the fingers of the right hand fall naturally into the groove of the rim. *Flyers*, the thin sprocket will be on your right (magneto chain drive).

The sprockets usually last for years, but can be replaced for a few shillings, and are only riveted on to the flywheel. (20-tooth only supplied.)

If main bearings or cups are worn, the cranks and crankcase must be returned to the WORKS for new parts to be fitted, as these are not supplied separately.

Big Ends

If your bushes or rollers show signs of pitting or " scaling " they should be replaced. (Works and London depot will rebush or exchange rods andcranks for you at a reasonable charge.)

Don't waste your time or money on oversize rollers—rebushing is not expensive, and the Scott engine, as an engineering job, surely deserves a better fate than faking up big ends ! ! When you realise that explosion force does not wear the bushes *evenly*, you *must* see that the oversize rollers are altogether wrong ! !

GENERAL NOTES ON SCOTT ENGINES

Air Leaks

These can generally be found by squirting petrol around the various joints ; pulling off each plug lead separately will instantly show which cylinder is weak, although a blown carburetter (induction pipe) washer *may* lead you badly astray (check this first) !

Intermittent firing or cutting out on one side may be due to cracked pick-ups (H.T.), but more elusive is the burnt contact-breaker points, or loosening of same ; early Lucas Magdynos are peculiarly sensitive on these points. Too wide a gap at the plug or magneto points is another cause.

Plugs for Scott Engines

A very debatable point this ! but a just golden rule. *If you are satisfied with your present plugs*, DON'T *change, stick to that type*. Apart from this, here are the recommended types.

GENERAL AND TOURING
    Champion No. 13 (for 1929–31 Flyers, No. 7).

FAST TOURING
    K.L.G. H.S. 3.
    Lodge H.H. 1.
    Champion Aero A (for 1927–8 Flyers and T.T. Replicas only).

SPECIAL HINTS ON SCOTT ENGINES

Fig. 11.—Lifting Super Engine out of Frame.

SPECIAL HINTS ON SCOTT ENGINES

Fig. 12.—SHOWING REMOVAL OF KICK-STARTER DEVICE.
Lifting gear with screwdriver and sliding off device.

SPECIAL HINTS ON SCOTT ENGINES

Racing

K.L.G. 268 and Champion Aero A.

Warning

Plugs with a longer reach than ⅜ inch must not be used; damage to pistons is the penalty!

Timing

Take out plug, set piston at top of stroke, retard ignition lever fully, set contact-breaker points just fully opened. If you have timed off the wrong cylinder, this will be denoted by a backfire in the silencer; it is then necessary to change over the plug leads.

Oil

Use Castrol XXL (or "runners up" Castrol XL, Duckhams' Adcol R.R.).

Petrol

Any good brand of No. 1 (OR BETTER STILL 50 per cent. petrol to 50 per cent. pure benzole). For T.T. Replicas, ethyl.

Decoke new engines, 1,500 miles; afterwards, 2,000 to 4,000 miles, according to model.

Scott Radiator

Perished hoses and rubber pads for bolts should be renewed, and in the event of a new hose weeping, a few turns of insulation tape round the brass water pipes will cure this.

The water system should be flushed out occasionally with warm water and soda to remove any deposit.

To prevent freezing in cold weather add about a pint and a quarter of ordinary commercial glycerine to the radiator water. If you cannot get glycerine, empty the radiator by the drain tap in the cylinder, but make sure that it *is* empty, as if there is a rust deposit at the cylinder end it is quite likely that it will block up the drain tap.

For a small honeycomb leak, stop this up with a piece of chewing gum (*after* you have chewed it!)—this is quite a good tip, as you can get this anywhere on the road, where you probably could not get Plasticine. Have the leak repaired as soon as possible (corrosion sets in very quickly and spreads) by a skilled radiator repair man. DON'T TACKLE IT YOURSELF.

Silencers for Scott Machines

The Howarth silencer, fitted to Flyers, etc., is very prone to choke up after the oil pump has been set on the liberal side (such as a new machine

SPECIAL HINTS ON SCOTT ENGINES

or rebore), and it is advisable to take this to pieces (three) and clean out thoroughly after 600 miles; easiest method is to burn it out over an ordinary gasring or blowlamp.

In any case, clean regularly every 1,000 miles.

For increased efficiency and to minimise back pressure, you may increase the small ¼-inch hole at the end of the cone (inside portion) to about ⅜ inch, and on the Flyers, which already have the expansion chamber at the front, the outer baffle of the inside part may be entirely removed, *but* this latter idea is not conducive to real silence, although careful driving (i.e. no hectic blinding in first or second gears !) will see you through.

Oil Pump Setting (Pilgrim)

Oil pump settings are usually a nightmare to the " new owner," and the " so many drops per minute " idea bewilders him more than ever, so we suggest the following as a more certain method.

On new (or rebored) engines, set the pump to give one drop of oil at every third pulsation at the " beak," i.e. one, two, then drop.

After running in, it can then be reduced to one drop at every fourth pulsation, i.e. one, two, three, then drop. (Or even less by that time, as obviously you will have got into the " swing " of things.)

The exhaust, of course, is a reliable guide—excessive blue smoke means too much, absence of smoke not enough.

A faint haze at low speeds (lift the half-compression lever momentarily and it should give an extra " puff ") is fairly safe, but just remember that if you are too generous in adding oil to your petrol, you may be smoking profusely, but not getting enough oil to the mains and big ends via the oil pipes ; so be very careful on this point.

A Useful Repair Hint

To replace worn engine chains, it is easier to attach new chain to old one and " follow on." If no old one is available, remove top engine plates, smear first dozen links of chain with stiff grease and thread over engine sprocket (this allows the chain to cling to the teeth instead of " piling up " at the back of crankcase). In the case of 1931 Flyers and Supers, this greasing is not necessary, as a chain guide is now provided.

SUNBEAM MOTOR-CYCLES

USEFUL NOTES ON ENGINE DISMANTLING, ADJUSTING AND TIMING

By H. G. Gale

Side-valve Models

TO remove cylinder, take out screws supporting front of the silencer, and loosen pin supporting the back of it. Undo union attaching exhaust pipe to cylinder, allowing exhaust pipe to drop down out of the way. Remove carburetter, valve covers (see Fig. 1), high-tension wire, valve caps and compression plug. Take off the nuts on the studs holding cylinder base to crankcase. Lift the cylinder to clear the studs and tappets, turning it round so that valve chamber is on left side. Turn the engine by revolving back wheel with one of the gears engaged till piston is at lowest point with connecting rod in backward position (see Fig. 2). The cylinder will now lift off the piston.

Overhead Valve Models

The cylinder head can be removed without disturbing anything else, but accessibility is improved by removing the tank. In this case first detach petrol pipe, remove gear rod from change-speed lever and withdraw Bowden cables from under tank. Raise saddle, and then undo the four pins which hold the tank on to the frame brackets, and it will then lift off. Next remove sparking plug, exhaust pipe, etc. Slacken the locking nuts at the base of the two push-rod tubes, and screw these tubes down into the crankcase, till they are clear of the rocker box above (see Fig. 3). Take out the four pins which attach the two side plates of the rocker box to the cylinder head. Undo the four long sleeve nuts which hold the head down to the barrel. The head can now be lifted off for decarbonising, etc. The method of compressing the valve springs is shown in Fig. 4, and in those cases where hairpin valve springs are fitted instead of the coil pattern, a special tool of a different type is supplied by the makers for dealing with them. If it is desired to remove the piston the cylinder barrel can be lifted straight up and away from the four long holding-down studs. The cylinder head fits on to the barrel by a plain joint. This is ground-in in the same way as the valves. No gasket is used (see Fig. 5). When the rocker box is replaced, the spring washers on the four pins which hold the rocker-box plates to the cylinder head must not be omitted, and it is

Fig. 1.—Dismantling Side-valve Engine.
After removing exhaust-pipe union and carburetter, take off the valve covers as shown.

SUNBEAM MOTOR-CYCLES

essential that the push-rod tubes are not screwed up too tightly against the rocker box, otherwise distortion of the box may be caused. The rocker box should not be opened unless absolutely necessary, e.g. to replace a rocker (see Fig. 6). If opened, the joints must be carefully made with goldsize in order that they may be air- and oiltight.

Fig. 2.—DISMANTLING SIDE-VALVE ENGINE.

Next remove high-tension wire, valve caps, compression plugs and cylinder-base nuts, then lift the cylinder clear as shown above. Note that the piston is at the lowest point.

Pistons

The gudgeon pin in early models was fully floating with brass ends, but in the later models the pin is held in position by a small spring clip at each end. Either clip can be removed (see

Fig. 3.—DISMANTLING OVERHEAD-VALVE ENGINE.
This shows the removal of the push-rod tubes.

Fig. 4.—A Useful Tool for Compressing Valve Springs on O.H.V. Engine.

Fig. 7), as the gudgeon pin can be pushed out from either end.

If the piston rings are removed, it should be noted that the bottom one is a scraper ring, and care must be taken to replace it the proper way, i.e. with the wider part uppermost (see Fig. 9).

Tappets on Side-valve Models

The exhaust tappet should be adjusted so that there is just a little play when the engine is hot. If adjusted when cold the clearance should be six to eight thousandths of

Fig. 5.—Ground-in Joint of Cylinder Head, O.H.V. Engine.
Note that no gasket is used.

Fig. 6.—Interior of Rocker Box, O.H.V. Engine.

The rocker box should not be opened unless it is necessary to replace a rocker. The joints must afterwards be remade with goldsize in order that they may be air- and oiltight.

SUNBEAM MOTOR-CYCLES

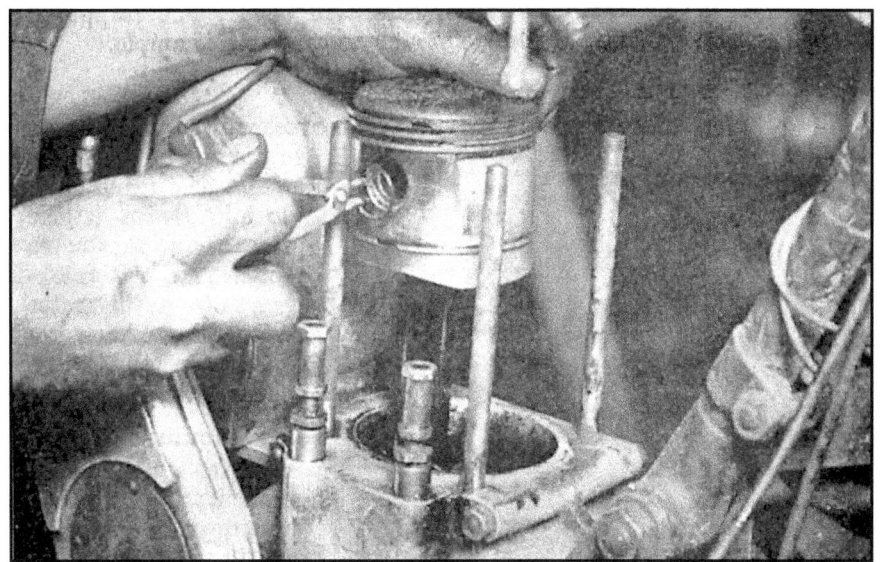

Fig. 7.—GUDGEON-PIN REMOVAL.
This shows how the spring clip securing the pin must be first taken out.

Fig. 8.—HOW THE SUNBEAM TIMING WHEELS ARE MARKED.
The punch marks on the centre pinion should register with those on the cam wheels, as shown above.

an inch. No appreciable gap at all is needed on the inlet tappet if adjusted when cold. The thickness of a cigarette paper is ample.

Tappets on Overhead Valve Models

The adjustment is effected at the end of the overhead rocker direct on to the end of the valve stem. The adjustment for inlet valve is the same as for side-valve models, i.e. the thickness of a cigarette paper; the exhaust requires ten to twelve thousandths of an inch.

Valve Timing

The cams are marked, and there is no advantage in replacing otherwise than as marked — the punch marks on centre pinion registering with those on the cams (see Fig. 8). The centre pinion is held on engine shaft by a key and lock nut (see Fig. 10).

Magneto Timing

This should be timed with the magneto control at full advance, the magneto points just about to break (see Fig. 11). The following figures give the distance which the piston should then be before top dead centre, and also the degrees if dial marking is used:

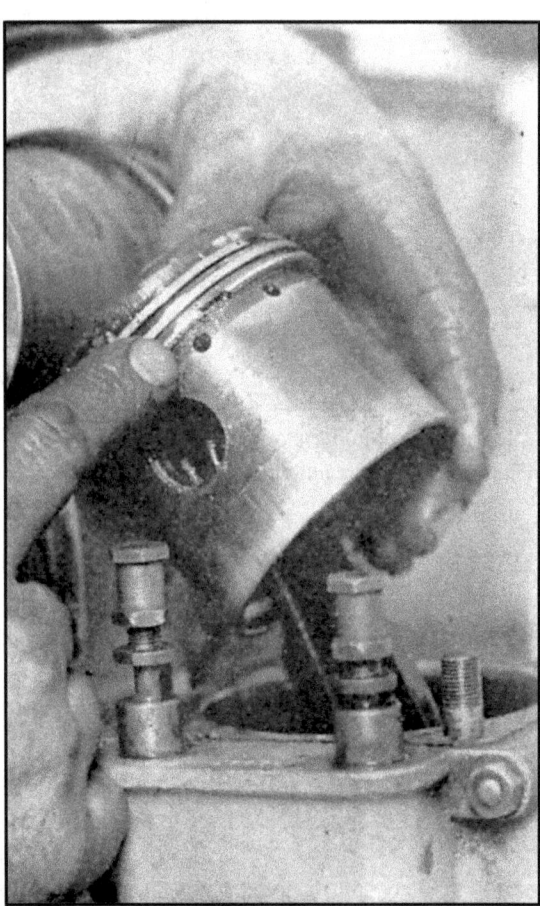

Fig. 9.—Replacing the Scraper Ring.

If the piston rings are removed, care must be taken to replace the lower ring (which is the scraper ring) with the wide part uppermost.

$2\tfrac{3}{4}$-h.p. Model 10: $\tfrac{5}{16}$ inch, or 30°.
$3\tfrac{1}{2}$-h.p. Longstroke: $\tfrac{7}{16}$ inch, or 35°.
$3\tfrac{1}{2}$-h.p. O.H.V.: $\tfrac{9}{16}$ inch, or 43°.
$3\tfrac{1}{2}$-h.p. O.H.V. T.T.: $\tfrac{5}{8}$ inch, or 50°.

Fig. 10.—Method of fitting the Centre Timing Pinion.

This pinion is held on the engine shaft by a key and lock nut. It is advisable to use a ring spanner for turning this nut. Before replacing the pinion make sure that the timing marks on it correspond with those on the cam pinions (see Fig. 8).

SUNBEAM MOTOR-CYCLES

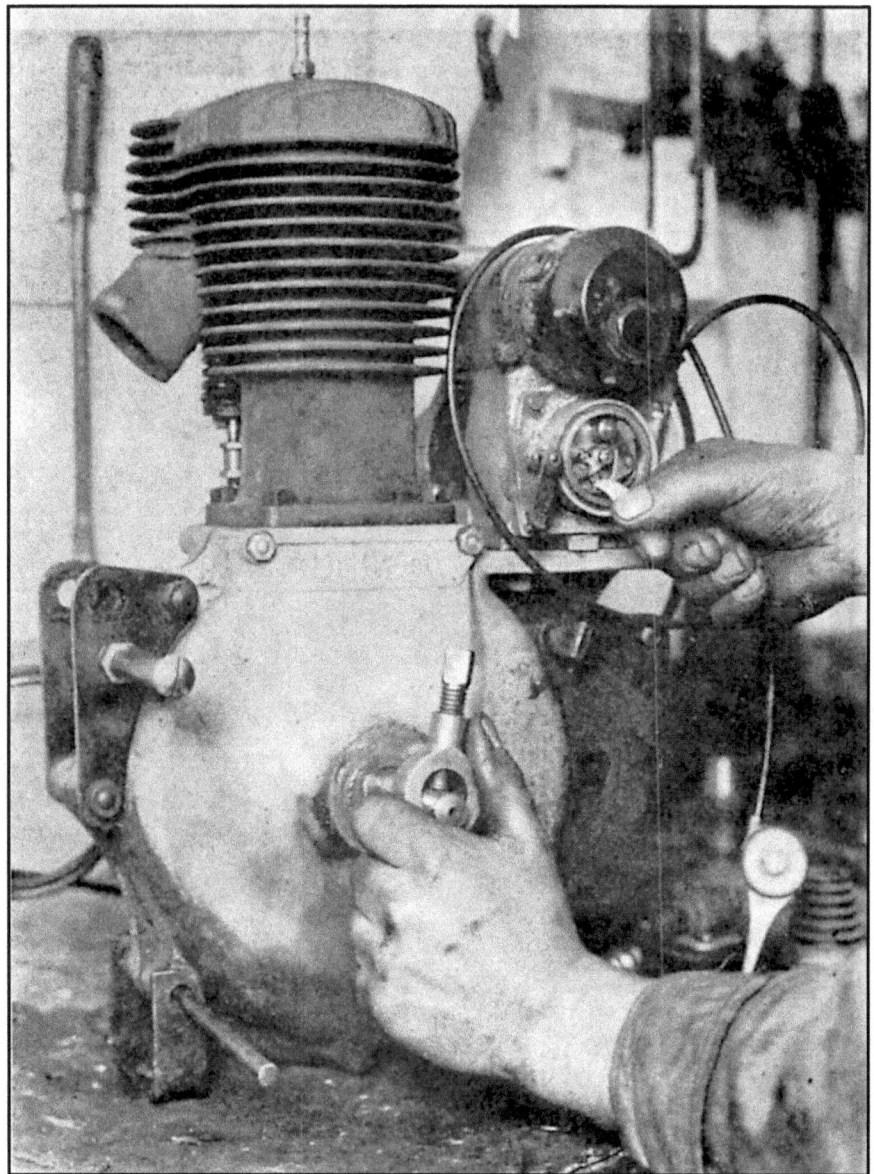

Fig. 11.—Timing the Magneto.

First set the magneto control at full advance. The magneto points should "break" at the following angles before top dead centre:

2¾-h.p. Model 10 . . . 30°	3½-h.p. O.H.V. .	. . 43°
3½-h.p. Longstroke . . . 35°	3½-h.p. O.H.V. T.T. .	. . 50°

If the later model is used for racing with a mixture of 60 per cent. benzol and 40 per cent. petrol, the ignition advance may be increased to ¾ ; or to 1 inch if alcohol fuel and a special piston is used.

A special tool is supplied for the removal of magneto driving pinion. This takes the form of a bolt which is screwed into the pinion after the removal of the lock nut. In the earlier models it is necessary to remove the magneto chain cover, but in later models access to the driving pinion can be obtained through an inspection port in the chaincase cover.

The magneto driving chain is adjusted by sliding the magneto backwards on its platform after slackening the holding-down bolts.

"SUNBEAM" TIMING CHART

1931

MODELS.	INLET.		EXHAUST.		IGNITION MAX. ADV.	Tappet Clearance.	
	Opens before T.D.C.	Closes after B.D.C.	Opens before B.D.C.	Closes after T.D.C.	Before T.D.C.	Inlet.	Exhaust.
Lion . . .	0°	60°	60°	17°	35°	·004″	·006″
No. 10 . .	30°	60°	60°	30°	35°	·002″	·008″
No. 90 . .	30°	60°	60°	30°	44°	·002″	·012″
No. 9 . .	30°	60°	60°	30°	41°	·002″	·012″
1930							
No. 80 . .	30°	60°	60°	30°	45°	·002″	·012″
No. 90 . .	30°	60°	60°	30°	44°	·002″	·012″
Lion . . .	0°	60°	60°	17°	35°	·004″	·006″
No. 9 . .	30°	60°	60°	30°	41°	·002″	·012″
No. 8 . .	30°	60°	60°	30°	43°	·002″	·012″
Nos. 5–6 .	0°	60°	60°	17°	35°	·004″	·006″
Nos. 1–2 .	0°	60°	60°	17°	35°	·004″	·006″
1929							
No. 80 . .	30°	60°	60°	30°	45°	·002″	·012″
No. 8 . .	30°	60°	60°	30°	43°	·002″	·012″
Nos. 5–6 .	0°	60°	60°	17°	35°	·004″	·006″
No. 9 . .	30°	60°	60°	30°	41°	·002″	·012″
No. 90 . .	30°	60°	60°	30°	44°	·002″	·012″
Nos. 1–2 .	0°	60°	60°	17°	35°	·004″	·006″
No. 7 . .	0°	45°	50°	15°	30°	·004″	·006″
1928							
No. 7 . .	0°	45°	50°	15°	30°	·004″	·006″
No. 8 . .	12°	52°	55°	20°	43°	·002″	·012″
No. 9 . .	15°	55°	55°	20°	41°	·002″	·012″
No. 90 . .	30°	60°	60°	30°	44°	·002″	·012″
Nos. 5–6 .	0°	60°	60°	17°	35°	·004″	·006″
Nos. 1–2 .	0°	60°	60°	17°	35°	·004″	·006″
1927							
No. 90 . .	15°	55°	55°	20°	44°	·002″	·012″
Nos. 5–6 .	0°	60°	60°	17°	35°	·004″	·006″
No. 9 . .	15°	55°	55°	20°	41°	·002″	·012″
Nos. 1–2 .	0°	60°	60°	17°	35°	·004″	·006″
No. 80 . .	12°	52°	55°	20°	45°	·002″	·012″

TRIUMPH ENGINES

By J. Earney, M.I.M.T.

THIS chapter deals with points peculiar to Triumph machines, and is supplementary to the details given under the various general headings.

1·74-H.P. MODEL

The " baby " of the Triumph range, the Junior Model X. engine, is a two-stroke type, and is designed in one unit with the gearbox.

Decarbonising

Dismantling the cylinder and piston is a very simple matter, and for this reason decarbonising can be carried out frequently. There is a tendency for piston rings to gum up and stick in the grooves in a two-stroke engine, and this trouble will be eliminated if this minor operation is often carried out. Remove the cylinder by disconnecting the carburetter, plug and other parts and undoing the four base nuts. (NOTE: two long nuts should be fitted on the flywheel side.) Lift the cylinder up and forwards, at the same time withdrawing the piston downwards (Fig. 1). Scrape all carbon from the head and ports. Do not forget the transfer port on the right-hand side of the cylinder and the underside of the piston.

Compression Release Valve

It is not always necessary to remove the release valve when decarbonising, but should this leak when the engine is running, the valve should be ground in. If the large hexagon nut is unscrewed, the complete assembly can then be removed. Extract the split pin and the valve can be taken from the seating. Thoroughly clean the various parts, lightly grind in the valve and reassemble.

Piston Details

The most important point is to see that the piston is fitted the correct way round. The short vertical wall of the piston crown should face the right-hand side of the machine and the long sloping side towards the left-hand side or the exhaust port (Fig. 2). This brings the stops in the ring grooves towards the rear. The gudgeon pin is a push fit in the piston.

Removing Unit from Frame

Remove clutch cover and kick-starter crank, undo clutch mainshaft nut (left-hand thread), and withdraw kick-starter ratchet sleeve and

REPAIRS TO TRIUMPH ENGINES

Fig. 1.—Decarbonising the 1·74-h.p. Triumph.

After disconnecting the carburetter, plug, etc., remove the four cylinder-base nuts, lift the cylinder up and forwards, at the same time drawing the piston downwards as shown above.

REPAIRS TO TRIUMPH ENGINES

fittings. Screw in the plug (provided in tool-kit), and withdraw the clutch as a complete unit. Disconnect the rear driving chain. The clutch-thrust bearing and cam lever can be taken off the shaft (Fig. 3). Undo the engine plates and the crankcase can be taken from the frame.

Flywheel Unit

Remove the cover and unscrew the mainshaft nut (left-hand thread). Screw the special plug (supplied with the tool-kit) into the flywheel and force the latter off the mainshaft. The back plate with the coils, etc., can be withdrawn from the crankcase by removing the two screws.

Ignition Timing

The correct ignition timing is $\frac{9}{64}$ inch advance. Note the engine rotates clockwise, i.e. backwards. If the engine is rotated until the piston is at the top of its stroke and the flywheel refitted with the mark on the rim at one with a similar mark on the back plate, the timing will be correct (Fig. 4).

Fig. 2.—DECARBONISING THE 1·74-H.P. TRIUMPH.
When reassembling see that the piston is fitted the correct way round. The long sloping side should face the exhaust port.

REPAIRS TO TRIUMPH ENGINES

Fig. 3.—Dismantling the Clutch-thrust Bearing.
Examine the thrust washer for wear. It should be renewed if this is serious.

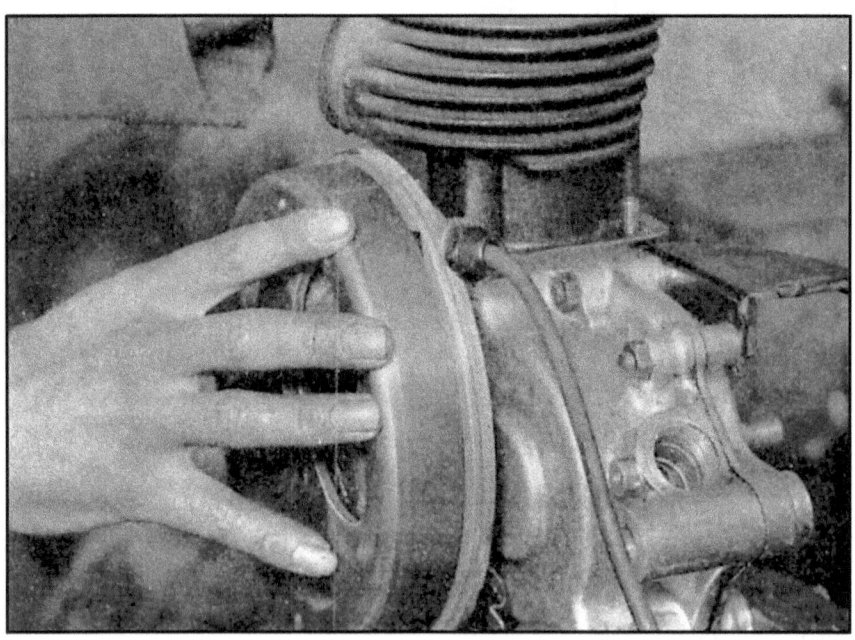

Fig. 4.—Timing the 1·74-h.p. Triumph.
Arrange the engine with the piston on T.D.C. Then refit the flywheel with the mark on the rim corresponding with the mark on the back plate as shown above.

REPAIRS TO TRIUMPH ENGINES

Important !!

The ignition system will not function if the headlamp is disconnected or bulb broken unless the lighting terminal is earthed. The clip supplied in the tool-kit or a length of cable can be used (Fig. 5).

Contact Points

These should be set to ·012 inch when fully open. Always set by a feeler gauge, as this system is very sensitive to this adjustment. It is not necessary to remove the flywheel, as the contact breaker is readily accessible between the spokes of the flywheel after the cover has been removed.

Lubrication

The "Petroil" system of lubrication is employed. Never run on neat petrol. The proportion of half a pint of oil to one gallon of petrol is recommended. This should be thoroughly mixed and shaken up in a can before putting into the tank. Always turn off the petrol if the machine is to be left standing, and if for a fairly long time it is advisable to run the carburetter dry. Rock the machine from side to side before starting again, thus avoiding the possibility of the mixture settling.

Fig. 5.—IF THE HEADLAMP BULB IS BROKEN.

In this case the ignition system will not act unless the lighting terminal is earthed by means of a short length of cable as shown above.

REPAIRS TO TRIUMPH ENGINES

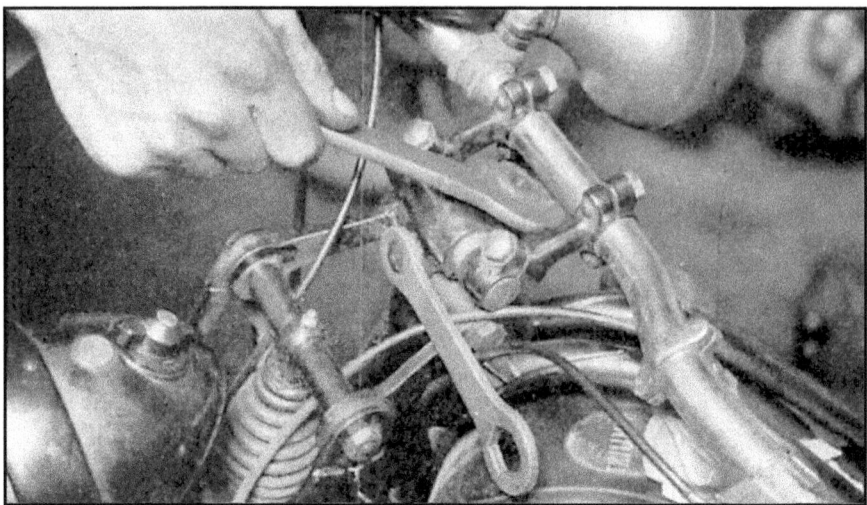

Fig. 6.—Adjusting the Steering Head.

Place the machine on the stand, remove the cap and setscrew on the steering pillar and slacken off the pinch bolt on head clip. Take up endplay by screwing down the slotted lock ring. Do not overdo this so that there is binding, or races will become pitted. Tighten the pinch bolt and refit cap and setscrew.

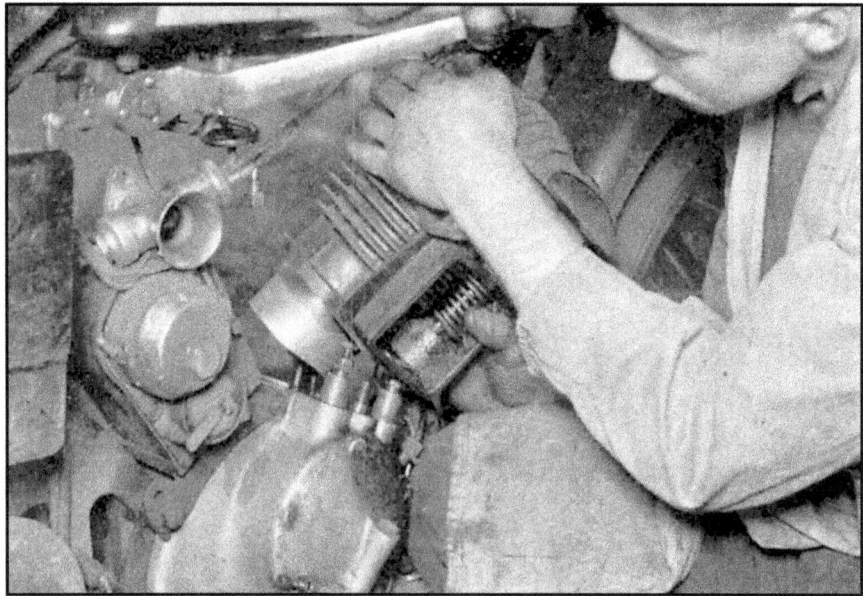

Fig. 7.—Removing the Cylinder on a Triumph N.S.D. Model.

After detaching the carburetter, exhaust pipe, tappet cover, etc., unscrew the base nuts, and lift the cylinder to expose the gudgeon pin. Then lift the cylinder and piston clear of the frame.

REPAIRS TO TRIUMPH ENGINES

Fig. 8.—Timing Gear on N.S.D. Model.

REPAIRS TO TRIUMPH ENGINES

Fig. 9.—Dismantling the Oil Pump (N.S.D. Model).
First loosen the central lock nut and setscrew, remove the three pump-cover screws, and then withdraw the oil pump complete as shown.

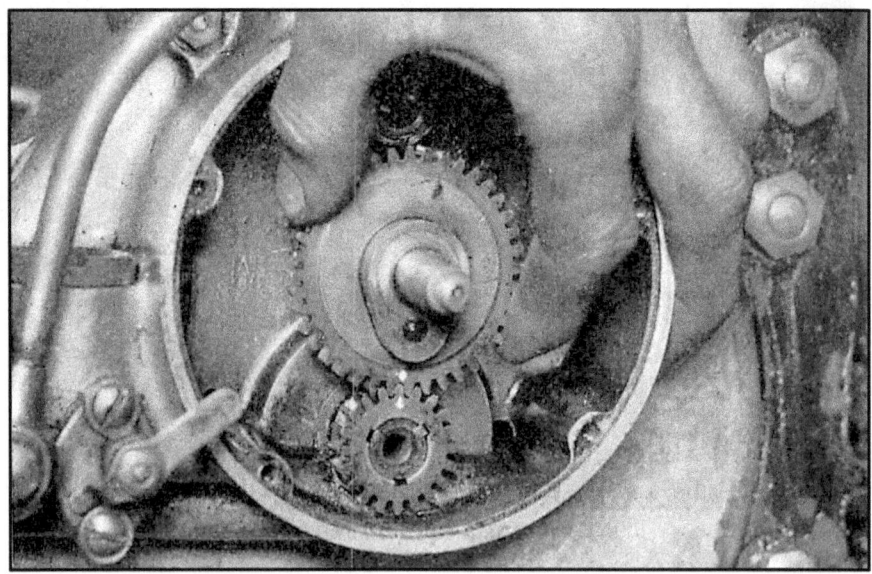

Fig. 10.—Reassembling the Timing Gear (N.S.D. Model).
This picture shows how the timing-gear teeth are marked for correct meshing.

REPAIRS TO TRIUMPH ENGINES

Fig. 11.—Reassembling the N.S.D. "De Luxe" Model.
The piston and rings must first be assembled in the cylinder as shown above.

SIDE-VALVE MODELS

How to remove Cylinder on N.S.D. "De Luxe" Model

After detaching the carburetter, exhaust pipe, tappet cover and sundry fitments, unscrew the three cylinder-base studs and lift the cylinder upwards and forwards as far as possible. Withdraw the piston until the gudgeon pin is exposed, when the latter can be pushed out. The cylinder with the piston inside can then be lifted clear (Fig. 7). On other models the cylinder can be lifted without removing the piston.

Dismantling Timing Gear

Remove screws and pipes, etc., as necessary. Note on the N.S.D. "De Luxe" model the oil-feed nozzle is a left-hand thread. The two magneto sprockets on the N.S.D. N. and Q.A. types should be pulled off with a drawer, and the timing cover lifted off. On C.N. and C.S.D. models the oil indicator and decompressor knob will come away with the cover. Do not lose the ball and spring from the regulator hole. The cam and levers can be extracted (Fig. 8). Note the oil-pump driving worm is screwed on the mainshaft with a left-hand thread. If it is required to remove the oil pump, the central lock nut and setscrew should be loosened, and the three pump-cover screws removed. The oil pump can then be withdrawn complete by applying pressure to the pump spindle in the timing case (Fig. 9). When reassembling, do not forget

REPAIRS TO TRIUMPH ENGINES

the ball and spring in the exhaust rocker. The mainshaft pinions are secured by a lefthand locking nut. Note the pinion has three keyways, each one giving a slightly different position

Fig. 12. — INSERTING THE GUDGEON PIN (N.S.D. MODEL).

The makers supply a tool which simplifies this operation. This is in the form of a slotted tube, which is temporarily inserted when the small end and the gudgeon-pin holes are in line.

of the teeth in relation to the flywheel position. The recommended position is marked on the cam and the

Fig. 13. — INSERTING THE GUDGEON PIN (N.S.D. MODEL).

The gudgeon pin is then pushed into position from the left-hand side of the machine, forcing the tool out on the opposite side. Note the slot in the tool should always face downwards to clear the stud between the tappets when being pushed out.

pinion. The tooth of the pinion so marked should be meshed with the marked space between the two teeth on the cam pinion (Fig. 10).

Big-end Bearings

Roller bearings are fitted to the big-end bearings in all models. The crankpin is riveted to the driving-side flywheel. When fitting a new crankpin, take care it is a tight fit in the flywheel. Thoroughly cleanse the hole, the flange of the pin and flywheel face from oil, press the crankpin home and re-rivet. This repair should only be undertaken by a skilled man, as it will be realised that a tiny error on the crankpin will put the mainshafts out of alignment. It is advisable therefore to trust this work to a good repair shop. The flywheels are drilled in the C.N. and C.S.D. models and a ⅜-inch rod can be used to correct the alignment. An unworn valve stem of this size can be used if a steel rod is not available.

Fig. 14.—Assembling the N.S.D. "De Luxe" Model.
Do not forget to adjust the tappets—using a feeler gauge to give a clearance of ·002 inch.

Notes on Reassembling

A simple check on the alignment of the mainshafts can be carried out when the flywheels are fitted into the crankcase. Hold the crankcase faces together by the hands, and obtain assistance to revolve the flywheels

REPAIRS TO TRIUMPH ENGINES

by the connecting rod. If the mainshafts are out of alignment, the crankcase faces will tend to open and close as the flywheels are rotated. When these are found to be in order, one-half of the case can be lifted off, the faces thoroughly cleaned and painted with gold-size or suitable jointing compound and finally bolted together.

Refitting the Cylinder and Piston

On most models this is a comparatively simple job. Care should be taken to fit the gaps of the piston rings on the opposite sides at the front and back of the piston. Make sure the cams are not lifting and the tappets are down before tightening the cylinder holding-down nuts.

On the N.S.D. "De Luxe" model, it is necessary first to insert the piston with rings into the cylinder (Fig. 11). Then rotate the flywheels until the connecting rod is at the bottom of the stroke, leaning towards the front

Fig. 15.—DETACHING CYLINDER HEAD O.H.V. MODEL T.T.
Use a spanner or screwdriver as shown above to depress the valve end of the rocker so that the push rods can be removed.

REPAIRS TO TRIUMPH ENGINES

of the crankcase. Loop a length of cord over the connecting rod so that this may be manœuvred into position when the piston is being fitted. Although this job can be done single-handed, it is advisable to obtain assistance to hold the cylinder with piston in position against the front down tube. Withdraw the piston from the cylinder until the gudgeon-pin hole is exposed, when with a little patience and " juggling " with the cord the small end can be coaxed to line up with the gudgeon-pin holes in the piston. The pin can then be inserted and the cylinder lowered on to the crankcase. Tighten the holding-down nuts and adjust tappets, and then complete reassembling (Fig. 14).

O.H.V. ENGINE, MODEL " T.T. "

Detaching Cylinder Head

Proceed in the usual way by removing such parts as carburetter and pipes, etc. Then loosen the push-rod tube clips and slide these down. Remove the outer rocker covers, and the rocker and push-rod ends will be exposed, together with the adjusting nuts, etc., for taking up the valve clearance. It is always necessary to dismantle the push-rod tubes this far to adjust the tappets, which, by the way, should be set at ·003 inch when the valves are closed with the engine cold. A lever or a long screwdriver should be brought to bear on the valve end of the rocker, depressing the valve and raising the push-rod end of rocker sufficiently to remove the push rod (Fig. 15), and after the yoke at the bottom has been removed the tube with the push-rod complete can be taken away. The cylinder-head bolts are inserted half-way down the cylinder barrel, upwards, into the cylinder head. Unscrew these six bolts progressively round the cylinder, say half a turn at a time, and the head can be lifted off. The valves are secured by the usual split cotters.

Rockers

These operate on roller bearings, and can be inspected by removing the end-plate screws. Take care the two inside thrust washers are not mislaid.

Timing Gear

This is dismantled in a similar way as to the side-valve models with right-hand magneto drive. The mainshaft pinion, however, is secured by a left-hand screw.

Big-end Bearings

The crankpin has parallel ends, and is nutted to both flywheels. Two rows of rollers (twenty-four in all) are fitted without cages. The remarks regarding alignment refer equally to this model as well as to the side-valve type, i.e. one of the valve stems can be used to put through the holes in the flywheel to check the alignment.

REPAIR NOTES ON VELOCETTE ENGINES

By A. E. Field (*Veloce Ltd.*)

OVERHEAD CAMSHAFT MODELS

Dismantling

IF a complete overhaul is desired the engine must be removed from the frame of the machine, but this is unnecessary when decarbonising. The method of removing the engine is quite obvious and simple, no detailed description being necessary. A simple tool for removing the finned exhaust-pipe nut can be forged from a piece of round bar, as shown in Fig. 3. Such a tool will prevent damage to the fins of the nut. In the absence of such a tool a soft metal punch should be applied at the base of the fins, and a few sharp blows with a hammer will effect the desired result.

This is Most Important—Mark the Parts

It is as well to point out here that all Velocette engines are assembled with the utmost care at the hands of skilled fitters. As they are not mass produced it is desirable to replace each part in its original position. To simplify this work it is therefore desirable to mark such parts as cylinder head bolts, cylinder nuts, vertical shaft couplings, etc., when dismantling, and take note of their positions.

Shock Absorber

The shock absorber should be withdrawn from the engine shaft at this stage. First remove the small $\frac{1}{4}$-inch $\times$ 40T[1] screw securing the locking plate. The large hexagon nut should now be unscrewed in an anticlockwise direction as shown in Fig. 4. The construction of the shock absorber is shown in Fig. 5, from which it will be seen that unscrewing the locking and withdrawal nut will pull the shock absorber complete from the taper of the mainshaft.

How the Cambox is removed

Drain the oil from the bottom bevel gear casing and oil sump by removing the two drain plugs—one underneath the bottom bevel gear casing and the other at the bottom of the crankcase on the timing side. Unscrew the two gland nuts on the vertical shaft cover. Slide the lower nut a little way up the shaft cover and spring the small jump ring out of its groove, sliding this up the shaft cover also. The cover can now be

[1] "T" is an abbreviation for "threads per inch."

VELOCETTE ENGINES

pushed down into the bottom bevel gear housing, thus exposing the top vertical shaft coupling. The four bolts securing the cambox should now be removed, when this can be lifted clear of the cylinder head and placed on one side to receive attention later.

Cylinder Head and Barrel

Remove the sparking plug and unscrew the four cylinder-head bolts, after which the cylinder head with valves can be lifted clear. Remove

An Interesting Oiling System

The oil passes by gravity to the oil-feed pump B. It is forced up the vertical shaft cover D into the top bevel gear casing E. The pressure is controlled by the valve A, and should be from 8 to 12 lb. to the sq. inch. The supply of oil to the big-end bearing, piston and cylinder barrel is controlled by a valve C (see also Fig. 2). Oil is admitted to the cambox by way of two oil grooves, one in the camshaft and one in the large bronze camshaft bearing. Once every revolution of the camshaft, these two oil grooves coincide, forming a continuous oilway (see Fig. 1A). Surplus oil from the cambox is carried away by the oil pipe to the crankcase and oil sump. Oil which collects in two pockets at each end of the cambox is carried by small oil pipes to the inlet valve guide, and to the shock absorber and primary chain. Splash lubrication is used for the big end and cylinder barrel.

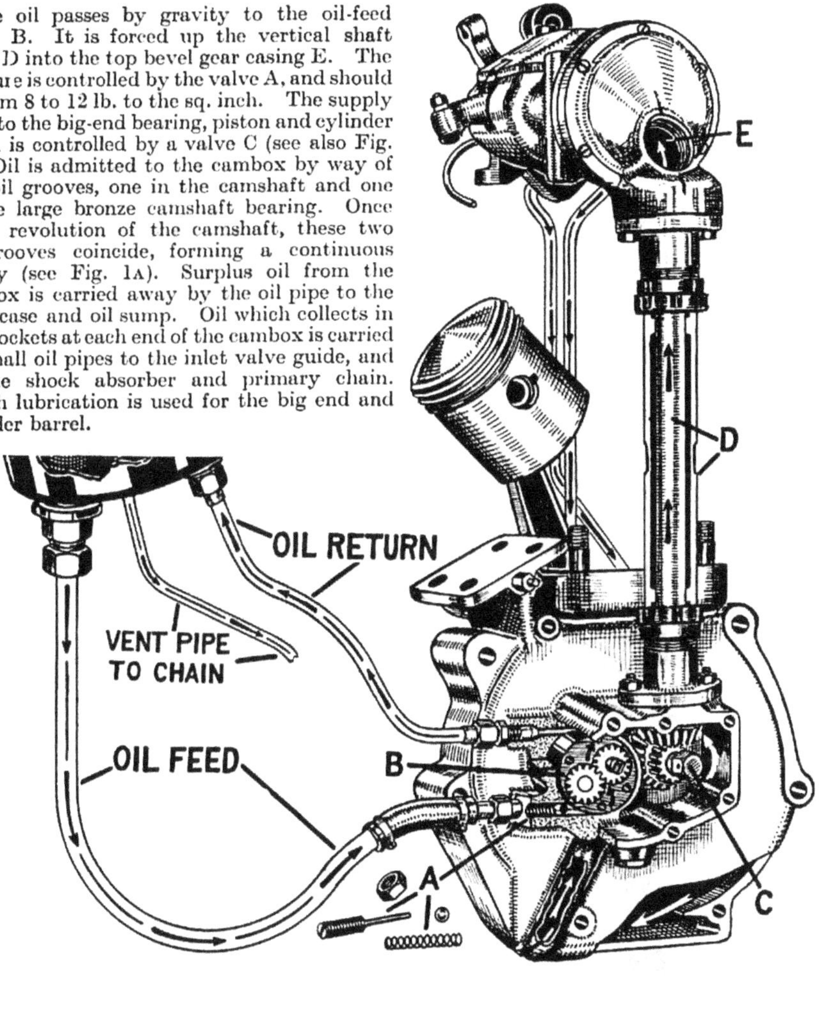

Fig. 1.—Illustration showing the Oiling System of the Overhead Camshaft Four-stroke Engine.

VELOCETTE ENGINES

the vertical shaft with cover and couplings, taking careful note (with the aid of marks) of the top and bottom of the shaft and couplings. After unscrewing the four cylinder holding nuts, the barrel can be lifted from the studs in the crankcase, care being taken to support the piston to prevent it from swinging against the four crankcase studs.

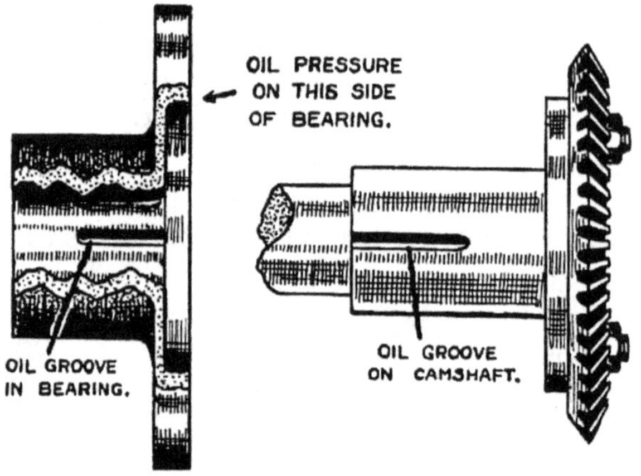

Fig. 1A.—Showing Part of the Camshaft with its Oil Groove, and the Corresponding Oil Groove in the Large Bronze Bearing of the Overhead Camshaft Machine.

When in position the two grooves should overlap ⅛ inch.

Pistons

Before attempting to remove the piston or circlip, it is advisable, when decarbonising, to place a duster over the orifice of the crankcase.

On late models the gudgeon pin is secured in the piston by means of two small spring rings known as circlips. A spoke ground to a sharp point is useful as a circlip remover. A small slot is provided in one piston boss to facilitate this operation. After removing one circlip the gudgeon pin can be pushed out from the opposite side of the piston. In the case of a standard or low-compression piston it is advisable to note on which side of the machine the circlip slot was present, in order that the piston may be replaced the same way round in the cylinder barrel. This is unnecessary with high-compression pistons, as a recess is present on the piston crown to provide clearance for the exhaust valve.

Magneto Chain Cover

The magneto chain cover and chain should now be removed. The front portion of the cover is held by two small screws. Slacken off the

Fig. 2.—Arrangement of the Ball Valve in the Timing-side Crankshaft.
Note the taper seating and oilways in the nut, and the drilled crankshaft.

VELOCETTE ENGINES

nuts securing the chain sprockets. The sprockets can be withdrawn from their taper seatings by supporting them with a spanner and giving the end of their respective spindles a sharp blow with a hammer, as is shown in Fig. 6. This procedure is unnecessary in the case of the dynamo sprocket on the K.T.P. machine, which is fitted with a key and keyway on a plain shaft, and can be withdrawn after removing the nut without the application of force. The rear half of the magneto chaincase can now be removed.

Coil Ignition is fitted on K.T.P. Models

In the case of the K.T.P. machine, which is fitted with coil ignition, the dynamo chaincase is manufactured in one piece with the bottom bevel gear cover. Its removal is effected as follows :

Unscrew the top and bottom inspection covers, and the bolt which is situated just above the lettering on the cover. Having loosened the dynamo drive sprocket, remove the six small screws and one $\frac{5}{16}$-inch screw and washer that secure the cover to the crankcase. It will be necessary to rotate the bottom sprocket in order to obtain access to all the screws through the holes in the sprocket. The cover complete with chain, sprockets and dynamo driving gear can now be withdrawn, taking care to remove the pump driving piece from the dynamo driving gear.

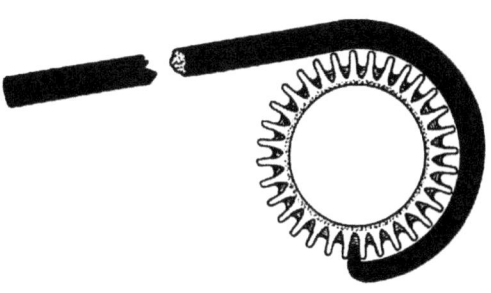

Fig. 3.—A SIMPLE "C" SPANNER FORGED FROM ROUND STEEL ROD FOR REMOVING AND REFITTING FINNED EXHAUST-PIPE NUTS.

On machines with magneto ignition the bottom bevel gear cover should now be removed by unscrewing the small retaining screws. The magneto driving gear and pump driving piece are then free for removal.

Now remove the magneto (or dynamo in the case of the K.T.P.) by unscrewing the four nuts underneath the platform. With the K.T.P. machine it is only necessary to remove the dynamo clip bolt.

Bottom Bevel Gear

It is now necessary to take out the bottom bevel gear with its housing by unscrewing the two retaining nuts and pulling the housing off the studs in the crankcase.

Crankcase Details

The ball valve nut (C in Fig. 1) should now be removed. As it has a left-hand thread it should be unscrewed in a clockwise direction. The

VELOCETTE ENGINES

Fig. 4.—WITHDRAWING THE SHOCK ABSORBER COMPLETE FROM THE CRANKSHAFT OF THE OVERHEAD CAMSHAFT MODEL.

¼-inch steel ball should be taken from the ball valve nut, and the spring and tongued washer from the crankshaft. For withdrawing the half-time gear from the crankshaft a gear puller is useful. If such a tool is not available leverage should be applied to the back of the gear by means of a screwdriver inserted through the bevel gear housing hole in the top of the case. The bevel gear on the crankshaft can now be withdrawn, taking care to remove any shims that may be present behind the gear.

The two halves of the crankcase can now be parted by unscrewing the nuts on one side, and withdrawing the crankcase bolts from the opposite side.

Removing Main Bearings

Remove the disk valve complete from the driving-side crankcase. The driving-side main bearing is removed by inserting two steel pegs in the holes provided, and tapping them lightly with a hammer. The removal of both the

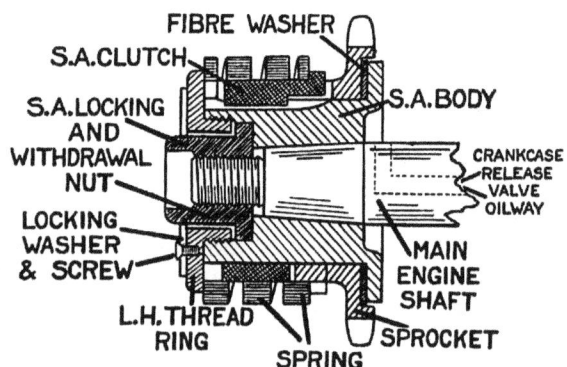

Fig. 5.—SECTIONAL DRAWING OF THE SHOCK ABSORBER OF THE OVERHEAD CAMSHAFT ENGINE.

VELOCETTE ENGINES

driving- and timing-side main bearings can be simplified by warming the crankcase over a gas ring.

Oil Pump

The oil regulator screw should now be unscrewed from the timing-side half crankcase, and the ball and spring withdrawn. To examine the oil pump the four retaining screws must first be removed. As the pump body is necessarily a tight fit in the hole in the crankcase, difficulty may be experienced in withdrawing it. A simple pump-removing tool can be easily made from a flat strip of steel having two ¼-inch clearance holes 1⅜ inches between centres, and two long ¼-inch bolts threaded ¼-inch × 26T for nearly their whole length. Two ¼-inch × 26T nuts

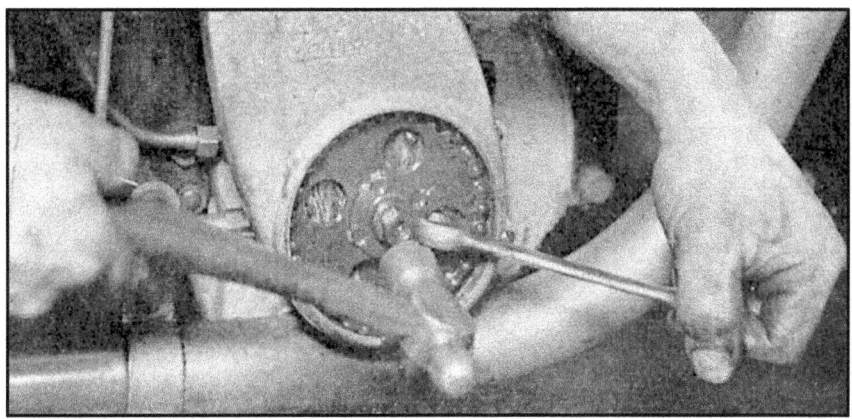

Fig. 6.—Illustration to show the Correct Method of Supporting the Dynamo Drive Sprocket of the K.T.P. Model, with a Spanner, when Withdrawing it from the Taper Spindle of the Driving Gear.

are screwed on to the bolts. Two of the holes in the pump body should be tapped out with a taper ¼-inch × 26T tap for about three threads. The bolts can then be screwed into the holes in the pump body and the strip of steel allowed to rest against the bevel gear casing. By screwing the nuts against the steel strip evenly, each one being turned at the same time, the pump will withdraw without damage. The pump-removing tool fitted to the pump is shown in Fig. 7. Warming the crankcase will assist the removal of the pump.

The timing-side main bearing can be pushed from its housing through the bevel gear casing. Heating the crankcase slightly will simplify removal.

Taking apart Flywheels

We can now give attention to the flywheels. To part these it is first necessary to unscrew the small crankpin nut locking pins. A box

VELOCETTE ENGINES

spanner of the correct size is necessary to slacken the crankpin nuts. The crankpin is securely held in the flywheels by a slight taper, and should be driven out with a rawhide mallet or lead hammer to prevent damage.

At this stage we have the engine entirely dismantled with the exception of the cambox, which will be dealt with later.

It is absolutely essential that all the parts be thoroughly washed with petrol before examination and reassembly.

How to inspect Big-end Bearing for Wear

We will begin by examining the big-end bearing. The track of the crankpin and outer ring in the connecting rod should be ex-

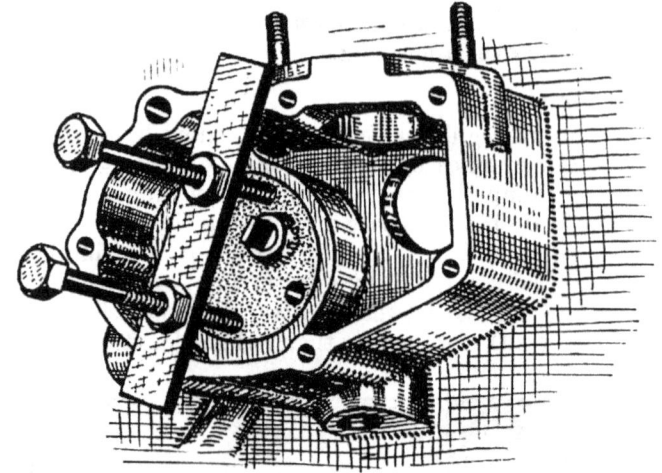

Fig. 7.—A Simple Oil-pump Extractor, made from a Piece of Flat Steel, Two ¼-inch Bolts and Nuts.

Fig. 8.—Method of Truing up the Crankshafts of the Overhead Camshaft Engine with "V" Blocks and a Dial or Clock Indicator.

VELOCETTE ENGINES

amined for pit marks. These can be seen more easily with the aid of a magnifying glass. The rollers should also be subjected to examination. If no pit marks or "flats" are present, and no up-and-down play is apparent in the assembled bearing, then it can safely be refitted. Should the tracks of the crankpin and outer ring be in good condition, but play be apparent in the assembled bearing, it may be found that a new set of rollers will put this right. Rollers of standard size, ·0005-inch and ·001-inch oversize, can be obtained from Messrs. Veloce Ltd. If the tracks of the crankpin or outer ring are pitted, it is advisable to replace the whole bearing. The outer ring is a press fit in the connecting rod.

Checking Small-end Bearing

The fit of the gudgeon pin in the small end of the connecting rod should now be tried. Any wear on the gudgeon pin will be noticeable by the formation of ridges corresponding to the ends of the bush. The small-end bush is a press fit in the con rod. Should a new bush be fitted, the oil hole must be filed in the top to correspond with the oil hole in the connecting rod *after* pressing into position. A small round file will be necessary for this work.

Clear Oilways

Ascertain that the oilways in the timing- and driving-side crankshafts are clean and free from obstruction. The latter, in conjunction with the boss cast on the driving side of the crankcase, form the crankcase release valve, which is in the form of a "timed port."

Fig. 9.—SUPPORTING THE CYLINDER BARREL WHILE INSERTING THE PISTON OF THE OVERHEAD CAMSHAFT MACHINE.

Assembling Big-end Bearing

The crankpin can now be fitted to one flywheel and secured by the crankpin nut. Support the flywheel on the bench with the crankpin

VELOCETTE ENGINES

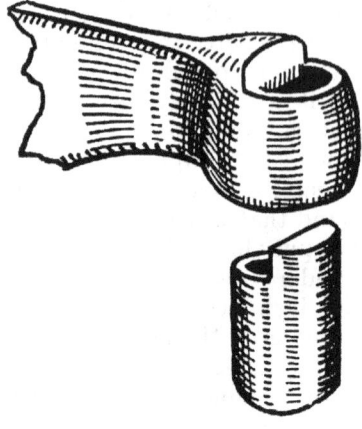

Fig. 10.—ROCKER END, SHOWING DETACHABLE CAM FOLLOWER OR SKID.

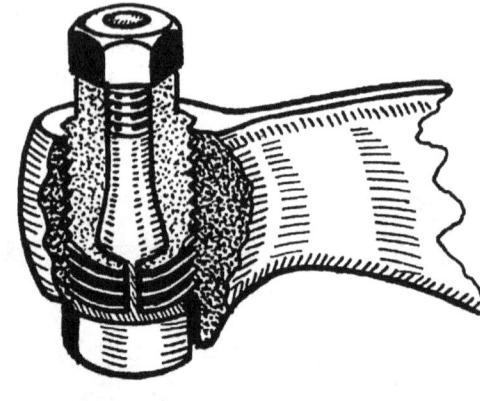

Fig. 11.—SECTIONAL VIEW OF THE ROCKER END, SHOWING THE ARRANGEMENT OF THE TAPPET IN THE SPLIT ADJUSTING SLEEVE.

projecting upwards. By exercising care the rollers can be placed in position without the aid of grease. The con rod with outer ring fitted can now be placed over the rollers. At this stage a small quantity of clean oil (of the same grade as that to be used) should be poured over the bearing; but be sure to remove all traces of oil from the taper of the crankpin and the taper hole in the flywheel. The other flywheel can now be placed in position, and the crankpin nut fitted and tightened securely. Any undue force used in tightening the crankpin nuts may result in the flange of the crankpin being crushed, causing the rollers to be pinched endways. This will, of course, cause exceedingly rapid wear of the bearing.

Aligning Flywheels

The timing- and driving-side main bearings that are to be used should now be placed on their respective crankshafts, and the assembly placed on "V" blocks. A dial or clock indicator is allowed to rest on the timing-side crankshaft at the place where the bevel gear is

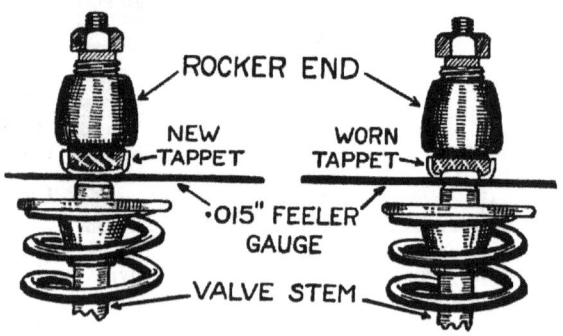

Fig. 11A.—DIAGRAMMATIC VIEW OF TWO ROCKER ENDS WITH TAPPETS.

This diagram shows clearly the care that should be exercised in inserting the feeler gauge between the valve stem and a badly worn tappet.

VELOCETTE ENGINES

fitted. The flywheels are now revolved by means of the connecting rod, as shown in Fig. 8. The point at which the shaft is "high" should be noted and the assembly removed from the "V" blocks. The rim of the flywheel should be jarred with a rawhide mallet or lead hammer at a place corresponding to the position where the shaft was "high." The driving side should now be checked in the same manner, and the operation repeated alternatively on the timing side and driving side until the shafts run dead true. If the shafts are out of truth, it is more important to get the timing-side shaft to run true than the driving side. An error of ·002 to ·003 inch will cause incorrect mesh of the bottom bevel gears. Do not forget to refit the two crankpin nut locking screws.

Fig. 12.—Illustration showing the Piston at Top Dead Centre, with the Slot in the Vertical Shaft in Line with the Crankshaft, for timing the Valves of the Overhead Camshaft Engine.

A Cause of Oil Flooding

Thoroughly clean the oilways in the timing-side half crankcase. Examine the timing-side main bearing, and if upon revolving it is found to be "rough" or the centre portion shows a considerable amount of play, it is advisable to renew it. Do not forget to refit the shim behind

VELOCETTE ENGINES

the bearing to prevent oil from flooding the crankcase. The bearing is a tight press fit in the housing, and the fitting of this is simplified by warming the crankcase.

Oil-pump Gears

The oil pump, which is of the gear type, should now be examined. The teeth should mesh nicely, and their sides should be flush with the ends of the pump body. The narrow gears constitute the delivery pump, and the wide gears the return pump. If an excessive amount of foreign matter has been allowed to pass through the oil pump with the oil, the gears and body will possibly be damaged. In this case the pump complete should be returned to Messrs. Veloce Ltd. for attention.

Reseating Oil-regulating Ball Valve

After assembling the pump, insert the brass shim in the pump hole. The pump itself with cover can now be pressed into position and the retaining screws replaced. The regulating ball valve should now receive attention. If there is doubt as to the efficiency of the seating of the ball, a new seating can be easily made by placing the ball in position, and with the aid of a punch and hammer lightly tapping the ball against the seat. A *new* $\frac{1}{4}$-inch steel ball (ordinary $\frac{1}{4}$-inch ball bearing) should then be placed in position and the spring and regulating screw inserted. Care should be taken to ensure that the ball is on its seating and the spring pressing against it. The lock nut should be left loose for adjustment of the oil supply when the engine is running. Should the springs of the two ball valves become mixed, the stronger spring is for the regulating screw, while the weaker spring is for the crankshaft ball valve.

Fitting Flywheels into Crankcase

The driving-side main bearing should now receive the same attention as the timing-side bearing. In this case no oil-retaining shim is necessary, but after a trial it may be necessary to remove the bearing to fit packing shims to take up endplay on the crankshaft. Upon fitting the flywheel assembly to the two halves of the crankcase and bolting up the latter, test the crankshaft for endplay. It is not desirable to have more than ·0015 inch, as more will interfere with the mesh of the bevel gears. Packing shims to take up endplay can be obtained from the makers, having thickness of ·003 and ·005 inch. These must be inserted between the driving-side main bearing and the crankcase. When fitting packing shims care must be exercised to see that the flywheels are *not binding, due to the entire absence* of endplay on the crankshaft.

Disk Valve

The disk valve should now receive attention. This should be airtight when blown through in one direction, and give a clear passage

VELOCETTE ENGINES

when blown through in the opposite direction. If it is not airtight in one direction oil will be prevented from draining from the cambox due to blowback from the crankcase. This will cause serious oil leaks from the cambox. When refitting in the crankcase, do not omit the small fibre washer.

The drain plugs should now be refitted to the timing-side half of the crankcase.

Refitting Bottom Bevel Gears

All is now ready for the fitting of the bottom bevel gears. If any shims were removed from the crankshaft behind the bevel gear, these should be refitted. The bevel gear can now be placed in position on the shaft, taking care to engage the key with the keyway. The half-time gear is then pushed on to the shaft as far as it will go, followed by the tongued washer of the ball valve shown in Fig. 2. The ball-valve spring should then be inserted in the crankshaft. If in doubt as to the efficiency of the seating in the ball-valve nut, this should be treated in the same manner as the oil-adjusting ball valve. A little grease applied to the ball will assist in holding it to its seating while the nut is placed in position. Take care not to dislodge the ball or buckle the spring during this operation. The nut should now be screwed up tightly in an *anticlockwise* direction. The bottom vertical shaft bevel gear and housing should now be examined. The gear should be quite free to revolve, but no up-and-down play should be present. If play is present, the gear should be carefully supported at the teeth end, while the sleeve should be pressed down the shaft of the gear from the top. Should it be necessary to fit a new housing, the gear can be pressed out of the small sleeve which secures it in the housing, when it can be readily removed.

Very Accurate fitting Required

To ensure quiet running the bevel gears must be carefully meshed until there is only about ·0005 to ·001 inch play between the teeth. If the teeth are too tight in mesh the gears will whine. This very fine adjustment is obtained by fitting very thin paper packings (obtainable from the makers) between the gear housing and the crankcase. It is important that the teeth of one gear should mesh for their entire length with the teeth of the opposing gear. As a guide, the ends of the teeth on one gear should be level with the ends of the teeth on the opposite gear. It is advisable to try the housing in position, tightened down with the nuts, with one packing only, at first. If the teeth are too deep in mesh they are noisy when the crankshaft is revolved quickly by means of the connecting rod. In this case more thin paper packings must be inserted between the housing and the crankcase. Should more than three paper packings be required, it is advisable to remove the (or a) packing shim from behind the bevel gear on the crankshaft. This

VELOCETTE ENGINES

increases the clearance between the teeth and allows the number of paper packings to be reduced. On the other hand, if too much clearance is present between the teeth, the insertion of an extra shim behind the gear on the crankshaft will decrease the clearance. From this it will be seen that with the use of packing shims behind the gear on the crankshaft, and very thin paper packings beneath the bevel gear housing, the gears can be very finely meshed. Packing shims of ·005 and ·0085 inch thickness are obtainable from Messrs. Veloce Ltd. for use behind the crankshaft bevel gear.

Details before fitting Cover

Having meshed the bottom gears the crankcase can be laid on its side with the bevel gear casing upwards. The pump driving piece should now be fitted to the projection on the oil-pump spindle. The magneto driving gear should be a good fit in the bush in the bottom bevel gear cover. Undue play in this bearing will result in oil leakage from the magneto chaincase.

Fig. 13.—ILLUSTRATION SHOWING THE TOP COUPLING IN POSITION IN THE VERTICAL SHAFT, AND THE SLOT IN THE BEVEL GEAR OF THE CAMBOX IN LINE WITH THE TWO STUDS OF THE BEVEL GEAR HOUSING, FOR TIMING THE VALVES OF THE OVERHEAD CAMSHAFT ENGINE.

VELOCETTE ENGINES

Should a new bush be necessary, it should be pressed into the cover, and if a reamer is not available the spindle of the gear should be carefully lapped into the bush with very fine grinding compound. Care should be taken to see that all traces of grinding paste are removed with clean petrol. A good quantity of oil should now be poured into the bevel gear casing, and the paper washer, and cover with gear, placed in position. Be sure to engage the gear with the oil-pump driving piece. The use of a good jointing compound, such as gold-size, in addition to the paper washer, will ensure an oiltight joint. The screws holding the cover should be tightened down evenly.

Refitting Magneto—A Note on the Driving Chain

The magneto should now be fitted and secured tightly to the platform with the four nuts. Before fitting the cylinder barrel it is advisable to try the adjustment of the magneto chain (although the timing of the magneto should be left until later), as it is easier to get at the magneto holding nuts before the cylinder barrel is fitted. Should the chain be slack when placed in position, packings of thin metal or paper should be placed between the magneto and the platform. The chain should *not* be adjusted too tightly, as owing to the expansion of the crankcase, due to heat transmitted from the cylinder when the engine is running, the chain tightens.

Mounting the Dynamo on K.T.P. Machines

In the case of the K.T.P. machine, the dynamo having been placed in position, the chain should be inserted in the chain cover. The sprockets can then be inserted in the large inspection hole, and engaged with the chain. The dynamo driving gear should be fitted and located in the bore of the large sprocket. A screwdriver or bar should be inserted in the top inspection hole and threaded through the bore of the small sprocket to hold it in place till it is started on the armature spindle. The case, complete with chain and sprockets, can then be placed in position, care being taken to ensure that the dynamo driving gear engages with the oil-pump driving piece. To adjust the dynamo chain unscrew the bolt of the dynamo clip, and by rotating the dynamo the chain can be slackened or tightened as desired, the armature spindle being eccentric to the dynamo case. The chain is in correct alignment when the dynamo bears hard against the back of the chain cover.

Refitting Piston Assembly

A new paper cylinder base washer should now be placed in position on the crankcase.

The piston should now receive attention. Should new piston rings be necessary, the ends should be checked, and if necessary carefully

VELOCETTE ENGINES

filed until a gap of ·010 inch for the top ring and ·008 inch for the second and scraper ring is obtained when the rings are inserted in the cylinder barrel. When the rings have been fitted in their correct grooves the piston can be placed in position on the connecting rod. Ascertain that the circlip removal slot is on the same side of the machine as it was when taking down. In the case of pistons for use with alcohol fuels, a recess is present in the piston crown. This should be at the *front* of the piston to provide clearance for the exhaust valve. The gudgeon pin and circlip should now be fitted, taking care to see that the circlip is pushed right into its groove in the piston boss. It is desirable to have the gudgeon pin a tight fit in a new piston, as when the engine is running, the piston expands more, due to heat, than does the steel gudgeon pin. With a new piston the gudgeon pin can be more easily fitted or removed after warming the piston.

The piston and rings should be smeared with clean oil, and the ring gaps spaced equidistant around the piston.

Fig. 14.—THE CAMBOX IN POSITION, WITH THE CHISEL MARK ON THE CAMSHAFT IN LINE WITH THE TWO CHISEL MARKS ON THE BEVEL GEAR HOUSING, AND THE COUPLING SLOT IN THE VERTICAL SHAFT IN LINE WITH THE CRANKSHAFT.

VELOCETTE ENGINES

Fig. 14A.—Adjusting the Points of the Contact Breaker of the K.T.P. Model.
The coil and condenser of the coil ignition system can be seen on the underside of the tank.

VELOCETTE ENGINES

Cylinder Barrel

The cylinder barrel should be supported in one hand, and the piston guided into the barrel with the other hand, as shown in Fig. 9. When in position on the crankcase studs, tighten up the cylinder base nuts evenly, each one a little at a time.

And Head

The cylinder head, having been cleaned and the valves ground in, can now be fitted. Should the joint show signs of leaking it should be ground on to the cylinder barrel before the latter is fitted to the crankcase. The joint is actually on the narrow face, and there should be a suspicion of clearance on the broad face to enable the head to be pulled down tightly at the joint. This slight clearance can be obtained by grinding the narrow face with fine grinding compound, and at the same time using coarse grinding compound for the broad face.

The cylinder-head bolts should be tightened so that each one exerts equal pressure. They should be screwed up, each one a little at a time when nearly home.

Camshaft Box on Late Type

Having reached this stage we can now give attention to the cambox. Take out the screws securing the small-end cover, when this will be free for removal. Unscrew the nut on the end of the camshaft. To prevent the camshaft revolving during this operation, it should be held by inserting the end of a spanner in the coupling slot of the bevel gear. The top cover should now be taken off and the rockers removed. The latter is effected on late machines by unscrewing the hexagon caps on the ends of the rocker pins, when the pins with end caps can be withdrawn, leaving the rockers ready for lifting out of the cambox.

Early Models

On early machines the fixing bolt in the centre of the rocker pin should be unscrewed with a screwdriver, and the rocker pin prised out by inserting the screwdriver between the flange at its end and the bronze rocker-pin bush. The bevel gear housing with bush should now be removed, and the seven screws holding the bevel gear casing taken out. The bevel casing can then be removed, after which the camshaft with large bronze bearing and large bevel gear can be pushed out of the cambox from the ballrace end. A shim ·010 inch thick is fitted between the ballrace and the shoulder on the camshaft, and this should be removed to prevent it being lost. By unscrewing the brass-retaining ring the ballrace can be removed for inspection. Remove any shims that may be present behind the ballrace to prevent their being lost.

VELOCETTE ENGINES

Removing Cams

Carefully clean all the parts, when they are ready for inspection. Should the cams (which are in one piece) show signs of excessive wear, they should be replaced. To remove the cam a good hand press is necessary. Should this not be available it is advisable to return the camshaft to the makers, as to attempt to remove the cam without proper tools will possibly cause damage to the camshaft. To replace the large bronze bearing it is also necessary to remove the cam. If, due to wear, this bearing shows considerable play, it is advisable to replace it, as a badly worn bearing will cause excessive oil leakage from the cambox.

Rebushing Rockers

The bushes are pressed into the rockers, and if new ones are fitted do not omit to drill the oil holes *after* they are in position in the rockers. The cam followers or skids are detachable from the rockers, and can be removed with the aid of a suitable punch and a few sharp blows with a hammer. If new skids are fitted, they must be square with the axis of the rockers. If returned to the makers, they can be ground when in position for a small charge. The rocker end and detachable skid are shown in Fig. 10.

Removing Tappets

The tappet is secured in the rocker by the effect of its tapered shank expanding the split adjusting sleeve in the threads of the rocker end. A partly sectioned rocker and sleeve with the tappet fitted is shown in Fig. 11. Before the tappet can be removed or adjusted it is necessary to slacken the lock nut and force the tappet down off its taper seating by giving the stem a sharp blow with a light hammer. The sleeve can then be unscrewed from the rocker. Should the tappet be badly worn, where it has been in contact with the valve stem, it should be replaced (see Fig. 11A).

It should be noted, before replacing the camshaft in the cambox, that the stud holes in the large bevel gear are elongated. This allows the gear to be rotated slightly to obtain an accurate setting of the valve timing.

Important to make Good Joints

It is important that a good joint be made between the large bronze bearing and the cambox and bevel gear housing. If necessary the bearing should be ground on to the face of the bevel gear housing with fine grinding paste. It is also advantageous to use liquid jointing compound such as goldsize at this joint. To prevent oil leakage it is also advisable to fit new felt strips to the top cover and felt washers to the rocker pins.

Reassembling Cambox

The cambox is now ready for assembly. The ball bearing should be placed in position, not forgetting to replace any shims that may have

VELOCETTE ENGINES

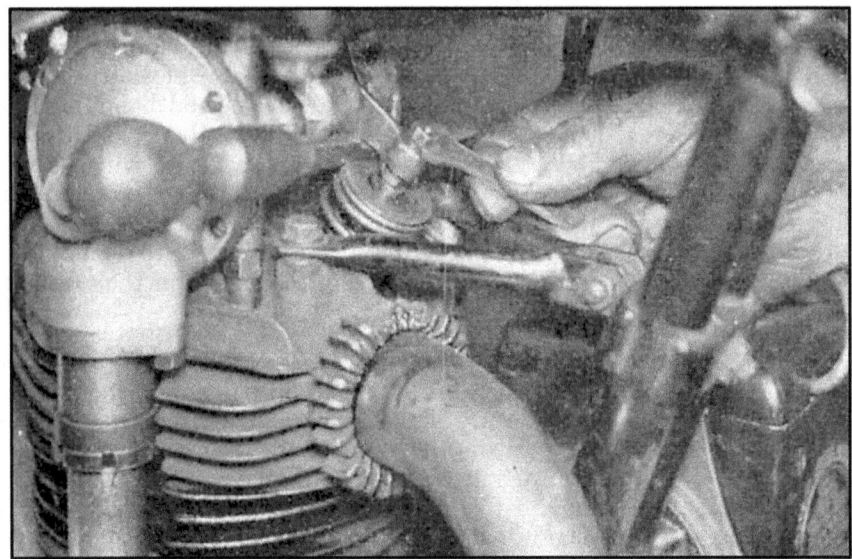

Fig. 15.—METHOD OF ADJUSTING THE TAPPETS ON THE OVERHEAD CAMSHAFT MODEL.
Note the screwdriver inserted between the rocker and the valve-spring top washer, to provide clearance.

been present behind it. The retaining ring should then be screwed up tightly. After replacing the ·010-inch shim on the camshaft, this, complete with bearing and gear, can be placed in position. Apply liquid jointing compound to the face of the bevel gear casing and tighten this against the bronze bearing by means of the seven small screws.

Meshing Bevel Gears

A small space should exist between the cambox housing and the bevel gear housing when the screws have been tightened. This ensures that the bearing is clamped securely between the two aluminium parts. The top vertical shaft bevel gear and housing should now receive the same attention as those at the bottom of the vertical shaft. They can then be fitted to the cambox housing. The same process of meshing the gears must be carried out with the cambox as with the crankcase. The same thin paper washers are used, and shims can be fitted behind the ballrace. Shims ·003 inch, ·005 inch and ·010 inch thick can be obtained for this purpose from Messrs. Veloce Ltd. Having meshed the bevel gears, the rockers can be replaced in the cambox and the rocker pins fitted and secured. The nut on the end of the camshaft should be quite tight. If a new paper end cover washer is to be used, see that it does not cover the oil holes in the end of the cambox and the cover. Liquid

VELOCETTE ENGINES

jointing compound should also be used for this joint. Having refitted the end cover, a small quantity of clean oil should be poured over the cams and rocker bearings, after which the top cover can be refitted.

Fitting Vertical Shaft

The vertical shaft should be cleaned, oiled and replaced in the shaft cover. Should the couplings be a slack fit in their respective slots they

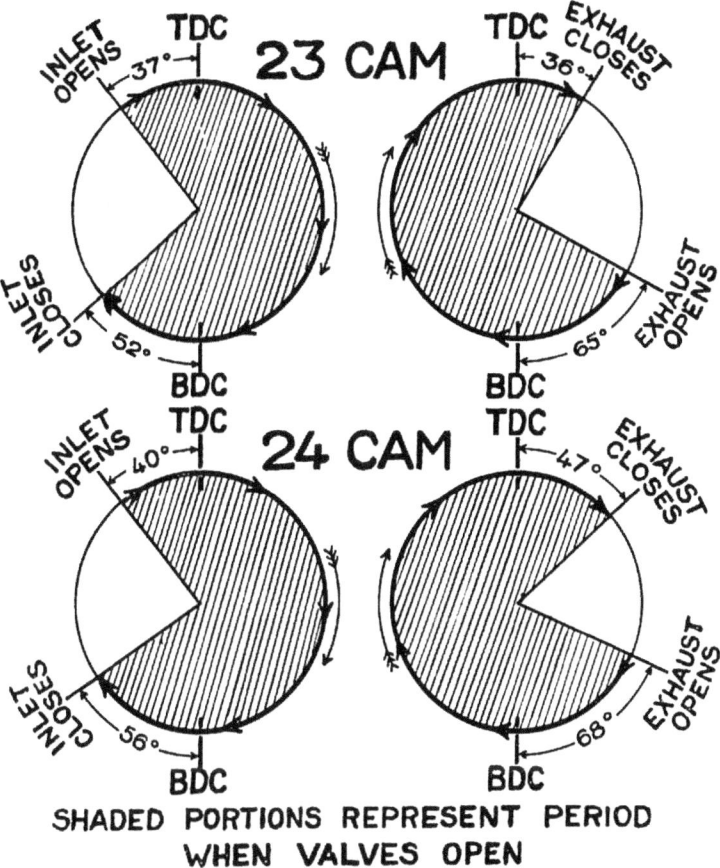

Fig. 16.—Timing Diagram for the O.H.C. Machine, showing Correct Timing for the No. 23 (Standard) and No. 24 (Racing) Cams.

Measurements taken with ·012-inch tappet clearances on both inlet and exhaust valves.

should be replaced, as if loose they will cause the engine to be noisy. If the slots are worn, oversize couplings should be obtained from the makers, and they should be filed with a smooth file until they are a

VELOCETTE ENGINES

tight push fit in the slots. If the slots of the shaft or gears are worn they can be reground by the makers. The gland nuts should be fitted to the shaft cover and packed with asbestos string. This is best done by wrapping three turns of $\frac{1}{8}$-inch asbestos string around the cover for each nut, and, with the aid of a screwdriver, push the string into the nuts. It only remains to slide the jump ring on to the vertical shaft cover, when the engine is ready for timing the valves and final assembly.

A Useful Note

It will be found that, by revolving the crankshaft, the slot for the coupling in the bottom bevel gear changes its position each time the piston is brought to top dead centre. By revolving the crankshaft twenty-two times the same position can be arrived at. This is due to an odd number of teeth being employed on one gear and an even number on the other gear. This allows any wear, due to lifting the valves, to be distributed over all the teeth.

The crankshaft should be revolved until the piston is *exactly* at top dead centre, and the coupling slot in the gear *exactly* in line with the two studs which locate the bevel gear housing. The bottom coupling and the vertical shaft and cover can now be placed in position. The slot in the top of the vertical shaft will then be in line with the crankshaft, and the piston at top dead centre, as shown in Fig. 12.

Timing the Valves

The cambox must now be set. Upon looking through the inspection plug hole and revolving the camshaft, a chisel mark will be seen near the centre of the gear. Two other chisel marks are present on the outside of the bevel gear casing, one above and one below the inspection hole. The camshaft should now be turned until the chisel mark is *exactly* in line with the chisel marks on the outside of the casing, and at the same time the slot in the gear is in line with the two studs that locate the bevel gear housing. The correct position of the slot is clearly shown in Fig. 13. The top coupling is now fitted in the slot of the vertical shaft, and the cambox can be placed into position. At this stage the piston should be at top dead centre, the slot in the top of the vertical shaft in line with the crankshaft and the three chisel marks exactly in line, as is shown in Fig. 14. If this work has been carried out accurately the valves are correctly timed, and the cambox can be secured by inserting the four bolts and tightening them evenly.

The vertical shaft cover should now be lifted and the jump ring pushed into its groove. The cover should then be pushed down till the ring rests on the bottom bevel gear housing. The gland nuts should now be tightened up. The engine should now be laid on its side and clean oil poured into the top bevel gear casing, after which the inspection plug can be replaced.

VELOCETTE ENGINES

Timing the Magneto

It is now necessary to retime the magneto. Fit the rear half of the magneto chain cover and place the chain and sprockets in position. Tighten the nut on the armature spindle of the magneto, thus securing the top sprocket. The engine should now be turned until the piston is $\frac{7}{16}$ inch before top dead centre with both valves closed. The magneto spindle is now turned till the contact-breaker points are just breaking with the contact breaker cam in the fully advanced position. The bottom sprocket should now be locked into position and the front half of the cover fitted.

Or Contact Breaker for Coil Ignition

In the case of the KTP, which is fitted with coil ignition, the contact breaker is fitted on the end cover of the cambox (see Fig. 14A). Its removal can be effected by screwing a $\frac{3}{8}$-inch × 26T bolt into the cam. The effect of the bolt bearing against the end of the camshaft is to withdraw the cam from the taper.

When More Advance is Allowed

Slightly more ignition advance is allowed with coil ignition. The cam should be secured to the camshaft, so that the points of the contact breaker are just breaking with the piston at $\frac{5}{8}$ inch before top dead centre, and the contact breaker-control in the fully advanced position.

Dismantling Shock Absorber

The shock absorber can now receive attention. By referring to Fig. 5 its construction can be clearly seen.

To dismantle the shock absorber it is only necessary to unscrew the left-hand ring. This is actually a circular nut having a left-hand thread, so that to unscrew, it must be turned in a clockwise direction. The spring can now be removed, and the shock absorber clutch withdrawn from the splines of the shock-absorber body. The sprocket and fibre washer can now be lifted off the body. Should the teeth of the sprocket show considerable wear, it is advisable to obtain and fit a new sprocket. The splines of the shock absorber body and clutch should also be subjected to examination. After a considerable period of service, it is advisable to replace the spring.

Reassembling

The parts having been thoroughly cleaned and lubricated can be reassembled in the following manner:

The fibre washer is placed in position on the body and the sprocket fitted. The clutch is now fitted to the splines of the body and the spring replaced, so that the projection at the one end of the spring engages

VELOCETTE ENGINES

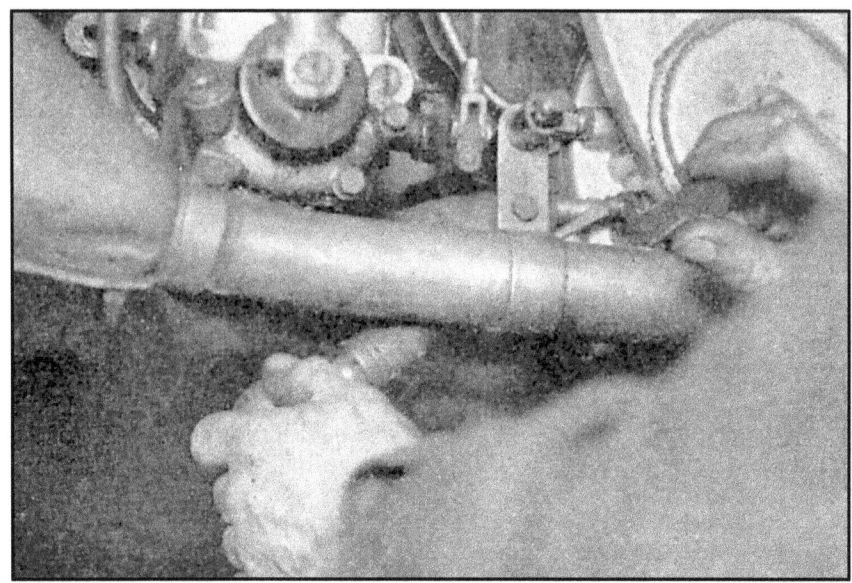

Fig. 17.—Turning the Oil-adjusting Screw of the Overhead Camshaft Engine with a Screwdriver, while holding the Lock Nut with a Spanner.

with one of the projections on the outside of the clutch. The locking (and withdrawal) nut is now placed in its recess in the body, and the left-hand thread ring engaged with the thread in the recess of the body and screwed up tight in an anticlockwise direction. No difficulty is experienced in starting the thread of the left-hand thread ring, as it is not necessary to compress the spring.

Fitting to Engine Shaft

The shock absorber is now ready for fitting to the engine. See that the taper hole of the body and also the taper of the crankshaft are quite clean. Now place the shock absorber complete in position and screw up the lock nut in a clockwise direction. It is extremely important that this nut be *screwed up tightly*, and the spanner should be jarred with a hammer for final tightening. The locking plate should now be replaced, and the $\frac{1}{8}$-inch × 40T screw tightened up.

Tappet Adjustment

The tappet clearances should now be set. For touring purposes the recommended clearances are ·015 inch exhaust and ·012 inch inlet. The clearances should on no account be reduced below those given above. It should also be remembered that an error of ·002 to ·003 inch will affect the valve timing to the extent of about 10 degrees on flywheel

VELOCETTE ENGINES

movement. To adjust the tappets a screwdriver should be inserted between the rocker and the valve spring top washer, as shown in Fig. 15. The lock nut should now be unscrewed two or three turns, when a sharp blow on the top of the tappet stem will release it from its taper seating in the adjusting sleeve. The sleeve can now be turned in the desired direction, and allowance should be made for the effect of tightening the lock nut, which draws the tappet into the sleeve, expanding the latter against the threads in the rocker end. It is advisable to again check the tappet clearances after the engine has been run for a short time, as with use the tappet is driven very slightly into the sleeve.

Checking Valve Timing

The timing can now be checked if desired. The engine should be turned to top dead centre with both valves open, and a piece of spoke or rod inserted in the plug hole and allowed to rest on the piston top. A mark corresponding to top dead centre should be made on the rod against some fixed point, such as the bottom of the cambox end cover. The crankshaft should now be revolved slowly backwards until play can be just felt on the inlet tappet. At this stage another mark should be made on the rod corresponding with the same fixed point on the engine. The crankshaft is now revolved forwards, taking the piston over top dead centre until play can be felt on the exhaust tappet, when a third mark should be made on the rod. If the engine is timed correctly, the distance on the rod between the mark made when play was apparent on the inlet tappet and the top dead centre mark, should be approximately the same as the distance between the mark made when play was just apparent on the exhaust tappet at top dead centre mark. This is known as " sharing the overlap of the cam." It will be seen, then, that the inlet valve should open approximately the same distance before top dead centre as the exhaust valve closes after top dead centre.

NOTES ON TUNING THE O.H.C. ENGINE

Valve Timing

For racing and competition purposes it is advisable to time the engine by the degree method. A circular disk marked off in degrees should be placed on the engine shaft and a pointer (made from a piece of wire) fixed underneath one of the cylinder base nuts with its free end resting near the edge of the disk. The correct timing for both the No. 23 (standard) cam and No. 24 (racing) cam is given in degrees in the timing diagram Fig. 16. The measurements are taken with a tappet clearance of ·012 inch on both valves, and it is extremely important to remove the exhaust rocker while the inlet valve is being tested, and the inlet rocker when attention is given to the exhaust valve. This procedure enables the position at which a valve opens or closes to be exactly ascer-

VELOCETTE ENGINES

tained. When using the degree method of timing, all "backlash" or play in the camshaft drive should be taken up, otherwise it will not be possible to obtain the figures given in the timing diagram. It must also be remembered that a worn cam cannot give correct timing. The skids in the rockers must also be correct and square with the axis of the rockers. For racing purposes it is advisable to return the rockers to the makers in order that the skids can be ground true.

Cams

Two cams are supplied by the makers—the 23 cam, such as is fitted to machines for standard use, and the 24 cam for racing purposes, and which is a standard fitment to the KSS and KTT. Very little advantage is obtained when using the 24 cam in conjunction with a silencer, as it is designed for use with a straight through exhaust pipe. The length of this pipe is extremely important, and when in position it should extend to the rearmost portion of the back wheel.

Compression Ratio

This is altered by fitting various pistons. Compression plates cannot be used owing to the bevel gear drive. Increasing the compression ratio, provided a suitable fuel and sparking plug are used, will result in increased power output. Pistons interchangeable in all machines with the exception of the KTT can be obtained with the following compression ratios from the makers:

	Compression Ratio.	*Correct Fuel.*
K & KSS.	5·5 to 1 (standard).	Pure petrol.
	6·75 to 1 (KSS).	50/50 petrol-benzol mixture.
	8·5 to 1.	Discol P.M.S.2.

If Discol P.M.S.2 is unobtainable, a good grade of special racing fuel should be obtained.

Pistons for the KTT machine are obtainable as follows:

	Compression Ratio.	*Correct Fuel.*
KTT model only.	6 to 1.	Pure petrol.
	7·25 to 1.	50/50 petrol-benzol mixture.
	8·5 to 1.	Discol P.M.S.2.
	10 to 1.	Discol R.D.1.

Ignition Timing

This should be accurately set to give 38 degrees (or just under $\frac{7}{16}$ inch) advance for petrol or benzole mixture, and 42 degrees (or just over $\frac{7}{16}$ inch) for alcohol fuels. Greater ignition advance will not increase the power output, but will cause overheating and pre-ignition.

VELOCETTE ENGINES

Tappet Clearances

For racing purposes the *minimum* tappet clearances are ·012 inch inlet valve and ·018 inch exhaust valve. For long-distance racing the clearance should be slightly increased.

Sparking Plugs

These should be chosen with care for the purpose for which they are to be used. For high-speed touring a first-class plug, such as a K.L.G. 246, is eminently suitable. A K.L.G. 396 is to be recommended for short-distance work, such as grass track racing with compression ratio not exceeding 8·5 to 1. For long-distance road racing a K.L.G. 356 or 464 are suitable. The 464 stands less heat, but more oil than the 356. For sustained full throttle use, such as track work, a K.L.G. 341 or 348 should be used. These two plugs oil up very easily, but withstand great heat.

Polishing Ports

It is advantageous to grind out and polish the ports of the cylinder head, but it should be borne in mind that the shape and streamlining of the ports is of far greater importance than a high polish. No advantage is to be gained by polishing the flywheels and interior of the crankcase, as the flywheels are clear of the oil in the sump and therefore oil drag is negligible.

REPAIR AND MAINTENANCE OF VELOCETTE ENGINES—TWO-STROKE G.T.P. TYPE

The G.T.P. engine can be decarbonised without removing it from the frame. For overhauling, it is, however, necessary to remove it, and this is done in the following manner :

Removing Flywheel

Remove the top portion of the chainguard and primary chain. The flywheel must now be removed, and this is done by unscrewing the large hexagon nut in the centre. Hold the rim of the flywheel, and unscrew the nut with a spanner in an anticlockwise direction. This nut, in addition to being a locking nut, is also a withdrawal nut, and after being unscrewed for a turn or so it will appear to tighten up again. By jarring the spanner with a hammer the nut can be unscrewed still further, when the flywheel complete with sprocket and belt pulley will be withdrawn. Now remove the exhaust pipes, carburetter, oil-feed pipe, sparking plug, and disconnect the contact-breaker control wire. The small bottom portion of chainguard should now be removed. Support the engine and take off the front engine plates. Withdraw the rear

VELOCETTE ENGINES

engine bolts, leaving the engine plates and dynamo attached to the frame. The engine can now be removed complete.

Order of Dismantling

The order of dismantling is as follows: unscrew the four cylinder-head bolts, when the cylinder head can be lifted clear of the barrel. Remove the four cylinder-base nuts and lift the barrel clear of the crankcase studs. Be sure to support the piston when withdrawing it from the barrel to prevent it swinging against the connecting rod or crankcase studs. If the engine has not been removed from the frame and the cylinder is being removed for decarbonisation it is advisable to place a clean duster over the orifice of the crankcase to prevent the entry of dirt or foreign matter. This is shown in Fig. 18. The gudgeon pin is secured in the piston by means of circlips, and a slot is provided in one piston boss to facilitate its removal. A spoke ground to a sharp point makes a very useful circlip remover. The gudgeon pin can now be pushed out from the opposite side of the piston as shown in Fig. 19. The piston can now be removed from the con rod.

Removing Contact Breaker

The contact-breaker cover should now be taken off. It is now necessary to remove the contact-breaker cam. This is fitted on a taper on the end of the crankshaft, and, after removing the small locking pin and washer, can be withdrawn by screwing an engine bolt into the cam. The cam is tapped out for this purpose, and the effect of the engine bolt being screwed through the cam against the end of the crankshaft pulls the cam off the taper. Remove the small oil pipe and the six small pump-cover screws, when the pump can be withdrawn. Remove the crankcase bolts, when the two halves of the crankcase can be parted, and the crankshaft assembly can be removed complete. The contact breaker can be taken off the pump side crankcase by unscrewing one small set pin.

Taking apart Crankshaft

The crankpin is a tight press fit in the balance weights, and is best removed by the use of a hand press. In the absence of a press the crankpin can be driven out with a soft metal punch and hammer. If the track of the crankpin is pitted a new one should be obtained. Should new rollers be required, these can be obtained from the makers of the machine, and, in addition to standard size, rollers ·0005 inch (or ½ thou.) and ·001 inch oversize can be supplied. The large end of the connecting rod forms the outer race for the bearing, and should this be badly worn, a new connecting rod can be obtained at small cost. Before commencing to assemble the big end, examine the small-end bush and gudgeon pin. The small-end bush is pressed into the connecting rod,

VELOCETTE ENGINES

and should a new bush be fitted, do not omit to make the oil hole at the top, corresponding with the oil hole in the connecting rod, *after* the bush has been pressed into position.

Reassembling

Before assembling the big end, see that all the parts are thoroughly clean, and the oilway in the driving-side crankshaft is clear and free from obstruction. The crankpin should then be pressed into one of the balance weights until the end is exactly flush with the part of the balance weight surrounding it. It will be noticed that a slight recess is present on the face of the balance weight, and the crankpin *must* not be pressed to the depth of this recess, or the flanges on the crankpin will be crushed, causing the rollers to be pinched endways. The rollers should now be placed in position, and the connecting rod placed over them, after which the other crankshaft and balance weight can be placed lightly on the crankpin. Apply a straightedge at two or three places across the edges of the two balance weights to get them approximately true. The other end of the crankpin should now be supported while the top balance weight is pressed into position. Be careful to see that the ends of the crankpin do not protrude from the balance weight. If the balance weights are placed on a flat plate and the crankpin pressed in as far as it will go, the position of the crankpin and width of the assembly will be correct. The assembly should now be trued up in " V " blocks,

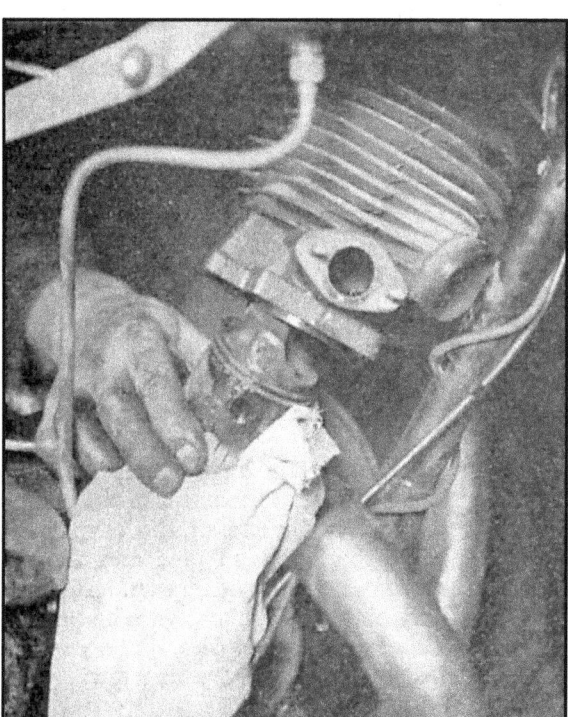

Fig. 18.—REMOVING THE CYLINDER BARREL FROM THE ENGINE OF THE G.T.P. MODEL.

Note the duster on the top of the crankcase to prevent the entry of dirt and foreign matter.

VELOCETTE ENGINES

using an indicator on the crankshafts in the same manner as the flywheels on the o.h.c. machine illustrated in Fig. 8.

Examining Main Bearings

The bronze main bearings are a press fit in the halves of the crankcase, and should it be necessary to replace them, the new ones should be carefully reamered out after pressing into position. Any undue wear in the main bearings will be detrimental to crankcase compression and suction. It is also essential to see that the oil hole in the driving-side bush coincides with the oilway in the crankshaft, and also that the oil hole in the pump-side bush coincides with the oilway that is drilled from inside the top of the crankcase. It will be noticed that a small screw is fitted to each half of the crankcase to locate the bushes in their correct positions. The exact dimensions of the oil grooves in the timing-side bush must be adhered to, particularly in length.

Check Endplay

See that the oilways in the crankcase are quite free from obstruction, when the crankshaft assembly can be placed in position in one half. The joint of the

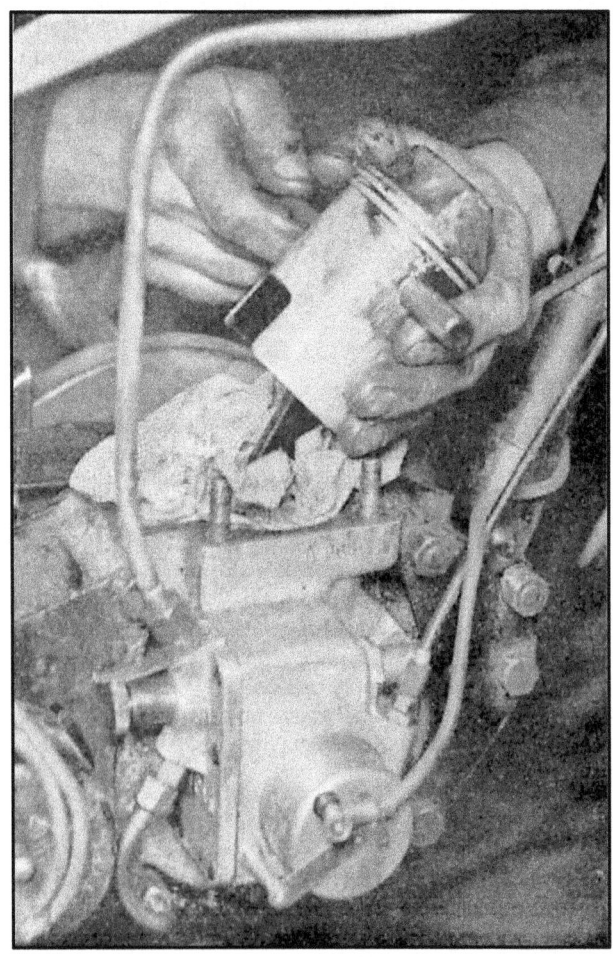

Fig. 19.—REMOVING THE GUDGEON PIN ON THE G.T.P. MODEL.

VELOCETTE ENGINES

crankcase should now be smeared with liquid jointing, the crankcase bolts inserted and the nuts tightened securely. Test the crankshaft for endplay. It is as well to remember that a small amount of endplay is not only desirable but essential. Should the play be excessive, it can be taken up by fitting a thin steel shim (or shims) between the driving-side balance weight and the crankcase. Shims for this purpose can be obtained from the makers.

In the unusual event of the oil pump requiring attention, it should be returned complete to Messrs. Veloce Ltd.

See that the ball valve is clean, but on no account alter the strength of the spring.

The oil pump can now be placed in position, and in addition to the paper washer the use of liquid jointing compound will ensure a good joint. The six screws should be screwed up tightly.

Fitting Piston and Rings

The piston with rings can now be fitted to the con rod. The cut-away part of the skirt is at the *back* of the piston. After inserting the con rod, see that the circlip is pushed right down into its groove in the piston boss.

Checking Connecting Rod for Truth

The alignment of the connecting rod should now be checked by placing a steel rule or straightedge across the top of the crankcase in line with the crankshaft. The piston should be lowered till the bottom of the skirt comes into contact with the straightedge, and it should touch on both sides of the skirt without being strained. If it does not, the con rod must be set (or bent) slightly to obtain the desired result. It is also advisable to check the position of the skirt in the bore of the crankcase. The piston should be movable sideways in the small end of the con rod an equal distance either side of the centre line.

The cylinder-base paper washer is now placed in position, and the cylinder lowered gently on to the piston. Care should be taken when inserting the piston to prevent damaging the rings. After locating the barrel on the four studs screw down the nuts evenly, each one a little at a time.

Refitting Cylinder Head

Should the cylinder-head joint show signs of leaking, it should be ground on to the cylinder barrel before the latter is fitted. Fine grinding compound should be used, and the joint is made on the broad face.

The cylinder head can now be placed in position, and the four bolts inserted and tightened up evenly, each one a little at a time.

VELOCETTE ENGINES

Timing Details

The contact breaker can now be fitted, and the cam, and its locking pin and washer, placed loosely in position, when the engine is ready for timing.

Fig. 20 is a timing diagram to which it will be necessary to refer. The engine should be turned till the piston is at top dead centre, as in Dia. 1. A pointer " P," made from a small piece of wire, is attached to some fixed point on the engine and allowed to rest against the rim of the flywheel. A mark "A" is made on the flywheel rim opposite the pointer when the piston is at the top dead centre. A further mark " B " is now made at a distance " X " (in the case of the G.T.P., $X = 2\frac{3}{4}$ inches) along the rim of the flywheel from the mark "A." The engine flywheel is now turned backwards until the mark " B " is opposite the pointer as in Dia. 2. With the engine in this position the contact-breaker cam should be set so that the points of the contact breaker are just breaking, with the contact breaker rotated to the fully advanced position. The cam locking pin should now be tightened securely and the contact-breaker cover replaced, when the engine is ready for fitting to the frame.

Refitting Engine into Frame

After replacing the engine in the frame the flywheel should be refitted in the following manner. First place the dynamo belt on the flywheel pulley. The belt cover plate is now placed in position, and the flywheel fitted to the crankshaft. Tighten the flywheel lock nut as tight as possible, using a hammer to finally turn the spanner. Slack off the dynamo clamping nut and rotate the dynamo, when the belt can be slipped over the dynamo pulley. As the armature spindle is eccentric to the dynamo casing, it is only necessary to rotate the dynamo to adjust the tension of the belt, as shown in Fig. 21.

The oil pipes, sparking plug, carburetter, exhaust pipes and chain cover can now be replaced.

NOTES ON THE G.T.P. ENGINE

Oil Adjustment

The oil adjusting screw should be set so that there is a faint blue smoke at the exhaust at all times.

Contact Breaker

Should the contact breaker become flooded with oil, the oil grooves in the pump side main bearing and crankshaft should be examined. These should register to form a continuous oilway once every revolution. If they are obstructed or do not coincide, the oil in the pump casing cannot be sucked into the crankcase, with the result that the casing becomes flooded with oil, and this leaks into the contact breaker.

The points of the contact breaker should be kept clean, and adjusted

VELOCETTE ENGINES

to the correct gap, i.e. ·018 inch. An incorrect gap is often found to be the cause of very erratic running.

Exhaust System

Periodically the exhaust pipes and silencers should be cleaned out. Should the holes in the baffles of the silencers or of the small cone at the end of each exhaust pipe become choked with carbon, considerable loss of power will be inevitable.

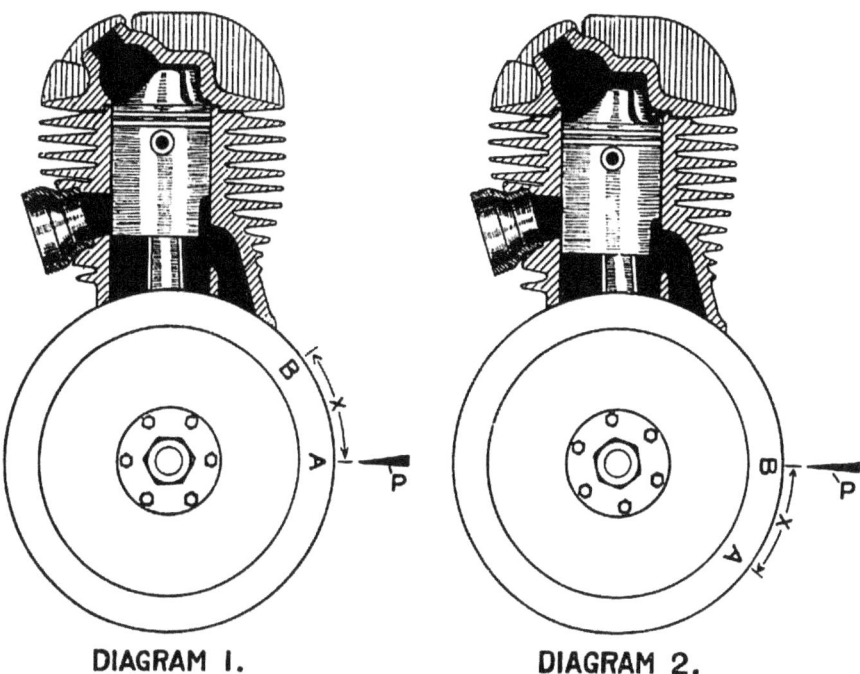

DIAGRAM 1.   DIAGRAM 2.

Fig. 20.—Timing Diagram for the Two-stroke Models.

The silencers should not be tampered with, with a view to increasing the speed of the machine. The standard silencers are the result of much careful experimenting on the part of the makers, and have been found to be the most efficient for silencing, and at the same time obtaining the best power output from the engine.

TWO-STROKE ENGINES WITH OVERHUNG CRANKSHAFT— " U " TYPE

It is proposed to take the " U " model as a typical example of this type of engine which was produced by Messrs. Veloce Ltd. until the end of 1928.

VELOCETTE ENGINES

OILING SYSTEM OF "U" MODEL

The oiling system on these engines is automatic, oil being drawn by crankcase suction through a filter at the bottom of the sump, via a small tube to an oilway cast in the crankcase running round the bronze main bearing. This oilway leads to the taper seating of the needle valve at the top of the main bearing. From this point oil enters a port in the drilled crankshaft once every revolution, and is sucked through the oilway in the shaft, and by way of an oil groove to the big-end bearing. Oil thrown off from the big end lubricates the cylinder barrel and piston.

The supply of oil to the engine is controlled by the adjustable needle valve. This needle has a quick thread, and is screwed on to or off its seating by a small handle working on a quadrant on the top of the crankcase.

Dismantling Cylinder and Piston

The cylinder barrel is removed in the same manner as the G.T.P. engine. The majority of the "U" engines are fitted with a cast-iron piston, which is attached to the con rod by a gudgeon pin having one aluminium button only. The piston is recessed on one side to take this button.

Fig. 21.—METHOD OF ADJUSTING THE DYNAMO DRIVING BELT OF THE G.T.P. MODEL BY ROTATING THE DYNAMO IN THE REAR ENGINE PLATES.

The gudgeon pin should be pushed out from the end opposite to the button.

The gudgeon pin of the aluminium piston is secured by circlips in the same manner as the o.h.c. and G.T.P. machines.

Overhauling Release Valve

A release valve is fitted at the top of the cylinder barrel, and this can be removed by first unscrewing the large retaining nut, when the cable and release-valve operating mechanism can be withdrawn. The

VELOCETTE ENGINES

release valve can now be driven out of the barrel by inserting a punch or rod through the sparking-plug hole, and tapping lightly with a hammer. It is very important to prevent the valve from leaking, as this will soften the springs. If a leakage occurs between the release-valve body and the cylinder barrel, a new copper and asbestos washer should be fitted. If the valve itself leaks, grind it into the seating of the body in the same manner as a valve of a four-stroke engine. A tube leads from the release valve to the exhaust port, and this should be decarbonised frequently. If the plug at the top of the cylinder over the tube is removed, the tube can be cleaned with a piece of stiff wire. If the tube becomes choked the valve will become inoperative.

Removing Connecting Rod

To remove the connecting rod the crankcase outer cover should be unscrewed, and the crankcase inner block can then be pulled out. This block is a push fit in the crankcase, and is located in its correct position by a stud at the bottom of the crankcase. It is not necessary to remove this stud to pull out the inner block.

The connecting rod is secured to the crankpin by a screw which has a left-hand thread, therefore, to remove it, it must be turned in a clockwise direction. The left-hand pin and washer having been removed, the con rod with big-end rollers can be taken off the crankpin.

Detaching Flywheel

The screws supporting the magneto chain cover should now be removed, and the sprocket withdrawn from its taper on the armature spindle. The flywheel, complete with driving sprocket, magneto chain cover and sprocket can be withdrawn by unscrewing the hexagon locking and withdrawal nut in the same manner as on the G.T.P. machine.

Stripping Crankshaft

The crankshaft can now be withdrawn from the crankcase. Access to the oil-sump filter and small oil pipe is obtained by removing the large drain plug from the bottom of the crankcase.

The parts should now be cleaned and thoroughly examined. Taking the crankshaft first, the shaft and crankpin are a press fit into the balance weight. Should it be necessary to fit a new crankshaft, see that the oil groove at its end corresponds with the oil groove of the balance weight.

Main Bearing

The shaft should be a good fit in the main bearing. If the bearing is badly worn it should be replaced, as it will affect the oiling system in addition to crankcase compression and suction, and also cause serious oil leakage behind the flywheel. This bush is a tight press fit in the crank-

VELOCETTE ENGINES

case, and is additionally secured by a peg made from a piece of brass rod threaded $\frac{1}{4}$ inch × 20T. This peg can be removed with a screwdriver through the drain-plug hole.

Fitting a New Bearing

Before attempting to press the bush out of position, remove the oil regulator and needle valve. This can be done by unscrewing the small set pin which secures the handle, which can then be pulled off the needle. The top gland nut should now be unscrewed, when the needle valve can be unscrewed and lifted out of the guide.

After pressing a new bearing into position the hole must be drilled and tapped for the peg. This can then be inserted and tightened up with a screwdriver. The hole for the needle valve must now be carefully drilled, and a small seating cut for the needle. The bearing should now be carefully reamered out so that no sideplay is apparent, while the crankshaft revolves freely.

Magneto Driving Sprocket

The magneto driving sprocket is screwed on to the flywheel by a left-hand thread, and it must be removed by unscrewing in a clockwise direction. To remove the driving sprocket the locking ring must first be removed. This ring has a left-hand thread, and must be turned in a clockwise direction to unscrew. The tongued washer can now be withdrawn and the driving sprocket unscrewed. This also has a left-hand thread, so to remove, unscrew it in a clockwise direction.

Refitting the Flywheel

After fitting the crankshaft all traces of oil must be removed from the taper of the shaft and bore of the flywheel, when the flywheel should be replaced, and the locking nut tightened very securely. A slight amount of endplay is desirable, and, should the flywheel bind against the end of the new bearing, the end face of the latter should be skimmed down very slightly in a lathe, or the bearing eased by careful filing.

Care of Needle Valve

The needle valve should now be refitted and adjusted in the following manner: screw in the needle, taking care that the point does not project too far through the guide, otherwise the point will be damaged.

Set the quadrant in its correct position, and repack the gland nut with asbestos string to prevent leakage. This gland nut must not be packed too tightly, but it is very important that no air leakage occurs, as this will affect the oiling system.

The handle or lever should now be placed on the needle in the " fast " (or full on) position, and the small set pin should be tightened slightly.

VELOCETTE ENGINES

Now turn the lever towards the " off " position until the needle can be felt to bear against its seating. If the set pin is not screwed in too tightly, the lever or handle can be slipped round on the needle until it is in the " off " position. The set pin can then be tightened securely. A test can be made by attaching a piece of rubber tubing to the oil tube in the sump and blowing through it to ascertain that the valve is shutting off properly.

Reassembling

The big-end rollers can now be placed in position with the aid of grease, and the con rod refitted, after which the locking screw and washer can be placed in position and the screw tightened securely by turning in an anticlockwise direction.

The crankcase inner block should now be pushed into position, together with its thin packing washer, after which the cover plate can be refitted and screwed up tightly.

Refitting Piston

The piston can now be fitted, and the alignment checked as per the instructions given in the G.T.P. section. In the case of cast-iron pistons, be sure that the aluminium gudgeon-pin button bears against the cylinder wall opposite the inlet port. This is extremely important, as otherwise the gudgeon pin is liable to foul the inlet port.

The cylinder barrel can now be refitted, and the release valve, with copper asbestos washer, placed in position. This should be secured by tightening up the large release valve nut.

Retiming Engine

The engine is now ready for timing. The method employed is exactly as given for the G.T.P. engine, with the exception that the measurement " X " on the timing diagram (Fig. 20) is $2\frac{11}{16}$ inches.

NOTES ON THE " U " MODEL ENGINE (Refer to page 270)

Should the engine receive too much oil, and adjustment of the regulator does not curtail the supply, the needle valve should be reset, as it may not be bearing against the taper seating in the bush when the lever is in the " off " position. See instructions on assembling the needle valve.

It is necessary to vary the supply of oil to the engine for the purpose for which the machine is to be used. If it is found that insufficient oil reaches the engine when the regulator lever is in one notch, while in the next notch the engine receives too much, another notch can be filed in the quadrant in between the two, and the regulator lever placed in this position. A faint blue smoke should be apparent from the exhaust at all speeds.

AUTOBOOKS WORKSHOP MANUALS

ALFA ROMEO GIULIA 1300, 1600, 1750, 2000 1962-1978 WSM
BMW 1600 1966-1973 WSM
BMW 2500, 2800, 3.0 & 3.3 1968-1977 WSM
BMW 316, 320, 320i 1975-1977 WSM
BMW 518, 520, 520i 1973-1981 WSM
FIAT 1100, 1100D, 1100R & 1200 1957-1969 WSM
FIAT 124 1966-1974 WSM
FIAT 124 SPORT 1966-1975 WSM
FIAT 125 & 125 SPECIAL 1967-1973 WSM
FIAT 126, 126L, 126 DV, 126/650 & 126/650 DV 1972-1982 WSM
FIAT 127 SALOON, SPECIAL & SPORT, 900, 1050 1971-1981 WSM
FIAT 128 1969-1982 WSM
FIAT 1300, 1500 1961-1967 WSM
FIAT 131 MIRAFIORI 1975-1982 WSM
FIAT 132 1972-1982 WSM
FIAT 500 1957-1973 WSM
FIAT 600, 600D & MULTIPLA 1955-1969 WSM
FIAT 850 1964-1972 WSM
JAGUAR MK 1, 2 1955-1969 WSM
JAGUAR S TYPE, 420 1963-1968 WSM
JAGUAR XK 120, 140, 150 MK 7, 8, 9 1948-1961 WSM
LAND ROVER 1, 2 1948-1961 WSM
MERCEDES-BENZ 190 1959-1968 WSM
MERCEDES-BENZ 220/8 1968-1972 WSM
MERCEDES-BENZ 220B 1959-1965 WSM
MERCEDES-BENZ 230 1963-1968 WSM
MERCEDES-BENZ 250 1968-1972 WSM
MERCEDES-BENZ 280 1968-1972 WSM
MINI 1959-1980 WSM
MORRIS MINOR 1952-1971 WSM
PEUGEOT 404 1960-1975 WSM
PORSCHE 911 1964-1973 WSM
PORSCHE 911 1970-1977 WSM
RENAULT 16 1965-1979 WSM
RENAULT 8, 10, 1100 1962-1971 WSM
ROVER 3500, 3500S 1968-1976 WSM
SUNBEAM RAPIER, ALPINE 1955-1965 WSM
TRIUMPH SPITFIRE, GT6, VITESSE 1962-1968 WSM
TRIUMPH TR4, TR4A 1961-1967 WSM
VOLKSWAGEN BEETLE 1968-1977 WSM

VELOCEPRESS AUTOMOBILE BOOKS & MANUALS

ABARTH BUYERS GUIDE
AUSTIN-HEALEY 6-CYLINDER WSM
AUSTIN-HEALEY SPRITE & MG MIDGET 1958-1971 WSM
BMW 600 LIMOUSINE FACTORY WSM
BMW 600 LIMOUSINE OWNERS HAND BOOK & SERVICE MANUAL
BMW 2000 & 2002 1966-1976 WSM
BMW ISETTA FACTORY WSM
BOOK OF THE CARRERA PANAMERICANA - MEXICAN ROAD RACE
COMPLETE CATALOG OF JAPANESE MOTOR VEHICLES
CORVAIR 1960-1969 OWNERS WORKSHOP MANUAL
CORVETTE V8 1955-1962 OWNERS WORKSHOP MANUAL
DIALED IN - THE JAN OPPERMAN STORY
FERRARI 250/GT SERVICE AND MAINTENANCE
FERRARI 308 SERIES BUYER'S AND OWNER'S GUIDE
FERRARI BERLINETTA LUSSO
FERRARI BROCHURES AND SALES LITERATURE 1946-1967
FERRARI BROCHURES AND SALES LITERATURE 1968-1989
FERRARI GUIDE TO PERFORMANCE
FERRARI OPP, MAINTENANCE & SERVICE H/BOOKS 1948-1963
FERRARI OWNER'S HANDBOOK
FERRARI SERIAL NUMBERS PART I - ODD NUMBERS TO 21399
FERRARI SERIAL NUMBERS PART II - EVEN NUMBERS TO 1050
FERRARI SPYDER CALIFORNIA
FERRARI TUNING TIPS & MAINTENANCE TECHNIQUES
HENRY'S FABULOUS MODEL "A" FORD
HOW TO BUILD A FIBERGLASS CAR
HOW TO BUILD A RACING CAR
HOW TO RESTORE THE MODEL 'A' FORD
IF HEMINGWAY HAD WRITTEN A RACING NOVEL
JAGUAR E-TYPE 3.8 & 4.2 WSM
LE MANS 24 (THE BOOK THAT THE FILM WAS BASED ON)
MASERATI BROCHURES AND SALES LITERATURE
MASERATI OWNER'S HANDBOOK
METROPOLITAN FACTORY WSM
MGA & MGB OWNERS HANDBOOK & WSM
MG MIDGET TC, TD, TF & TF1500 WORKSHOP MANUAL
OBERT'S FIAT GUIDE
PERFORMANCE TUNING THE SUNBEAM TIGER
PORSCHE 356 1948-1965 WSM
PORSCHE 912 WSM
SOUPING THE VOLKSWAGEN
SOLEX CARBURETORS (EMPHASIS ON UK & EU AUTOMOBILES)
SU CARBURETORS (EMPHASIS ON UK AUTOMOBILES)
TRIUMPH TR2, TR3, TR4 1953-1965 WSM
TUNING FOR SPEED (P.E. IRVING)
VEDA ORR'S NEW REVISED HOT ROD PICTORIAL
VOLKSWAGEN TRANSPORTER, TRUCKS, STATION WAGONS WSM
VOLVO 1944-1968 ALL MODELS WSM
WEBER CARBURETORS (EMPHASIS ON ALFA & FIAT)

BROOKLANDS BOOKS & ROAD TEST PORTFOLIOS (RTP)

AC CARS 1904-2009
ALFA ROMEO 1920-1933 ROAD TEST PORTFOLIO
ALFA ROMEO 1934-1940 ROAD TEST PORTFOLIO
BRABHAM RALT HONDA THE RON TAURANAC STORY
BUGATTI TYPE 10 TO TYPE 40 ROAD TEST PORTFOLIO
BUGATTI TYPE 10 TO TYPE 251 ROAD TEST PORTFOLIO
BUGATTI TYPE 41 TO TYPE 55 ROAD TEST PORTFOLIO
BUGATTI TYPE 57 TO TYPE 251 ROAD TEST PORTFOLIO
DELAHAYE ROAD TEST PORTFOLIO
FERRARI ROAD CARS 1946-1956 ROAD TEST PORTFOLIO
FIAT 500 1936-1972 ROAD TEST PORTFOLIO
FIAT DINO ROAD TEST PORTFOLIO
HISPANO SUIZA ROAD TEST PORTFOLIO
HONDA ST1100/ST1300 PAN EUROPEAN 1990-2002 RTP
JAGUAR MK1 & MK2 ROAD TEST PORTFOLIO
LOTUS CORTINA ROAD TEST PORTFOLIO
MV AGUSTA F4 750 & 1000 1997-2007 ROAD TEST PORTFOLIO
TATRA CARS ROAD TEST PORTFOLIO

VELOCEPRESS MOTORCYCLE BOOKS & MANUALS

1930'S BRITISH MOTORCYCLE GEARBOXES & CLUTCHES (BOOK OF)
AJS SINGLES & TWINS 250cc THRU 1000cc 1932-1948 (BOOK OF)
AJS SINGLES 1955-65 350cc & 500cc (BOOK OF)
AJS SINGLES 1945-60 350cc & 500cc MODELS 16 & 18 (BOOK OF)
ARIEL 1939-1960 4 STROKE SINGLES (BOOK OF)
ARIEL LEADER & ARROW 1958-1964 (BOOK OF)
ARIEL MOTORCYCLES 1933-1951 WSM
ARIEL PREWAR MODELS 1932-1939 (BOOK OF)
BMW M/CYCLES R26 R27 (1956-1967) FACTORY WSM
BMW M/CYCLES R50 R50S R60 R69S (1955-1969) FACTORY WSM
BSA BANTAM ALL MODELS FROM 1948 ONWARDS (BOOK OF)
BSA SINGLES & V-TWINS UP TO 1927 (BOOK OF)
BSA SINGLES & V-TWINS 1936-1939 (BOOK OF)
BSA SINGLES & V-TWINS 1936-1952 (BOOK OF)
BSA OHV & SV SINGLES 250-600cc 1945-1954 (BOOK OF)
BSA OHV & SV SINGLES - 250cc 1954-1970 (BOOK OF)
BSA OHV SINGLES 350 & 500cc 1955-1967 (BOOK OF)
BSA TWINS 1948-1962 (BOOK OF)
BSA TWINS 1962-1969 (SECOND BOOK OF)
CATALOG OF BRITISH MOTORCYCLES (1951 MODELS)
DOUGLAS PRE-WAR ALL MODELS 1929-1939 (BOOK OF)
DOUGLAS POST-WAR ALL MODELS 1948-1957 FACTORY WSM
DUCATI 160cc, 250cc & 350cc OHC MODELS FACTORY WSM
HONDA 50 ALL MODELS UP TO 1970 INC MONKEY & TRAIL (BOOK OF)
HONDA 90 ALL MODELS UP TO 1966 (BOOK OF)
HONDA MOTORCYCLES 125-150 TWINS C/CS/CB/CA WSM
HONDA MOTORCYCLES 250-305 TWINS C/CS/CB WSM
HONDA MOTORCYCLES C100 SUPER CUB WSM
HONDA MOTORCYCLES C110 SPORT CUB 1962-1969 WSM
HONDA TWINS ALL MODELS 50cc THRU 305cc 1960-1966 (BOOK OF)
HONDA TWINS ALL MODELS 125cc THRU 450cc UP TO 1968 (BOOK OF)
INDIAN PONYBIKE, BOY RACER & PAPOOSE ILL PARTS LIST & SALES LIT
J.A.P. ENGINES 1927-1952 & MOTORCYCLES 1934-1952 (BOOK OF)
LAMBRETTA ALL 125 & 150cc MODELS 1947-1957 (BOOK OF)
LAMBRETTA LI & TV MODELS 1957-1970 (SECOND BOOK OF)
MATCHLESS 350 & 500cc SINGLES 1945-1956 (BOOK OF)
MATCHLESS 350 & 500cc SINGLES 1955-1966 (BOOK OF)
MOTORCYCLE ENGINEERING (P. E. Irving)
NORTON 1932-1947 (BOOK OF)
NORTON 1938-1956 (BOOK OF)
NORTON DOMINATOR TWINS 1955-1965 (BOOK OF)
NORTON MODELS 19, 50 & ES2 1955-1963 (BOOK OF)
NORTON MOTORCYCLES 1957-1970 FACTORY WSM
NORTON PREWAR MODELS 1932-1939 (BOOK OF)
NSU PRIMA ALL MODELS 1956-1964 (BOOK OF)
NSU QUICKLY ALL MODELS 1953-1963 (BOOK OF)
RALEIGH MOPEDS 1960-1969 (BOOK OF)
RALEIGH MOTORCYCLES 1919-1933 (BOOK OF)
ROYAL ENFIELD SINGLES & V TWINS 1934-1946 (BOOK OF)
ROYAL ENFIELD SINGLES & V TWINS 1937-1953 (BOOK OF)
ROYAL ENFIELD SINGLES 1946-1962 (BOOK OF)
ROYAL ENFIELD 736cc INTERCEPTOR FACTORY WSM
ROYAL ENFIELD 250cc & 350cc SINGLES 1958-1966 (SECOND BOOK OF)
RUDGE MOTORCYCLES 1933-1939 (BOOK OF)
SPEED AND HOW TO OBTAIN IT
SUNBEAM MOTORCYCLES 1928-1939 (BOOK OF)
SUNBEAM S7 & S8 1946-1957 (BOOK OF)
SUZUKI 50cc & 80cc UP TO 1966 (BOOK OF)
SUZUKI T10 1963-1967 FACTORY WSM
SUZUKI T20 & T200 1965-1969 FACTORY WSM
TRIUMPH PRE-WAR MOTORCYCLE 1935-1939 (BOOK OF)
TRIUMPH MOTORCYCLES 1935-1949 (BOOK OF)
TRIUMPH MOTORCYCLES 1937-1951 WSM
TRIUMPH MOTORCYCLES 1945-1955 FACTORY WSM
TRIUMPH TWINS 1945-1958 (BOOK OF)
TRIUMPH TWINS 1956-1969 (BOOK OF)
VELOCETTE ALL SINGLES & TWINS 1925-1970 (BOOK OF)
VESPA 1951-1961 (BOOK OF)
VESPA 125 & 150cc & GS MODELS 1955-1963 (SECOND BOOK OF)
VESPA 90, 125 & 150cc 1963-1972 (THIRD BOOK OF)
VESPA GS & SS 1955-1968 (BOOK OF)
VILLIERS ENGINE (BOOK OF)
VINCENT MOTORCYCLES 1935-1955 WSM

FOR A DETAILED DESCRIPTION OF ANY OF OUR TITLES PLEASE VISIT OUR WEBSITE
www.VelocePress.com

www.ingramcontent.com/pod-product-compliance
Lightning Source LLC
Chambersburg PA
CBHW050554170426
43201CB00011B/1688